INSIDE
THE
FOURTH
REICH

INSIDE THE FOURTH REICH

by
ERICH ERDSTEIN
with
Barbara Bean

St. Martin's Press
New York

for
Para Cacho Y Chinga

Copyright © 1977 by Erich Erdstein
for information write:
St. Martin's Press
175 Fifth Avenue
New York, N.Y. 10010
Manufactured in the United States of America
Library of Congress Catalog Card Number: 77-9153

Library of Congress Cataloging in Publication Data

Erdstein, Erich.
Inside the Fourth Reich.

1. War criminals—Germany. 2. Germans in South
America. 3. Erdstein, Erich. I. Bean, Barbara,
joint author. II. Title.
D804.G4E75   363.2'34'0924 [B]   77-9153
ISBN 0-312-41885-X

The man named Thompson leaned forward across the table in a London office building. It was the first week of October, 1968, and I had been in England less than a week. I arrived with only my life, one battered suitcase of documents, and a Taurus .38, with which I had shot and killed Dr. Joseph Mengele, the Nazi "Angel of Death."

Sunlight streamed through the slats of the Venetian blinds on the window behind the intelligence man, causing me to squint if I looked directly at him. I focused on a discoloration on the floor and wondered what had made the stain. The left side of my head pounded steadily, making it difficult to hear the soft voice that droned on with no inflection.

"You're sure it was Mengele?"

"Yes. He admitted that he was Joseph Mengele. We talked about his job in the camp." A stab of pain coursed through my jaw to my temple, the reminder of a face wound I had suffered over a year ago. It hadn't bothered me as much lately, and I had almost forgotten it except when I saw the scars in the mirror each morning.

"You're sure he was dead?"

I closed my eyes. Again this question, and again I saw it in slow motion: the choppy water, and the man

floating face down, tangled in the ropes . . . shots
. . . the twang as they hit the metal smokestacks . . . a
scream . . . the other prisoner lurching and falling . . . a
shout . . . turning . . . a boat flying the blue and white
flag of Argentina rounding the curve . . . the other boat
maneuvering close to the limp bodies in the water, haul-
ing them on board.

"Mr. Erdstein? . . ."

"He was dead." I tried to avoid moving my mouth,
but the pain ran through my jaw again, and the pounding at the base of my skull quickened. I cursed the man
and his bland English stare.

"How can you be sure?"

"I can't be sure . . . but I'm a cop. I've seen men die
before. I know how long he was in the water."

"Maybe you made a mistake about the time."

For a moment I was standing in a meatpacking
plant, holding a stopwatch, timing the movement of the
men as they plunged a hook deep into the bloody carcass,
threw the chain over the iron bar, and yanked it toward
the ceiling.

"No, I don't think so."

The neon lights buzzed, reminding me of some
other place, some other conversation. I tried to remember . . . in Buenos Aires, the chief of police. I couldn't
remember his name. Then I also sat in pain, and then,
too, I didn't know where I'd go next. Always running.
Always fleeing. Austria. Argentina. Uruguay. Paraguay.
Brazil.

"Mr. Erdstein? Did you hear me?"

"I'm sorry. What did you ask?"

"I'd like to get the whole story. Maybe you could start
from the beginning."

The beginning? The corpse of Eugene Parries
propped up against the bed, the belt twisted around his

neck. No, maybe before that; the war, the war to save democracy.

The beginning. A young Jew watching his house where men in black uniforms with red, white, and black armbands walked up and down with rifles clanking against their belts. That was the beginning.

1

I pressed my back flat against the wall of the coffeehouse to avoid being swept along with a couple trying to reach an empty table in the corner. The normally staid Victoria Coffeehouse was overflowing with people, some crowded around the small marble-topped tables, some moving restlessly from table to table, unable to sit. Their faces, like mine, were tense and worried. Their voices buzzed angrily. It was not the usual crowd of light-hearted Viennese, whiling away a long, gray Saturday afternoon over their coffee. On the opposite side of the smoky room, near the ornately carved walnut buffet that displayed the pastries, a group of rough-looking young men laughed boisterously, drawing glares from the other customers.

I glanced apprehensively toward the telephone booth. On a normal day the public telephone here was rarely used, but today—March 12, 1938—there was a line of people waiting to call friends or family, wanting to communicate the news: the Germans were invading Austria.

I had run the few blocks from the university as soon as I heard the news on the radio. Confused and alarmed, my first thought was to call my father. I knew I could

5

trust him to retain his icy rationality in any crisis. Usually it irritated me, but today I needed reassurance. The world as I had known it during my eighteen years was crumbling. Seemingly overnight the Austrian government had collapsed under Hitler's demand that it name the German puppet Seyss-Inquart Chancellor or face an invasion. Chancellor Schuschnigg had resigned last night in an emotional radio speech, and today Seyss-Inquart was flying to Linz to meet Hitler.

When the German Chancellor had started making threats about invading Austria, I was convinced it was mere bravado. Surely he wouldn't risk war by invading a country whose independence had been guaranteed by the Treaty of St. Germain and the League of Nations. He must know the British and French wouldn't stand for it. Yet he had dared, and there were no signs that anyone was coming to Austria's rescue.

Even more surprising was the collapse within Austria. Like most of my countrymen, I had never taken the Nazis seriously. They were a tiny, though noisy, minority, mostly scum who saw the movement as their only opportunity to gain power and prestige. Even Hitler was hard to take seriously; he was so obviously crazy.

Yet last night, I had been walking through the Karlsplatz, when I saw a hoard of Nazi thugs, drawn into the streets by the announcement of Schuschnigg's capitulation, swarming through the streets in a frenzy, locking arms, screaming over and over again: "Sieg Heil! Sieg Heil! Hang Schuschnigg!" And the police, astonishingly, did nothing. They even seemed to enjoy it.

At the table next to me, a woman was telling her friends about the Chancellor's speech. She repeated his final words, her voice breaking: "So I take leave of the Austrian people with a German note of farewell, uttered from the depth of my heart: God protect Austria!"

A mocking voice inside my head recalled the stirring

6

cry of the same Chancellor only a few months ago: "Red-White-Red until we're dead." Now the red and white flag of Austria was to be replaced by the swastika.

I took off my glasses and wiped them against my faded brown slacks as I considered my situation. I was an 18-year-old law student. I was Jewish. I had been an active, card-carrying member of the Social Democratic party since I was twelve, since the day 17,000 Austrian troops fired into Viennese workers' flats, killing 1,000 people and wounding four times that many. More than once I had seen government troops wade into a crowd of unarmed socialist demonstrators, slashing indiscriminately with their sabers. As the country's Christian Democratic government became more and more dictatorial, I became increasingly disillusioned with my country. But I knew that the still relatively mild dictatorship under which we now lived would be much worse with the Germans in control, especially for a Jewish socialist.

A socialist *snob*, I could hear my father correct me. He was right. I embraced the political philosophy of the left and sympathized with the working class, but enjoyed the luxuries and advantages my industrialist father's wealth brought me. We had become increasingly alienated. I accused him of being a member of the oppressor class at the same time that I spent his money extravagantly.

My thoughts were interrupted by a tap on the shoulder. I was next in line for the telephone. I stepped inside the booth and dialed the number of the celluloid factory where my father had his main office, directing the operations of five factories. When the secretary answered, I blurted, "I want to talk to my father."

Normally he didn't like being interrupted by calls from the family, and I was accustomed to holding the line while he finished the business at hand. Today, however, there was no delay. He picked up the phone immediately.

Again I didn't waste time on social amenities. "Have you heard?" I asked.

"I know. Leave."

"Leave?"

"Don't go home. They'll be waiting for you. Just head south, to the border."

His words weren't making sense. "Who, they?" I asked stupidly.

My father exploded. "They! Go!" he bellowed. He hesitated and his voice softened. "Erich, let us know where you are whenever you can."

My mind still couldn't grasp what he was saying. "I don't have any money. I don't have a passport. I don't have any clothes. How can I go?"

"GO!" the voice of paternal authority boomed. There was a click as he slammed down the phone.

I walked slowly out of the booth. A fellow student walked up to me and tried to start a conversation, but I brushed past him and walked into the raw March weather, pulled my heavy sweater around me, and headed automatically toward University Hall, where I had parked my car when I arrived for classes that morning.

The car was a beauty, a light green 1938 Auburn-Cord convertible, with gleaming wood dashboard, dark green leather upholstery, and all the latest gadgets. I jumped in, started the motor and drove out of the lot. I'd driven several blocks before I thought about where I was going. My eyes glanced at the gas gauge; it registered empty. Instinctively, I turned the corner and headed back to the neighborhood garage, only a block from home. The streets were empty and eerily quiet.

As I pulled up to the gas pump at the garage, the attendant looked at me strangely. I asked him to fill the tank and walked into the garage looking for Karl, the owner, who was a friend of mine and had always serviced the family's cars.

Trying to keep my voice casual, I told Karl I was late for an appointment and had inadvertently left home without any money. Could he lend me any? Before I could finish the sentence, he asked me how much I needed.

"How much do you have?" I asked.

"Four hundred shillings. Here take it."

That was almost one hundred dollars, and I offered to sign a receipt, but Karl just shoved the money at me. "Just take it and go. Go."

Karl was as insistent as my father. Alarmed, I hurried back to the car, and drove to the end of the curved driveway. I stopped at the curb. Down the street to the right I could see my house, Number Seven Esteplatz, a massive stone building. The curtains were drawn in our first floor apartment. On the sidewalk in front I saw men in black shirts with Nazi armbands. With a chill, I recognized the uniforms of the dreaded German SS, which I had seen before only in movie newsreels and magazines.

I turned the wheel sharply to the left, away from the home where I had lived for ten years, from my family—my father, my mother, and my younger sister Gertrude—and from my carefree life as a student. I turned into the Triester Strasse and drove south at a high speed, until Vienna was behind me.

The countryside seemed peaceful, as if people here were unaware that German tanks were rumbling across the border a few hundred miles to the northwest. The radio stations, now controlled by the Nazis, proclaimed that Austria had been saved from chaos. The Germans were putting a stop to the bloody Communist riots in Vienna. Hitler was on his way to his native land to receive the adoration of the grateful Austrians. Soon a plebiscite would give the Austrians a chance to choose a new government.

My foot pressed harder on the accelerator. The landscape flew by in a blur, as I rushed to put more distance between me and the Germans. I was surprised by the thoroughness of the takeover. I wanted to get away fast. I wouldn't be safe in Mussolini's Italy either; if I were arrested I might be turned over to the Germans. I had no papers except a crumpled driver's license, my student identification card and, of course, my Social Democratic membership card. I tore the party card into small pieces and threw it in a stream. It could only get me in trouble.

I decided my best chance was to go to Genoa, which had previously been part of Austria. There were many Austrians and German-speaking people there, and I would be less conspicuous than in other parts of Italy. Hopefully I could beg, borrow, or steal passage on a ship to somewhere.

The farther I drove, the more my panic subsided, giving way to my natural optimism. I became confident that I could get by on my wits and boundless charm. I was already looking forward to the adventures that lay ahead of me. Although I was sorry to leave my family, I had always been restless, feeling smothered by my mother and hampered by my strict father. As a boy, I rebelled by sneaking out in the middle of the night to joy ride on the trolley cars. In later years, I joined the turbulent street demonstrations that were common in that period.

I had always dreamed of travel, of escaping to lands where men were free, much freer than in autocratic Austria. I would lock myself in my father's study, listening to records and poring through travel books. My favorite was a book on the Amazon. I was fascinated by the wild jungle, the unpopulated wilderness. Now I was free to travel, no longer tied to my studies, to the grim instructors who demanded perfection, to the stifling protection of my family, to a predetermined future as a pale-skinned businessman chained to a desk, balancing the accounts and driving an army of oppressed employees.

Toward evening I approached the Italian border, which was marked by a small station alongside the winding road through the mountains. I couldn't see any custom officials or Austrian troops, only an SA stormtrooper, who was leaning against the hood of a car stopped at the stations; his flashlight was trained on the driver's papers. I knew if I stopped here, I was lost. The car ahead of me was waved on. I drove up to the hut slowly, then punched the accelerator and roared past the startled SA guard. His shouts were echoed by the Italian officials on the other side of the border, as I disappeared around the curve.

At the first opportunity, I turned off the main highway onto a dirt road and wandered through the countryside, looking into the rear view mirror, expecting to see pursuers. There were none. Finally, exhausted, I pulled the car into a meadow and fell asleep.

*   *   *

The next morning I woke at sunrise, with a stiff neck and an empty stomach that growled angrily. I looked out on a meadow where blades of grass were forcing their way through patches of snow. In the distance towered jagged, snow-covered mountain peaks. Feeling more confident after a night's sleep, I headed down the narrow road to a farmer's chalet. The farmer invited me to join his family at a breakfast of goat's milk, cheese, and thick-sliced brown bread. Like most of the farmers in this area, the parents spoke German and were glad to offer their hospitality to a wandering student.

11

It was easy to forget that I wasn't just a schoolboy on a lark, as I drove through the narrow, dirt-covered roads, past small chalets nestled at the edge of ice-blue lakes that reflected the magnificent mountains towering above. With Karl's money, I was able to buy gas and find meals and lodging with peasant families. When necessary, my fractured Italian seemed to be understood. I stuck to the side roads to avoid any run-ins with the Italian military or police, so the trip took almost four days.

The radio kept me informed about what was happening in Austria. I heard about Hitler's triumphant arrival in Vienna and listened in vain for retaliation by other European countries. From the Swiss radio stations I learned that Himmler's SS troops were arresting thousands of "unreliables" throughout Austria. This unreliable was suddenly glad he had left.

It was night when I reached the outskirts of Genoa; I pulled off the road and slept in the car, not wanting to take any risks so close to my destination. The next morning I drove into Genoa, around the hairpin curves that hugged the rocky coastline and down the narrow cobblestone street to the harbor. There was only one large ship in port, an impressive Italian ocean liner, the *Conte Grande*. A few inquiries confirmed that this was the only ship leaving port soon. Its destination: South America.

"That's for me," I thought, old photographs of the mighty Amazon flashing through my mind. Third-class passage to Rio de Janeiro was $300. I turned from the ticket office and cast a sad look at the Cord, my ticket to South America.

From my previous travels, I knew that the seaport would have a lively red light district, where I would find not only a fence who would buy my car, no questions asked, but where I could hope to disappear until the ship departed. The underworld of pimps, whores, and thieves was always antagonistic to the government—whether democratic or fascist. I could be fairly certain that they wouldn't turn me over to the police.

I parked my car in a dim alley near the docks and walked into the seediest bar on the block. After a few hours of wandering from bar to bar, sipping beer and making small talk with the bartenders and other customers, someone directed me to a slim, dapper-looking man sitting at a corner table. Luckily, the fence spoke German and after about fifteen minutes of haggling, we settled on a price: 40,000 lire, about $500. That was only about a tenth of what the car was worth, but I wasn't in a position to strike a hard bargain. At least I would have money for the ticket and a few necessities, plus a little money to start my new life. A half hour later I had the money in my pocket and watched sadly as the Italian drove off in my car.

My next problem was to find someplace to stay for four nights until the ship left. I knew that hotels registered all guests and would report any foreigners without proper papers to the police. I continued my rounds of the waterfront bars, and by late evening, I had been taken under the wing of a German prostitute named Carla, a cheerful dumpling who took pity on my sad story. Her pimp was out of town for a few days, and she offered to take me in.

Carla fussed over me like a mother hen, taking time between her busy evenings to initiate a naive student into some heretofore undreamed of sexual escapades. She also stuffed me with a hearty German dinner and washed my one set of clothes. The next day, feeling like a new man, I paid a visit to the Brazilian consulate to inquire about a visa. Playing the rich playboy, I told the kindly gray-haired attaché to whom I was referred that I was a student who wished to sail to Brazil, tour the country, and perhaps take a jungle safari.

13

The attaché's sleepy eyes roamed over me as I told my story. Quickly judging the true situation, he asked if I had a passport. Well, no, I didn't—just my student card; it was a sudden whim, this desire to travel to South America. He nodded sympathetically at this flimsy story. A half hour later I was leaving the building with an entry permit in hand. I couldn't believe my good fortune. Of course, it had cost me my remaining $200, since it was highly irregular to issue a visa without a passport, but I was on my way. I held the precious white card up to the sunlight, with its incomprehensible Portuguese text, my freshly inked fingerprints, and official-looking signatures on the dotted line.

I hurried to the travel agent's office to book passage on the *Conte Grande*. They asked if I had a visa, and I waved it in front of them proudly, not daring to let it out of my possession. In a few minutes, I possessed a third class ticket to Rio de Janeiro.

Four nerve-wracking days followed. I lolled around Carla's apartment by day and drifted through bars at night. The evening before the ship was due to leave, Carla told me her boyfriend was returning, so she bid me farewell and good luck. I was too keyed up to sleep, so I made the rounds of the bars until daybreak, then wandered among the fruit stands on the waterfront until it was finally time to board the *Conte Grande*.

Safely on deck, I paced nervously, sure that at the last minute police officials would run up the gangplank and haul me away. It had all been too easy so far. But my luck held. The ship steamed away on schedule, and I was on my way to the land of my dreams. Once the ship was well under way, I looked up the chief purser. Counting on my youth and charm, I confessed the truth: that I had just escaped from Vienna, had no luggage, no passport, and very little money. Once I was in Rio de Janeiro, I planned to look up some wealthy friends of my family, who had emigrated there and owned a large bookstore.

The purser, whose name was Luigi, talked to me for a while, sizing me up carefully as he stroked his pencil-thin mustache. I must have appealed to his fatherly instincts, because he ended our conversation by telling me, "Don't worry, son. I'll see you get there safely. I'll put you in a third-class cabin with some fellows about your age. They won't care if you have luggage or not. And I'll see that you get the essentials. If you need anything else while you're on board, just let me know."

The cabin to which he assigned me was cramped and dim, but a suite wouldn't have pleased me any more. True to his word, he had a package delivered to me containing a toothbrush, toothpaste, razor, soap, and a miscellaneous assortment of clean underwear.

Elated by my easy escape, I enjoyed the ocean cruise as if it were a well-deserved vacation. Luigi introduced me to several other officers who also befriended me, giving me a few extra pairs of white slacks and shirts and a battered pair of tennis shoes. My meals were included as part of the fare, but the officers usually invited me to eat with them in their mess, where the food was excellent. I spent the long hours of the ocean voyage playing *bellot*, a French card game that I had learned in the coffeehouses. When we crossed the Equator, I received the traditional baptism in the small basin reserved for first crossings.

The two weeks passed quickly, and I was refreshed, suntanned, and thoroughly cocky by the time the ship steamed into the beautiful harbor of Rio de Janeiro. I leaned over the railing, thrilled with my first glimpse of the gleaming Brazilian city, with its arcing white beach, modern buildings, and mountain peaks. I lined up eagerly with the rest of the passengers, clutching my entry permit in my hand, my ticket to a new life in Brazil.

At last my turn came, and the immigration official

took the permit without looking at me. As he studied it, his eyes narrowed. His eyes met mine, and he gave me a quick once-over. "Where did you get this? Did you draw it up yourself, or did some charlatan sell it to you? Let me see your passport!"

I stood dumb, staring back at him in disbelief. Luigi, who had been keeping an eye on me, rushed up to help. Acting as an interpreter, he explained to me that my entry permit was invalid, lacking the necessary stamps and proper signatures. Arguing heatedly with the customs man, he tried to convince him to let me enter the country. The customs official wouldn't budge. He just shook his head firmly, handed back the permit, and motioned for the next passenger.

The purser explained that, according to international law, the ship was required to take me along to the next port. "The company might not like it," he said, "but we can't just throw you into the sea. Don't worry. We'll think of something. I'll do what I can at Santos."

My spirits sank to a new low as we pulled away from the glittering Rio and headed back out to sea. At Santos, the coffee port, the scene was repeated, with an equally unyielding customs official. At least, I thought with grim resolve, if I had to return to Genoa, I would be able to strangle the kindly, gray-haired attaché in Genoa who had robbed me of $200.

At the ship's next two stops, Buenos Aires and Montevideo, the officials refused to even look at my Brazilian entry permit. The ship began its return trip; at our second stop in Montevideo, Luigi took me aside.

"Look Erich, you're going to be in trouble if you try to disembark at Santos or Rio; Brazil immigration is too tough. And after Brazil, our next stop is Africa. They'll pick you off the ship there and ship you back to Austria. Your last chance to disembark illegally is in Montevideo. Customs are a little more relaxed there and once you're

16

in the country, they won't kick you out." He burst out laughing, and I looked at him as if he were crazy. "Cheer up, at least you don't have to worry about smuggling off your luggage!"

That evening the purser and the crew members who had become my friends met me near my cabin. They were dressed in their casual, civilian clothes ready to head out for a night on the town. I was dressed in the cast-off white pants and shirt they had given me. They gathered around me, and, as they chattered in Italian and I said as little as possible, we sauntered down the ramp, past the customs official on duty. He smiled and nodded, recognizing the purser. Assuming we were all members of the crew, he waved us through the gate.

That night we celebrated in almost every bar in town, toasting liberally my safe arrival in South America.

As the crew started back to their ship, Luigi took me aside and suggested that I go directly to the Salvation Army mission. "They'll give you a solid meal and they won't ask any questions. If anyone does ask, just say you jumped ship."

I followed his directions and was greeted cheerily by a plump matron who fed me a thick, bland stew and led me into a large dormitory room, filled with Army cots upon which slept ragged men, some snoring loudly. I slept soundly during my first night in this new land, leaving tomorrow's problems to tomorrow.

2

By noon the next day I had landed my first job in South America. Not knowing any Spanish, I bought a copy of the *Buenos Aires Herald*, the only English-language newspaper serving the River Plate region. The want ads included a job for a time study man at the Swift meatpacking plant in La Plata, Argentina. Having no idea what a time study man did, I applied to the Swift office in Montevideo and was hired immediately. Evidently, well-educated young men who spoke English and were willing to move to the sleepy provincial capital of La Plata, about fifty miles south of Buenos Aires, were not easy to find.

Armed with a Swift employee identity card, a valuable piece of paper that allowed me to travel freely between Argentina and Uruguay, I left Montevideo on the overnight ferry that traversed the 120-mile stretch of the muddy Rio de La Plata between Montevideo and Buenos Aires. I was surprised that South America, at least this part of it, looked so much like Europe. The people were almost all of European descent, and even the trees were European imports. It wasn't the jungle my father's travel books had portrayed.

For eight months I worked at the Swift factory, diligently timing the movements of factory workers so

18

that management could evaluate their productivity. Since my Spanish was barely adequate, I spent most of my free time with the English and Americans, often playing bridge at the Swift company club.

I picked up the intricacies of time study and was soon making recommendations for improving the worker's productivity to my boss, whose name was Martin C. Martin. When Martin was transferred back to the United States, he recommended that I be given his job. The central office in Chicago routinely asked that my papers and job file be sent to the head office. Unfortunately, I had no papers to submit. The next morning I was called to the general manager's office to explain. He was shocked when I admitted that I did not have any papers, tongue-lashed me for cheating the company, and fired me.

I was surprised at the company's reaction, since no one had ever asked about my papers, but I left with few regrets. I was feeling more at home in South America, had mastered elementary Spanish, and had saved some money. In the confusion, I managed to hold onto my Swift identity card, which I used to return to Montevideo.

Even in the few months that I had been in South America, I knew that Uruguay was a country more congenial to my personality than Argentina. The two sister republics reminded me of Germany and Austria—the Argentine more hurried, cold, and severe than the more funloving Uruguayan. Within a few months of my return, I felt completely at home in the small but prosperous country. Montevideo, home to almost half the country's population, was a charming mixture of stately old Spanish colonial buildings and modern low-rise offices and apartment buildings lining narrow streets. The city itself jutted into the River Plate on a narrow peninsula, while to the northeast stretched miles of white, sandy beaches. An Argentine who joined me at the rail as we sailed into the harbor explained that according to legend the city was given its name by a Portuguese sailor, who upon spying the hill that guards the harbor cried, "Monte vejo eu!" ("I see a mountain!")

The Uruguayans were more democratically inclined than most South Americans and had instituted many liberal social programs similar to the New Deal reforms in the United States. Uruguayans enjoyed life to the fullest—savoring fine meals, long afternoons at the beach, and leisurely strolls through the city's beautiful parks.

It was in Montevideo that I began slowly to make friends among the South Americans as well as among the European and American communities. Before long, my Spanish had improved greatly, and I began to relax and enjoy life like a Uruguayan. I was not able to find a job, but I soon was making a living.

During this period, floods of homeless people were arriving in Montevideo each week from a Europe threatened by Hitler's expansionary aims. Most of them had had to leave their property behind and were anxious to sell the few luxury items, like cameras and jewelry, that they had managed to bring with them.

I became friends with several of these new immigrants who asked me to help them find buyers for their possessions. Through my connections at the Swift country club which I frequented in Montevideo, I was able to find buyers who were eager to avoid the heavy duties imposed on European imports. Word spread among the immigrants that I could get higher prices for their merchandise than they could get elsewhere, and I was soon conducting a brisk trade, making money by charging a ten percent commission.

When I earned enough to live on for several weeks, I relaxed and enjoyed myself until my money ran out again. Living in a rented house in the suburbs with two other bachelors, one a British bank manager and the other an assistant manager of an insurance company, I spent my spare time collecting new friends. It was easy to make dates with working girls, who were not chaperoned like the upper-class South American women. Often I met my roommates after work with our car full of girls. During the winter months we frequently entertained at home, moving our parties to the beach during the long summer weekends.

Despite my carefree life, I continued to worry about my family, with whom I had had no contact. My letters had been neither answered nor returned. From the refugees, I learned of the events that had taken place in Austria since the invasion. In the first weeks after the takeover, the Germans had arrested 78,000 people, and there were rumors that they were already constructing a concentration camp in Austria for political prisoners and Jews.

Hitler had quickly unleashed the SA and SS on the Austrian Jews. As stormtroopers stood guard and crowds of Austrians stood by and jeered, Jews were forced to scrub sidewalks and gutters and clean public latrines and SA and SS barrack toilets. I could not imagine that, with my father's connections, my family had been affected, nor could I picture my gentle, party-loving mother being forced to scrub toilets in her beautifully tailored dresses. Years later I was to learn that she was one of those humiliated in this way. My father's business was expropriated, and our family chauffeur was named as the new manager.

The immigrants also reported that their homes had been ransacked and their possessions seized. Businessmen had been forced to sell their firms at rock-bottom prices. A special SS agency, the Office for Jewish Emigration, had been established to sell permits to Jews wishing to leave. The administrator was a native of Linz named Karl Adolf Eichmann. Eichmann was a man I would hear of again, nearly twenty years later.

During these same months, in the summer of 1939, the newspapers and radio reported the inexorable march toward war: Hitler's threats and ultimatums, the ominous troop movements, the British and French leaders' desperate appeals for peace. As Czechoslovakia fell and Hitler moved on to Poland, I realized that war was inevitable, that Hitler would never be stopped except by armed force.

On September 1, 1939, the Germans marched into Poland, and the Allies finally had enough of appeasement. Two days later, Britain declared war on Germany. Although most South Americans worried about interruption of their trade with both sides in the conflict, the war itself was viewed as a European problem. As an Austrian and a victim of Hitler's aggression, I couldn't stand on the sidelines. On the day Britain declared war, I hurried to their embassy to volunteer for the fight.

There was a large group of people lined up in front of the high iron gates—British subjects, South American and European idealists, and even some mercenaries itching for a fight. When my turn came, a young British officer asked me why I had come. I want to fight Hitler, I replied, explaining my background. The officer appeared only mildly interested, until I mentioned that I had studied languages at the University of Vienna.

"How many languages do you speak?" he asked, his pen poised above the paper on the desk in front of him.

"German, of course, English and French fluently, Spanish adequately, plus some Italian. Languages have always come easily to me."

"Good, good," the officer nodded. "Come back in a few days. We may be able to use you."

I returned several times during the next few days,

eager to enlist, but in the general confusion no one seemed to know what to do with me. Finally someone explained that it would be too much trouble to ship me to England for training as a soldier; they had plenty of soldiers. But if I was willing to serve without pay as a messenger and translator, my services might be needed.

Soon I was carrying messages between the British and American and French embassies. As I made friends among the embassy staff, they began to trust me with slightly more important tasks. I began making daily reports on the attitudes of various ethnic groups in Montevideo. Because of my linguistic ability, I was asked to circulate among the German-speaking community and among the "natives" and report on their attitudes about the war. Surprisingly, very few British embassy officials spoke Spanish and even fewer fraternized with anyone but other Englishmen and Americans. In this early phase of the war, I and a few others like me served as the communications link between the British and the Uruguayans. Despite their separation from the people, both the British and the Germans realized the importance of South America, with its valuable exports of beef, tin, petroleum, wheat, and other raw materials.

The first three months of the war I was little more than an errand boy, but I appreciated the chance to be a part of the war effort, in even this small way. Then in December, there came a chance to prove my worth to the British; it was an event that was to change the course of the war in Uruguay and my future.

The excitement began on a warm summer night, December 13, 1939. I was dining late in the evening with one of my girlfriends in the outdoor restaurant in the middle of Parque Rodó, a beautiful downtown park. We sat at one of the secluded tables, surrounded by greenery. The lights strung overhead swayed in the cool evening breeze and romantic music from the radio drifted

23

through the park. We sipped our wine after a delicious meal of *parrillada*, a mixture of grilled meats and sausage that is a Uruguayan specialty.

Suddenly, an announcer broke into the music. In an excited voice, he announced that three British ships had attacked the German pocket battleship, the *Graf Spee*, about 400 miles off the coast of Uruguay. The wounded German ship was said to be heading for the port of Montevideo.

We downed the last of the wine, paid the bill, and raced for the harbor. As we were driving toward the quay, the lights of Montevideo were blacked out. At the harbor a huge crowd of people had already gathered and were chattering excitedly. Some people held portable radios up to their ears and shouted out the latest news bulletins as they were broadcast.

Shortly after midnight, a gasp went up from the crowd as the silhouette of the huge surface raider appeared on the horizon. I stood spellbound as the shadowy ship loomed larger and larger, wending its way through the darkened channel. Somehow it slipped into the only available docking space in the entire harbor. Like a ghost ship, the *Graf Spee* hugged the pier, silent and foreboding. Slowly, the crowd began to disperse, deciding that the excitement was over for the night. I too returned home, but spent a sleepless night. I could not stop wondering how the ship had maneuvered the narrow channel and managed to steer directly to the one empty berth. Did the crew have contact with someone on shore?

Over breakfast the next morning, I listened to the radio. By now there was information about the battle, which had been between the *Graf Spee* and three much smaller ships—two British cruisers, the *Ajax* and *Exeter*, and a New Zealand ship, the *Achilles*. The British, noting that in the past three months the *Graf Spee* had sunk nine

British cargo vessels carrying a total of 50,000 tons, praised the valor of their captains, whose ships had been greatly outgunned.

Behind the scenes, the Germans and British were fighting a furious tug-of-war over the Uruguayan government. According to international law, a ship could remain in a neutral port only 72 hours or be interned. The German ambassador, Dr. Otto Langmann, after personally assessing the damage, reported that it would be necessary to fly in technicians from Buenos Aires and asked for an extension of the time limit so that repairs could be made.

The British were in a quandry, hoping on one hand that the *Graf Spee* would either be interned for the duration of the war or stay long enough for British reinforcements to arrive. The *Achilles* had taken the wounded to the British base in the Falkland Islands, near the tip of South America; the *Ajax* and *Exter* were guarding the mouth of the River Plate, but could not hope to sink the *Graf Spee*. In their first encounter they had been lucky. Several larger British warships were steaming toward Montevideo, but it would take four or five days before they would arrive.

Hoping the *Graf Spee* would not realize that its enemy was powerless and escape, the British set up a smoke screen, demanding that the ship be allowed to remain in Montevideo for only 24 hours, citing the provisions of the Hague Convention, which stated that a belligerent ship could stay in a neutral port only 24 hours unless they needed more time to repair damage or wait out bad weather. The British contended the Germans could make their ship seaworthy in this amount of time. The damage was to the main gun turret, and repair to armaments was not allowed by the terms of the Convention.

The Uruguayans didn't want to offend either side,

but they were understandably nervous about the presence of the German ship in their capital. These fears were increased by the German's thinly-veiled threats that they might shell the harbor if not allowed to stay. Finally, on the evening of the 14th, Uruguay announced that the *Graf Spee* could remain 72 hours from the time of the announcement to make whatever repairs it could in that time.

The next day the Germans requested and received permission to bury *Graf Spee* sailors killed during the battle. On Friday afternoon, December 15, I stood in a crowd lining the *Avenida 18 de Julio*, Montevideo's main street, named for Uruguay's Independence Day. Behind a naval brass band came a procession of sailors carrying the coffins of the 37 men killed in action. As they passed, a few people nearby gave the Nazi salute. I was surprised at the strain shown by the pallbearers; they were sweating profusely and their backs were bent. It was a warm day, but not that warm.

At the cemetery just outside the city, the cortege came to a halt; the coffins were lined up in neat rows in front of Captain Langsdorff, who was dressed in his formal white uniform. His face was drawn, his voice strained as he gave the funeral oration. When he finished the coffins were lowered into the graves, while the German ambassador and other Reich dignitaries came to attention and raised their right arms in the Nazi salute. Langsdorff, looking grim, gripped the hilt of his sword and slowly raised his right hand to the peak of his cap in the traditional naval salute. The deviation did not go unnoticed, and rumors spread that the captain, although a member of the Nazi party, had become disillusioned with Hitler since the Führer's pact with Stalin.

After the funeral, I dropped by the British embassy to give my daily report, mentioning the Nazi salutes I had noticed from the onlookers and my belief that the ship must have had communication with people on shore. In discussing the day's events with the officer to whom I reported, I began to suspect even more strongly that the Germans had a good idea of what the British were proposing to the Uruguayan government; they had seemed to stay one jump ahead. I wondered aloud if perhaps this also explained how the Germans knew the port conditions so well, too. Perhaps they had broken the British diplomatic code.

This didn't seem to surprise the officer, so I went one step further and told him about my idea for dealing with the *Graf Spee*. I suggested sending a message in code reporting the imminent arrival of British warships in the River Plate, ships sent to capture the German battleship. If the Germans were indeed monitoring the coded messages, they might panic and leave before the 72-hour deadline.

Although I was not aware that the British actually preferred that the *Graf Spee* remain in Montevideo's harbor, the method I suggested hit a responsive chord. It was an indication of the disorganization and amateur nature of intelligence operations at this early stage of the war that a few hours later I was called in again. To my surprise I was taken into an office to meet with Mr. Griffiths, the chargé d'affaire. In their confusion the British were ready to listen to any plan, even if it came from a 19-year-old messenger boy.

I reiterated my idea and then sat quietly as Griffiths and the military attaché who had joined us discussed its feasibility.

They were interested in any ruse that would help convince the Germans that British ships were waiting to pounce on the *Graf Spee* should she decide to leave. After a great deal of discussion, it was decided to send a message from the British embassy in Montevideo to the British embassy in Buenos Aires reporting that the French ship *Richelieu* and the British aircraft carrier *Ark Royal* were in position outside the harbor. Trusted informants were asked to spread this misinformation among the populace, especially in the local German community.

I left the embassy dazed, swelled with pride that I had participated in the inner councils of British intelligence. With a new sense of exaggerated importance, I hurried down to the harbor, straight to the *Graf Spee*. Some Germans were milling around the pier, shouting up to the sailors. I struck up a conversation with them, posing as a German, hoping to learn something more that would be useful to the British.

On the evening of December 17, everyone waited nervously to see whether the *Graf Spee* would abide by the 72-hour deadline, which would expire at eight p.m. I went to the British embassy and joined several staff members on the roof, where we could get an unobstructed view of the harbor. There was a stiff wind, which angrily whipped the waters of the River Plate.

A crowd later estimated at over three-quarters of a million people lined the shore; hoards of newspaper reporters and radio commentators were on hand to provide first-hand accounts for the world's major news services. During the afternoon there were reports of movement of men between the *Graf Spee* and the *Tacoma*, a German merchant ship that had been interned in Montevideo when war was declared. At five p.m., Nazi banners were run up the foremast and mainmast, and sailors scurried to raise the anchor. Slowly the *Graf Spee* began to move out through the channel, seemingly headed southeast. My heart sunk; evidently the Germans hadn't fallen for our tricks; they were going to escape.

About fifteen minutes later, the *Tacoma* also sailed out of the harbor. None of us could believe that the Germans would defy the Uruguayan government by allowing the interned ship to leave Montevideo. As the

Graf Spee neared the mouth of the channel, she suddenly swung around to starboard. One of the officers said she now appeared to be facing west, and, as if to confirm this opinion, the battleship moved toward the pontoon that marked the entrance to the Buenos Aires channel.

It was becoming more difficult to see the ship clearly because the sun was setting behind it, obscuring the view. Someone thought they saw two smaller boats arrive from the west, and there seemed to be movement between the ships, but we couldn't tell what was happening.

At quarter to eight, the *Tacoma* started back toward the harbor. Now we were really confused. I turned to ask the man standing next to me what he thought was going on, when, just as the sun dipped below the horizon, my eye caught a brilliant flash of fire from the *Graf Spee*. A double explosion rumbled across the water toward us, and plumes of black smoke boiled up from the battleship. Another blast lifted the *Graf Spee* out of the water, then dropped her back, spewing flaming wreckage into the air and water. Before we could react, a third explosion blew off the main turret, and the great ship writhed like a wounded whale; vivid orange flames raced along the length of the ship.

Suddenly one of the officers broke the stunned silence with a whoop. "They fell for it! They scuttled the *Graf Spee*!" As the others began to comprehend what had happened, they began to shout, whistling and clapping each other on the back. The officer to whom I had initially suggested my plan wrung my hand and congratulated me. I was delirious; I had helped outwit the German Navy, tricking them into destroying one of their most valuable battleships to avoid its being captured by a phantom fleet.

The next day we learned that the *Graf Spee* crew had been transferred from the *Tacoma* onto two Argentine tugboats and a barge. Captain Langsdorff and a small scuttling party had set the charges, then transferred to the Argentine boats, too. The Germans believed that they would receive better treatment from the Argentine government, which was decidedly pro-German. The crew, however, was interned in the Naval Arsenal in Buenos Aires for the duration of the war, despite Langsdorff's attempts to free them. Failing to save his ship and his crew, Langsdorff laid out the Imperial German flag on his bed and shot himself.

3

The *Graf Spee* incident convinced the Uruguayan government to take seriously the rumors about the presence of a Nazi Fifth Column in their country. Several prominent citizens, including a university professor named Hugo Artucio, had reported that Germans in Uruguay were being pressured into cooperating with a Nazi party that was attempting to foster revolution. These persistent rumors had been brushed aside by the government until the *Graf Spee* affair suddenly brought the war closer to home.

During this same period, I had been trying to convince my friends at the British embassy that there was something suspicious about the abnormally heavy coffins of the *Graf Spee* crewmen. It was a mystery that had been nagging me ever since the day of the sailors' funeral.

Early in 1940 the British finally arranged for me to meet with Uruguay's national security police to see if they were interested in pursuing the matter. Although the police were alarmed, the government was not eager to offend the Germans by desecrating the graves of their war dead. After much discussion and tedious court proceedings, the police received authority to exhume one grave only to see if there was any substance to my suspicions.

On a gray, rainy morning, the police called me in to accompany them to the cemetery, undoubtedly so that I would be there to confront if the coffin contained only a corpse. The detail was carried out in secrecy, to avoid embarrassing the government if nothing was found. As we drove in through the cemetery gates, the captain in charge growled, "You better be right about these graves, Erdstein, or we're all going to look very foolish."

I didn't answer; we would know soon enough. But my confidence was fading, as I stood in the drizzle alongside the fresh gravesites. The captain selected one of the graves at random, and two of the cemetery groundskeepers dug in the wet mud, cursing softly. A winch was moved into position to raise the coffin to the surface. I nervously ground my shoe into the muck as they slowly pried open the lid.

I wasn't sure whether to look away or stare. I had never seen an exhumed body. Curiosity won, and I moved closer as they raised the lid and peered into the box. My heart stopped. Inside was a mound of guns—at least four machine guns and an assortment of hand guns, plus a supply of ammunition. There was a shout from the captain, who waved the wide-eyed groundsmen away. The other policemen surrounded me, clapping me on the back. I tried to appear suitably modest, disguising my shock at the sight of all those guns.

Subsequently, the other graves were exhumed; they too contained guns, not bodies. It was never discovered what the Germans had done with the corpses of the sailors killed in action. We could only assume that they must have buried them at sea before the *Graf Spee* reached Montevideo. The more urgent question now was: for whom were the guns intended?

Shortly after the discovery of the arms cache, in

May, 1940, the Uruguayan Congress appointed a special Senate Committee on Anti-National Activities. This committee had an executive arm charged with conducting a full investigation into Fifth Column activities. Because of my involvement in the arms case, I served as an unofficial liaison between this investigatory group and British intelligence. Because I was not a citizen of Uruguay, I could not be appointed to an official position.

I concentrated my search for Fifth Columnists at a café called the *Viejo Berlin* (Old Berlin), which I had already discovered in my work for the British was frequented by Germans and Uruguayans of German ancestry with Nazi sympathies. I became a regular at the café each evening, posing as an Austrian who was interested in National Socialism, but unsure about their programs and undecided about what side to take in the current conflict.

I was soon sought out by a group of men who tried to recruit me to the Nazi cause, appealing to my "Aryan" pride and to the inevitability of a German victory. Surely I would want to be on the winning side.

I smiled, appeared more naive than I was, chatted easily with the men, and nursed innumerable pitchers of beer. I was careful not to appear too eager for information, letting them work at convincing me and pretending to ignore much of their conversation. After weeks of this, I began to learn about the Nazi organization in Uruguay—the activities of groups like the Hitler Youth and the German Labor Front, the money and assistance given to the Nazis by German-owned businesses in Uruguay, and the plans Hitler had for South America. Slowly, my new friends lost their inhibitions about talking in front of me. I was accepted as one of the group.

I learned that if the Nazis had their way, Uruguay would become part of "Antarctic Germany," an agricultural colony of the Reich. According to the Germans, as

33

the Uruguayans began to appreciate the might of the German Reich and realize how much more efficient the Nazi regime would be than their own chaotic and corrupt democracy, they would rise and demand that Hitler serve as their Führer. The Nazis were spending a great deal of money in propoganda aimed at convincing the Uruguayans that their destiny belonged with Germany.

They talked of SA troops who trained in secret, ready to take over communication and police facilities. They bragged of men who were being trained as paratroopers to aid in a German invasion. They assured me the plans were detailed and ready to be implemented at a moment's notice.

Finally, after more than a month, I heard a name to connect with this vague boasting of domination and conquest. One of the group's regulars came in late in the evening, flushed with excitement. He had met one of the top leaders of the Uruguayan Nazi party, an impressive man he said.

"He said there would be important positions for men like me who were helping to realize the Führer's dreams in South America!" The nondescript shopkeeper glowed in anticipation of his bright future.

The next morning I hurried to the committee headquarters to report to my boss, Carlos Nogues, the head of the executive branch of the committee. Without delay, Nogues organized a special detail to raid the Nazi party leader's house.

This raid gave us the information we had been lacking. Although my friend had exaggerated the man's importance, we did find a notebook listing other Nazi party leaders. We interrogated him and were able to narrow down the list to the top officials. Immediately, we moved to arrest these men and capture whatever documents they had.

One of the most productive raids took place in Salto,

a small port city on the Uruguay River, which separated Uruguay and Argentina. Adolph Fuhrmann, a Salto photographer, was earmarked to become the head of the Gestapo in a Uruguayan puppet state. He was presently engaged in photographing all the key public buildings, military barracks, and port facilities in Uruguay to aid in a German invasion.

In his house were found documents outlining the Nazi plan for conquering Uruguay; correspondence between Fuhrmann and other Nazi officials; deeds for property that we later found out were adjacent to key army posts, police stations, railroad depots, and bridges; a file bulging with photographs of military targets; and information about Uruguay's troop dispositions which turned out to be amazingly accurate. Among the party documents was a circular stating that, upon the Nazi takeover, it would be "necessary to eliminate immediately all Jews, political leaders, and Free Masons."

On June 10, 1940, the plot was made public. The Uruguayans were shocked. They had had no idea of the threat to their independence and security. Most of them had not taken the Nazis or the war threat seriously. Now many people, including top government officials, feared that there would be a Nazi putsch. On June 19, the President issued a general mobilization order. The freedom-loving Uruguayans responded dramatically, hundreds of thousands lining up at the nearest government building to enroll as defense volunteers.

Then, inexplicably, the government wavered, releasing the Nazi leaders who had been arrested. Some said it had caved in under the heavy pressures brought to bear by powerful German commercial firms and by the German government. To further intimidate Uruguay, the Nazis instituted a criminal suit of slander against Professor Artucio, who had seriously damaged the Nazi propoganda efforts with his impassioned radio broad-

35

casts and public lectures. The move backfired; the suit was decided in favor of Artucio, and the next day, the Supreme Court of Uruguay ordered that the thirteen Nazi leaders be arrested a second time and charged with high treason against the state. We had kept an eye on these men, and once again moved swiftly to apprehend them. Only Julius Dalldorff, a press attaché at the German embassy in Montevideo, was able to escape under the protection of his diplomatic immunity.

*   *   *

Although the Uruguayan government had gained control over the Nazis in their own country, they remained concerned about subversion of neighboring states. The captured Nazi party documents showed that the organization operated throughout South America. Uruguay felt it had to maintain its official policy of neutrality, but the government secretly approached the British and Americans with a plan to work together to halt German interference in other Latin American countries. Great Britain and the U.S. enthusiastically endorsed the idea, since by 1941 the American government was as interested as Britain was in South America's political leanings and in its valuable natural resources.

Because of my work with the British and Uruguayans, I became a liaison between the Uruguayans and the other members of this loosely-organized alliance. My role in the *Graf Spee* incident, followed by the discovery of the arms cache, had established my reputation for analyzing political situations, ferreting out information, and working independently. I became a roving troubleshooter, sent wherever there was a need to get to the bottom of Nazi intrigue, to counter German propoganda efforts, or to sound out local opinion. Although I worked primarily for the Uruguayans, I was often loaned to the

British and Americans, and usually my expenses were covered by the nearest paymaster.

My first assignment outside Uruguay was early in 1941, when I was sent to the territory of Misiones in northern Argentina at the request of the British Trade Commission in Montevideo. The British firm of Liebig and Company was concerned about Nazi infiltration among the workers on their large *estancias*, or cattle ranches, in this region. The British asked me to visit the ranches, investigate Nazi activity, and report back on the political situation and on the loyalty of their managers. This remote area had a reputation for being hostile to foreigners, and I was assigned two guards carrying Mausers, who accompanied me when I traveled on horseback across the desolate stretches of plains between the ranches. The law allowed guns if carried in plain view, so I carried a .38 tucked in my belt, plus the .32 stuck down my boot.

Thanks to the bodyguards, I didn't run into any violence, but during my travels, I met someone who would prove to be worse trouble. In the small town of Apostoles, I was introduced to an Argentine school-teacher named Laura Silvera. Although I usually made it a practice to avoid the upper class South American girls because they were so well-chaperoned and chaste, I made an exception with Laura. Her parents were far away in Buenos Aires, and she was enjoying a newfound freedom. She was pleasant company in this remote part of the world. I had become spoiled by the abundance of pretty young women in Montevideo, and was lonely. Laura was beautiful with smooth, olive skin and large green eyes. In this small provincial town, I seemed a sophisticated, suave European. Laura was entranced, quit her job in Apostoles and followed me to Posadas, my headquarters between trips to the ranches.

Immediately after I submitted my report to the British Trade Commission, the American counsulate requested my services in the same area, just over the border in Paraguay. The United States was interested in purchasing *ramio*, a fiber needed to make parachutes, from a Dutch plantation deep in the semi-tropical forest. The Germans also had been bartering for the company's crop, and the U.S. authorized me to offer more money than the Germans if necessary.

I moved, with Laura in tow, to Encarnación, the provincial capital. From there I made several trips to the plantation, sleeping in a primitive hut on a cot under mosquito netting, attended by several servant girls. Because of my experience with Swift's, it was decided to send me as a technical advisor. My suggestions for improving the farm's productivity were well-received by the plantation manager and made it easier for me to convince him that his firm's interests lay with the Allies.

He had been assured by German representatives in Paraguay that they were certain to win the war, and he would be smart to go with the winner. I pointed out that the United States would soon enter the war and that meant the Allies would ultimately win. I also convinced him that not only would the Americans offer more for his crop, but that it would be cheaper for him to ship it to the U.S. By the end of my stay, I had secured the crop for the Americans.

From Encarnación, I was sent in spring of 1941 to Asunción, the capital of Paraguay. Once again, Laura followed close on my heels, showing up at my hotel and moving in with me. I had been warned not to expect a return to civilization on the level of Montevideo. Paraguay was one of the poorest and most primitive South American countries, and no greater contrast with Uruguay could be found. There was a handful of rich and educated people; most Paraguayans lived in abject poverty. Paraguayan girls were old at twenty, many with several children by the time they were fourteen or fifteen years old. Boys the same age were serving in the military, patrolling the streets in bare feet and lugging World War I Mausers that were often as tall as they were.

Only three or four streets in the center of the city were paved. Down the hilly cobblestone and dirt streets rumbled donkey carts and noisy, broken-down trucks called *camiones*, which were used as buses during the war and always jammed with people standing in the back. Since there was no gasoline, they ran on *gasogeno*, fuel produced by carbon bricks burned in huge iron kettles mounted on the cab of the trucks. I made the mistake of taking one downtown one evening, when I was dressed in my best white suit; I arrived at the casino covered with fine, black soot.

Despite the glaring poverty and unrelenting tropical heat, Asunción had a certain tropical charm, with its flaming orange *flamboyant* trees and vivid sunsets reflected in the Paraguay River. The people were easy-going and good-humored. Office hours ran from eight to eleven to avoid the sweltering afternoon sun. Although the nights were bitterly cold, as soon as the sun rose the temperature shot into the nineties.

Asunción was the spy center of South America, situated as it is near the center of the continent—with Brazil on the northeast, Argentina on the southwest, Bolivia on the northwest, and Chile not far to the west. The city in 1942 was swarming with British, German, American, and South American political operatives. Paraguay, like the other South American countries, was neutral, and any political activity by foreigners was illegal. Everyone just winked at the law and continued with his clandestine activities.

The country's president was a Guarani Indian named General Morinigo, who strutted around like a brightly-plumed parrot in his starched white uniform, weighed down by enormous gold epaulettes, shiny medals, and gaudy sashes that he draped across his chest. Less amusing to those of us on the Allied side were his pro-Nazi views. It was hard to influence Morinigo, since he spoke halting Spanish, preferring his native Guarani dialect. The Indian influence was still strong in Paraguay; it was the only country in which the natives had absorbed the invading Spaniards instead of the other way around.

Despite the miserable climate, I enjoyed life in Asunción. All the intelligence people frequented the same two social clubs and angled for information over the gaming tables. I often played poker at a table with Heinrich Thomas, the manager of the Banco Germanico and a German spy; Commander Parker, officially the naval attaché at the American embassy but in reality the chief intelligence officer; and Fernandez Chavez, the vice-president of Paraguay, who was pro-Ally. I enjoyed needling Parker, whose cover was comical; Paraguay was the only land-locked South American country. The only semblance of a seaport was the harbor on the Paraguay River, which led into the Paraná River, and eventually, after 500 miles, to the Rio de la Plata and the ocean.

I became good friends, too, with Chavez, a charming sophisticate, who smiled condescendingly at Morinigo behind his back. Chavez was in love at the time with a beautiful dark-haired, blue-eyed woman named Noemi, who was later discovered to be a drug smuggler.

By fall of 1942 I had been in Asunción a year and a half, and my work was going well. I had organized a number of Pan-American cultural centers, which through their social activities and meetings helped win friends for the Americans among the young, well-educated Paraguayans. Through Chavez I also gained entrance to the elite social circles. I reported daily to the American embassy, which provided me with a modest expense allowance that I cashed at the Banco de la República for a suitcase full of inflated Paraguayan pesos.

My good spirits were boosted by news from two fronts. One was the announcement in December, 1941, of the United States's entry into the war, which convinced me that the Allies would eventually win. The other was more personal, information from the British that they had located my family and were arranging for them to emigrate to Buenos Aires. I had requested the help of the British in locating my parents before I left Uruguay, but had not dared get my hopes too high.

Although everything seemed to be proceeding smoothly, trouble was brewing behind my back. Laura had written her parents a letter telling them she was married and living in Asunción. Alarmed, her father contacted the military police and asked them to find her and return her to them.

The chief of police, a pro-Nazi of German descent named Fuster, sent a detective to locate Laura. With very little effort, he traced her to my hotel. She panicked as soon as he began questioning her, singing freely. She told him everything she knew about me and my clandestine activities. The incident provided Fuster, who already was aware of my work, with an excuse to rid himself of an American operative. The ouster was abrupt.

I was playing cards late one evening at the *Club Centenario* with Parker, Chavez, and the German bank manager when the club manager came to the table and told me I had a telephone call. I excused myself and followed him out to the lobby. There was Fuster, flanked by two burly policemen with .38's sticking out of their belts. Fuster suggested I accompany him. I had no gun on me and wasn't about to start a scene at the Club. I walked out into the black, chilly night with them, and they shoved me into a police car.

We drove in silence to the police headquarters while

41

I tried to think of a way to get out of whatever trouble I was in. When we arrived at the headquarters building, I was bundled inside and tossed into a cell. Despite my angry shouts and threats, I was left alone for several hours.

As I was trying to think of how to get word to Chavez or the Americans, Fuster returned with his two friends, unlocked the cell, and led me back to the car.

"Where are we going? What's this all about?" I demanded. "I am a foreign citizen. You have no right to treat me this way."

Fuster merely grunted and told me I was being asked to leave the country because of my spying activities. I glared at his broad back and told him if he would just call Vice-President Chavez, a friend of mine, I was sure this matter could be cleared up in no time. There was no answer.

A few minutes later, we arrived at the harbor. Now I was scared, feeling the weight of the two burly guards on either side of me. Fuster turned off the ignition. The harbor was dark and deserted, and I could hear the waves lapping against the pier. I was convinced now that they had brought me here to shoot me and dump me into the river.

As we left the car, I pivoted on one heel, lowered my head, and charged into the guard behind me, then turned to swing at Fuster. The second guard jumped out of the car and over it, gave me a karate chop on the back of the neck, and I crumpled to the ground. Before I could get to my feet, he kicked me in the small of the back.

The other guard, the fat one, picked himself up off the ground and, at Fuster's orders, yanked me back to my feet. He held my arm tightly against my back and jerked it up toward my neck whenever I started to make a move. We walked down to the end of the pier; in the black water

I could see a small patrol boat. The two policemen picked me up by my arms and stepped into the boat with me. One pushed me down flat on my stomach in the bottom of the boat, with his .38 pressed against the back of my neck. The other started the motor, and we pulled away from the pier, leaving Fuster. I waited until we had pulled far enough away from the pier so that we were out of Fuster's range, then tried again to rear up against the guard. I felt a sharp pain at the base of my skull.

When I came to, the motor was still purring, the water slapping against the sides of the boat. My head ached. I could barely see out of the boat, but we seemed to be headed downriver past several small villages where a few lights burned. I asked the guard why he hadn't killed me.

He laughed. "I'm sorry, Señor, not to accomodate you, but it seems you have some important friends. Chief Fuster felt it would be better for all concerned if you just left town, voluntarily."

Several hours passed, and just as the faint light of dawn pierced the thick underbrush on the left bank, we approached the outskirts of a town. My friends pulled ashore in a quiet bay and pulled me to my feet.

"Here you are, Señor Erdstein. Good luck to you." The policeman burst out laughing and his companion joined in as he pushed off, leaving me standing on the swampy riverbank, rubbing the back of my neck.

I stood watching the patrol boat back away, pivot, and head back upstream. I looked down at my soiled suit, brushed myself off, and tried to straighten my clothes and smooth down my hair. I felt my pockets, but remembered that everything had been taken from me at police headquarters. Once again, I was in a strange part of the world, without papers and without money.

I scrambled up the riverbank and onto a dirt road that seemed to lead into town. To quiet my rumbling stomach I tore off some fruit from a tree in a farmyard. Following my instincts, I wandered to the center of town, catching out of the corner of my eye a sign on the train station: Formosa. So that's where I was—Formosa, Argentina, a small frontier town a few miles south of the border with Paraguay. An ancient-looking black locomotive with ten passenger cars was standing at the station. As I approached the tracks, the train started slowly out of the station. I ran and jumped onto the stairs and ducked inside. I didn't know where it was going, but I wanted to get farther away from Paraguay.

Glancing down the corridor, I could see the conductor entering the next car, so I turned the other way, and ducked into the lavatory-dressing room. I locked myself in one of the stalls until I was sure he was gone. At every stop, I returned to the men's room, successfully eluding the conductor.

After about an hour we pulled into a prosperous-looking little town called Basobilbaso, where we were scheduled to make a two-hour stop. I hopped off the train, hoping to find some food.

As I walked down the street leading away from the station, I saw that the stores all bore Jewish names—Weinberg, Rosenblatt, Stein, Goldfarb. I walked into the first store, a clothing shop called Weinberg's, where a woman was stocking the shelves.

She straightened up, smoothing down her dress and starched white apron. I noticed that her face looked kind, with warm, brown eyes. I greeted her in Spanish and asked if Mr. Weinberg was in. She shook her head as she looked me over, taking in every detail of my rumpled appearance. He was expected shortly, however. She was his wife; could she help?

I smiled what I hoped was a shy, boyish smile. "I'm in a bind, Señora. I'm a Jewish refugee from Germany and I've been on the run since 1939. I don't have any papers.

44

so I can't hold a job. I've been kicked out of several countries. I was just expelled from Paraguay, and I have no money, nothing. I hitched a ride on the train this morning, and when it stopped here, I got off . . ."

Mrs. Weinberg listened sympathetically to my story, clucking her tongue and shaking her head. A few brown curls fell over her eyebrows, and she swept them back in place. When I paused, not sure what to say next, she broke into rapid Yiddish. I only spoke a few words of Yiddish, but I could make out the gist of her conversation. I knew that she had asked my name.

I answered in German, and still not sure how much I should reveal, I told her my name was David Stein.

"David, sit down here in the back, rest yourself, and I'll get you something to eat," she answered in German. "Mr. Weinberg will be here very soon. He'll be able to help you. He's a good man." She bustled me into the back room, pulled out a chair and gently pushed me into it. She left the room, returning a few minutes later with a mug filled with steaming coffee and several slices of thick rye bread spread with butter. I wolfed this down gratefully.

After a few minutes, a thin, pale man came in through the back door. Mrs. Weinberg grabbed his arm and, motioning toward me, poured out my sad story, again in Yiddish. Mr. Weinberg nodded sympathetically, pulling up a chair next to mine. "What can I do for you, boy?" he asked.

I told him I wanted to go to Salta. Friends of my family lived near there, and I thought they would take me in. Actually, I knew Salta was a major city, far away from Paraguay and near the border with Bolivia in case I needed to escape from Argentina. From there I could easily contact my superiors in Montevideo.

Mr. Weinberg's face lit up at the mention of Salta. "Salta? Where exactly do they live?"

45

"Oh, I don't know. Somewhere near there. I only know their name."

"What's their name?" Mr. Weinberg asked. I made up the most common name I could think of—Goldberg—and was relieved that he merely shook his head sadly. He didn't know any Goldbergs in Salta. If I only knew where they lived, he could check. But such a common name . . .

He recovered quickly and clapped me on the back. "Well, come on. We'll do what we can for you." He led me out to the street and walked with me from store to store, relating my story to the other merchants. With each retelling, my story grew progressively sadder. Tired and hungry, I began to feel sorrier and sorrier for the poor refugee boy, the archetype of the wandering Jew.

At each store, the shopkeepers contributed to my welfare, giving me pants at one, three shirts at another, a spare sports jacket and tie, socks and underwear, even some money for the trip. A luggage store owner gave me a handsome leather suitcase to hold my new belongings.

Mr. and Mrs. Weinberg added to the purse and escorted me to the train station, where they bought me a ticket to Salta—not first class, too ostentatious . . . not third class, too condescending—but a proper second class seat. The kindly couple bundled me onto the train and hugged me goodbye. Mrs. Weinberg had tears in her eyes, and I must confess I was so carried away by emotion and my good fortune, that I had tears in my own. As the train chugged out of the station, I sat staring at my new belongings and my "pot" of 2,000 pesos—almost $400.

4

In Salta, I checked into the city's finest hotel, signing the register Erico Martin, tourist. After a hot bath, a leisurely dinner in the hotel restaurant, and ten hours' sleep, I was a new man.

I placed a call the next morning from a pay telephone to Batlle Pacheco, the president of the Senate Committee in Montevideo. He was astounded to hear from me and learn I was in Salta.

"Erico! We heard you were arrested. How did you get out of jail? How did you get to Salta?"

"Oh, I swam down the river to Formosa and took a train," I joked. I explained what had happened to me and asked what he wanted me to do now. He told me to stay in Salta. I would be contacted in a few days.

While I waited, I played the tourist. Salta is a beautiful city, set on a plateau and surrounded by mountains. The air is clean, thin, and invigorating, and the people attractive. My hotel faced the central Plaza, which is dominated by a huge Colonial cathedral.

Three days after my call to Pacheco, an OSS courier (ironically, an Argentine of German descent named Winkler) came to my hotel room with an assignment. He told me I was to stay in Salta, which was the hometown of

47

Robustiano Patron Costa, the democratic-conservative candidate for the Presidency in the upcoming national elections. The Allies and the Uruguayans were interested in Costa's attitude about the war. I was to be their liaison, reporting on the various political parties' positions and investigating any Fifth Column activity.

I told Winkler I would need a cover. He was prepared; I was to pose as a representative of a cattle-breeding magazine, a publication printed in the United States as a front for intelligence activities. Winkler told me I would be receiving copies of the magazines, as well as identity papers under the name Erico Martin. About a week later, I received the papers and several hundred copies of the magazine, which I read cover to cover, becoming an instant expert on cattle-breeding.

To smooth my entrée into Salta's social circles, I made the acquaintance of Patron Costa's niece, Estela Torino Lopez. I sought her out at one of the evening "promenades" that took place on the main Plaza. In this courting ceremony, the young men walk in a circle around the young women. This gives the young people a chance to look one another over. If a man finds a woman that pleases him, he walks alongside her, still under the strict eyes of the chaperones, of course.

On that warm summer evening, Estela was dressed in a pale pink flowered dress with a high neckline and a white lace shawl that modestly covered her bare arms. I noted her square, blank face and thick legs, covered by incongruously heavy stockings for the weather.

The first evening, I caught Estela's eye and nodded. The next evening I took her aside for conversation. Soon I was invited to call at her parents' turreted stone mansion, which faced the Plaza, proudly displaying the Torino family coat of arms on the door.

Estela was a talented musician and during my chaperoned dates with her, we often played piano duets.

The extent of our passion was to press our knees together as we sat side by side on the piano bench. Luckily, Estela was more interested in religion than sex. She was the president of the Catholic Action Council for all of Argentina. Because of her involvement in this group, she was visited almost daily by the Archbishop of Salta, Monseñor Roberto Tavella, who also happened to be Patron Costa's closest friend and a power behind the throne in local politics.

Tavella was a sophisticated, witty man who lived in luxury and kept several mistresses discreetly occupied. With his and Estela's help, I was accepted readily into Salta's social circles. By keeping my ears open and instigating political discussions as often as possible, I picked up valuable information and a good picture of the political structure. I found that Costa and his party were strongly pro-Ally, but that there was a military coalition that was extremely right wing and closely connected with German intelligence. The Argentine military had been trained by German advisors from 1915 to 1940, and its officers had been strongly influenced by the Nazi ideology.

Since there was no American representative in Salta, I relayed my information by telephone, mail, or courier. When I had information I thought the Allies or the Uruguayan government should know, I called the secret OSS number in Buenos Aires or contacted someone at the Senate Committee in Montevideo. If the message was complicated, I would ask that they have a courier contact me. The couriers, who were changed frequently, came to my hotel room or called me to arrange a meeting at a public place. Now and then I sent information through the mail, often by a picture post card. These were written in a very simple code, which I had memorized.

I was not a spy investigating military secrets; the information I was gathering consisted of names and political views—public knowledge for anyone who wanted to ask a few questions. I was valuable because the British and Americans generally did not speak the language and needed someone they could trust to maintain contact with the people. The Uruguayans had a small foreign service staff and also needed extra ears.

The police watched me constantly during my stay in Salta, suspicious of my sudden transition from tourist to magazine representative. They only called me in once, however, early in 1943. I stuck to my cover story, offering little information that wasn't specifically requested and taking care to point out that I was staying in Salta because I had fallen in love with Estela Torino Lopez. The mention of the prominent family brought the questioning to a swift close, and the police left me alone after that.

The main difficulty I had in Salta was caused by Estela's ardor. Once, for example, she insisted that I take communion with her during the Week of the Miraculous Lord, assuming that I was a Catholic. I couldn't bring myself to take communion and was not sure I would know what to do, having never been in a Catholic church before. I decided to prevent a possible fiasco by confessing my sins first.

Luckily I had a fresh "sin" to confess. A few weeks before a young Argentine soldier who had a crush on Estela insulted me, and I knocked him out. His honor offended, he challenged me to a duel with swords. Dueling had been part of the ritual of my college fraternity, so I was not inexperienced. I had been in only one actual duel before and had won. My second opponent was no more skilled than the first, and I won easily, giving him a nasty cut on the cheek and gaining new respect from Estela and her friends and relations. Now I conveniently remembered that dueling was a sin among Catholics.

50

Sure enough, when I confessed to a priest, I was promptly excommunicated.

Delighted, I rushed to Estela's house to break the bad news. She flew into a rage, marched over to the telephone, and called the Archbishop to demand an explanation. After a few minutes of rapid-fire Spanish, she handed me the receiver. Archbishop Tavella granted me absolution by telephone and reinstated me in the Church. I was flabbergasted. The day of the communion, however, I was mysteriously felled by a severe case of influenza and could not attend.

In March, 1943, having gained a comprehensive picture of Salta's political scene, I received orders to go to Tucumán, a city about 150 miles south of Salta and the center of the military movement about which I had been warning my superiors. I told Estela and her family that I had to leave for a few weeks for an assignment. She was sorry to see me leave, but gave me a letter of introduction to her friends, the Paz Posse's, a powerful Tucumán family. Dr. Paz was the owner of *La Prensa*, Argentina's most influential newspaper.

Estela and my other acquaintances in Salta sent reports of my congeniality to their friends in Tucumán, assuring an easy entrée into society. Soon I was dating several prominent political leaders' daughters and making new contacts.

Called the Garden of Argentina, Tucumán is an elegant and historic city, founded almost 400 years ago. Most of the buildings, including a distinctive cathedral rivalling Salta's, were built in the eighteenth century. Though not far from Salta, Tucumán's people are very different—darker, more violent than Salta's. I was amazed the first time I saw two Tucumános fight. They lowered their heads like two rams and charged each other.

Here, as in Salta, my hectic social life and the magazine cover gave me an excellent opportunity to meet most of the community's political and social leaders. I heard most of the political scuttlebutt and watched with concern the growing power of the fascist military group.

In June, 1943, only a few months after my arrival in Tucumán, there was a military coup engineered by the group I had been monitoring. Argentina's president was deposed, the elections were cancelled, and the Army named a new President, a General Rawson, who was soon replaced by a General Ramirez. The Secretary of Labor in the new government was a young Colonel who was very popular with the masses, *los Descamisados* "the shirt-less ones," as they were called. His name was Juan Domingo Perón.

After the coup, security was tightened throughout the country, and although still officially neutral, the government became increasingly pro-German. I realized the danger that placed me in, but somehow in the fantasy world of Tucumán, the threat seemed vague and distant. I was swept up in a series of parties and balls, teas and receptions, and late night gambling sessions. It was hard for me to remember that there was a war raging throughout Europe and the Pacific and that I was obstensibly a part of it. Often, I would be lulled into thinking I was still the Viennese playboy of my youth.

My stubborn optimism about the war was beginning to look less like wishful thinking and more realistic. Hitler's army had surrendered at Stalingrad in late January, the Americans and British were beginning the invasion of Italy, the Germans had lost supremacy in the air. The end seemed in sight.

On October 12, I went to a formal ball with a beautiful raven-haired girl named Lisalotte, the daughter of the general who commanded the Second Army. She had fair skin and flashing eyes and was fond of wearing huge white hats that framed her delicate face. I returned about two o'clock to my room at the Savoy Hotel, the faint buzz of champagne still warming my body. I had no trouble falling asleep that night to pleasant dreams of lovely girls dancing in shimmering pastel dresses.

As I floated to the surface of reality I realized someone was pounding on the door, shouting and threatening me. I reached out in the dark and pulled the lamp cord. The clock read four in the morning. I stumbled to the door, grumbling, my heart beating in terror. As I turned the lock, the door sprang open, and I was pushed flat against the wall by a burly policeman. At least fifteen plainclothesmen swarmed into the room, led by a tall, swarthy man whom I recognized as "El Negro" Uriburu, the chief of the Police of Investigation. He was of Spanish extraction; his nickname came from his dead, black eyes and dark skin, not his race. He was a relation of Patron Costa's, but was known to be a dedicated fascist.

Uriburu escorted me from the room after giving me a few minutes to dress. As we left, I tossed a glance back toward the policemen, who were methodically ripping apart my hotel room. I didn't have much to hide, except some fake identity papers. Those I had carefully slipped under the paper lining on the wardrobe shelf. I had several sets of papers by this time, some provided by the OSS and some that I had bought on the black market. If they found them, which I had a feeling they would, they could trace me back to Swift, to Paraguay, to places I would rather forget. I had kept them in case I needed to escape and used them when I traveled between countries to help cover my tracks. Now I regretted it.

Uriburu took me to the government house, where I was placed in a private cell in the basement. As he left me, he warned me that he was going to find out all about me.

My jailers allowed me to make a telephone call, and I phoned Lisalotte, hoping she could prevail upon her father to obtain a writ of *habeus corpus*. Since I had not been charged with a crime, the government could not legally hold me more than twenty-four hours. If a friend obtained a writ from a judge, the government had to produce me.

At this time, I was still fairly naive about the due process of law. I expected my stay in jail would be short, since I was fairly sure they didn't have enough evidence to hold me. Lisalotte assured me that I would be out of jail by the next evening.

Mid-afternoon I was taken from my cell and brought to Uriburu's office. I was relieved, having already decided that jail did not suit me. The chief sat in a large, overstuffed desk chair, stroking the worn leather arms menacingly as he spoke. "We know who you are, Erico. We've enjoyed having you here, but there are people in Buenos Aires who very much want to talk to you." He nodded toward the two guards who had brought me to his office. "These two men will accompany you to your hotel so you can pack your things. Oh, and don't try to escape. You'll be shot."

I was not allowed to make another telephone call. The nasty-looking Tucumanos, .45 automatics sticking out of their belts, steered me to my hotel. My room was in disarray. I ran my hand over the shelf paper as I emptied the wardrobe. My spirits sank lower; the papers were missing. When my suitcase was filled, one of the men handcuffed me to him and we left for the train station.

The eight-hour trip to Buenos Aires deepened my depression. The policemen chained me to the seat and sat guard over me. It was almost impossible to shift positions, and my back soon became cramped. When I went to the lavatory, the guard switched the handcuffs back to our wrists and accompanied me. Even in the dining car, I sat with one arm handcuffed to the seat.

Across from our seats in the second class car sat

54

three women, evidently a mother and two daughters, who were dressed in black mourning clothes. They were red-eyed when they got on the train and cried most of the way to Buenos Aires. They transferred some of their sympathy to me, and I wondered if the person they were mourning had been shot by the military. They shared some of their afternoon snack with me, glaring at my keepers as if to dare them to interfere. Despite my growing despair, I couldn't help being amused. Somehow my boyish demeanor always made people think the best of me. It was what had made it so easy for me to enter into the lives of complete strangers and have them confide in me. These women obviously assumed that I was unjustly accused.

When we debarked from the train in Buenos Aires there were two more policemen waiting to take me into custody. The two Tucumános handed me over and got back on the train, and the new caretakers shoved me into a car. My parents and sister had arrived in the city while I was in Tucumán. Now I was near them, but we might as well have been separated by an ocean still. The thought brought little comfort as we drove up in front of the dreaded Federal police headquarters in the Calle Moreno.

I had heard of the tortures and cruelties taking place here since the new military regime had seized power. It was even worse than I had imagined. My suitcase was confiscated, and I was taken to a large room in the basement filled with hundreds of prisoners in ragged clothes, lying on tattered newspapers on the tile floor. I learned to be thankful for the newspapers. Not only did they provide some comfort, but they kept me abreast of the news. There was only one wash basin and latrine for more than 150 prisoners. It was July—winter in South America—and the basement was damp and cold.

Meals were served in tin cups with a metal spoon and

consisted of thin soups, with a few pieces of indistinguishable solid matter floating on top. I became accustomed to the distinct taste of saltpeter, which was added to keep prisoners doped enough to avoid problems with fights and homosexuality.

Men were not removed for questioning, but were tortured in the main cell. One man from La Plata with whom I became acquainted had been thrown into prison for giving one peso to a Human Rights Commission of which the government disapproved. The guards applied the electric prod to his genitals to force him to tell the name of the person to whom he had given the money. When he refused to tell them, they threw cold water on him, then applied the prod again. His screams were cut short, still echoing through the dank cell. He was dead of a heart seizure.

Another man who lay next to me was the secretary of the Conservative Labor Union for public employees. He had recently had an appendectomy. Two guards beat him one day and kicked open his incision. Then they left and let him bleed to death slowly in front of us all.

I found it difficult to sleep. Several times a night when the alarm bells would clang, guards would rush in and line everyone up for questioning and beating. Often they removed prisoners, leading them kicking and screaming into the courtyard. Muffled orders preceded the sharp retort of the firing squad.

Although I was terrified at first that I would be shot or tortured, my turn never came, although I did undergo long interrogations. Who paid me? What had I said? To whom? Was so-and-so a spy? But not once was I touched. I assumed that the police knew that influential people were applying pressure for my release. I found out later that in addition to the writs of *habeus corpus* from my friends in Argentina, there had been inquiries from the Uruguayan embassy. Argentina, still officially neutral,

56

was not eager to offend its neighboring country by torturing or killing one of its government employees.

After more than a month in jail, my parents were allowed to visit me. Our first meeting in five years was a sad one. Separated by a metal grill, we sat wordless for several minutes. Then my mother began to sob and my father's eyes welled with tears. I could imagine how I looked—a pale skeleton with matted hair, my ragged clothing about to fall off after weeks of wear. There was little to say after my parents told me about their escape and their new life in Buenos Aires. There was good news; my younger sister, Gertrude, was happily married to an Argentine businessman. They told me they were doing everything they could to secure my release. Then my father slid several cartons of cigarettes under the grid. As I watched them leave, I knew why I had been allowed to see them. In my humiliation and despair, I felt like telling my captors whatever they wanted to hear just to get out of here.

But before I could be interrogated, I was moved again, this time to a prison in La Plata. Seizing on small comforts, I was overjoyed to see that this prison at least had mattresses on the floor. It took me only one night to become disillusioned. The mattresses harbored bedbugs, which kept me awake nights and drove me wild with itching. Luckily my stay in La Plata was short-lived. During the next several weeks, I was moved every few days, ending up back in Buenos Aires. Imprisonment was beginning to take its toll, when, one day, a guard smuggled me a note saying that I would be transferred to a new prison from which it would be easier to liberate me. I didn't know who had sent the note, but the next day I was transferred to the infirmary. I was surprised, since I hadn't complained of illness. I suffered from malnutrition, nervous tension, and depression, but I knew I was no worse off than the other prisoners. Remembering the note, I went without complaint.

After two months in Argentine prisons, the infirmary, Spartan though it was, looked like a luxury hotel to me. Instead of one large detention area, the infirmary had small, one-room cells for two prisoners. The rooms were clean, with whitewashed walls and tile floors. Best of all, each cell had a toilet, a washbasin, and two cots with blankets and no bedbugs. Before being taken to my cell, I was given a shower with antiseptic soap and a clean pair of pajamas.

My roommate was a pale, thin young man who was disinclined to talk. He sat staring at the floor and sighing, and I was almost relieved when a few days later he was taken away, still silent and uncomplaining. I wondered whether he was being returned to prison or would be set free—or shot.

Another cellmate arrived the next day and I could tell immediately he would be a contrast to the first. He strode into the room as if he were entering the presidential suite of the Hilton. He was short and stocky, with a head of thick black hair and shaggy eyebrows. I guessed he was in his mid-thirties. I introduced myself, and he smiled broadly and held out his hand. "Aristotle Onassis. Glad to meet you."

I had never heard of him, but it didn't take me long to figure out that he was rich. The guards were bowing and nodding as they scurried behind him, and by nightfall they had delivered several cartons of cigarettes, a radio, and a selection of expensive shirts and suits from his home. Obviously, my fellow prisoner was not going to be uncomfortable during his stay in jail.

After telling Onassis my story, I asked him why he was in jail. He told me angrily that he had been asked by Labor Minister Juan Perón's mistress, Eva Duarte, to sign a blank check for one of her favorite charities. When he refused, he was arrested and brought to jail, evidently until he was willing to sign the check. This was the first but not the last time I heard about Eva's influence over Perón, the government, and the Argentine masses.

The day passed quickly, as Onassis and I entertained ourselves by discussing politics and swapping stories of our adventures. It was Onassis who first convinced me with logic that the Allies would win. Up to now, I was sure that they would, but it was largely wishful thinking. I had no real reason in the early years of the war to think the Germans could be stopped. Onassis' reason for betting on the Allies was the strength of American technology. As he explained it, "The Germans shoot down three American airplanes, the Americans will send six more to replace them. If the Japanese sink two ships, the Americans will send four more to replace them. The Axis powers just can't keep it up as long as the Americans. And technology's the key to modern warfare." The genial Greek gestured expansively with his slim hands as he talked, breaking out in a booming laugh when something amused him. He chain-smoked, sharing his cigarettes freely.

Like me, Onassis had arrived in South America poor, young and inexperienced. He had been born in 1906 in the Greek colony of Smyrna in Asia Minor, which was then under Turkish domination. His father was one of Smyrna's leading merchants, owning a prosperous tobacco business. After World War I, the Greeks invaded and occupied Smyrna, only to be ousted by the Turks in 1922. In reprisal, thousands of Greek citizens were arrested, including Onassis' father, stepmother, and sister. Using the quick wit and charm that would serve him well his entire life, Onassis managed to gain access to his father's safe and used most of the contents to free his family from prison—only to be criticized for spending

59

too much money. Resentful, the teenage Onassis left for South America to make his fortune.

My story about my trip on the *Conte Grande* reminded him of his similar voyage aboard a rundown Italian steamer. To conserve his small amount of cash, he booked steerage and was assigned to a dormitory in the cargo hold, with one meal a day. Then he bribed the purser five dollars a day to let him stay topside, where he enjoyed the meals and comforts of the second class passengers, who were paying twenty dollars a day. During the twenty-one day voyage Onassis had saved $315, precious capital he used to enter the tobacco trade. By the age of 23, he was a millionaire.

Spying fresh opportunity when the war broke out, Onassis switched businesses, entering shipping through the back door by salvaging condemned ships, repairing them, and selling them at enormously high profit. By the time I met him he had a fleet of merchant ships, registered under various flags of convenience.

During the few days we shared a cell, Onassis brightened my spirits, providing an escape from the nightmare of the last few months. The second evening as we lay on our cots listening to the radio, Onassis sat up and proclaimed, "Let's go out."

I looked at him as if he'd gone crazy, but he ignored me, jumped up and called the guards. After a few minutes of spirited negotiations with one of the guards he had purchased us an escorted night on the town.

He selected a suit and told me to pick one I liked. Just putting on the expensive beige linen suit made me feel like a free man, although I suspect it looked rather comical hanging from my emaciated frame. Flanked by two guards, Onassis and I walked down the stairs, out the door, into the warm, clear evening.

We walked across the prison yard to a plain black car that was parked in the driveway. The guards put us in back; they sat in the front seat with one policeman driving, the other turned to keep an eye on us. We pulled up alongside the guardhouse, and the driver rolled down the window. My mouth was dry, and I pressed my hands together to keep them from shaking. A sentry stuck his head in, looked us over, and then waved us through the gate.

As we drove toward downtown Buenos Aires, I stared in amazement at the crowded streets, the flashing neon lights of the nightclubs and restaurants, the carefree people who mingled freely. The women were dressed in pastel and bright-patterned dresses, some sporting the new short length, some in more formal street-length gowns. I envied the young couples walking arm-in-arm and laughing. It was intoxicating and I thought of all the times I had driven by or been a part of similar scenes without seeing them at all.

As if in a dream, I followed wordlessly as we parked the car and walked into a bar called the Tabaris, which I had heard was the most popular gathering spot for the wealthy businessmen of Buenos Aires. We walked down a narrow stairway to the smoke-filled American bar in the basement. On a small center stage, showgirls were dancing in glittering sequinned gowns. Onassis was known here, and he soon was entrancing two beautiful bargirls as he leaned against the bar, with a drink in one hand and a cigarette in the other. The two guards hovered nearby, looked ill at ease in their poorly-fitting, cheap suits.

After several minutes of dazed disbelief, I recovered my composure, ordered a Scotch and water, and began to flirt with the bargirls. As we watched the comedians and dancers perform, Onassis explained that there were two tiers of private boxes above the stage for entertaining. The upper tier was the most deluxe, with private rooms containing tables and couches.

61

While I was trying to charm a lanky honey blonde, I heard behind me a woman's voice that had a distinct Viennese accent. I excused myself, and worked myself over to the girl, who told me she was a waitress, her name was Gretel, and she was indeed from Vienna. I looked over to make sure the guards were distracted and struck up a conversation with her. She was a petite brunette and a non-stop talker. Within a few minutes I had heard her life story, knew her likes and dislikes, and knew she was violently opposed to the new military government, considering it just as evil as the Nazis who had caused her to leave her homeland. I ordered several more drinks from her, keeping the conversation going. One of the guards glanced at me. I winked at him and raised my eyebrows towards Gretel; he smirked and turned his attention back to the scantily-dressed dancer on stage.

Speaking in the rapid Viennese dialect, I explained my situation to Gretel and asked her if she would be willing to help me. Her eyes widened at my story and she stared for a second as if she were trying to decide if I were telling her the truth. Then she said yes; she would do what she could. I gave her the telephone number of my contact in Montevideo, and asked her to call and report where I was being held. I had almost given up on the Uruguayan government and decided I was expendable, but was willing to take this last chance. If they moved quickly, they might free me before I could be moved again.

The message conveyed, I relaxed and decided to enjoy the rest of the evening, glancing at the guards now and then, dreading the signal that it was time to go. It came about three o'clock in the morning and, as we left, I glanced back at Gretel, who smiled as if to reassure me. We drove back through the empty streets; I tried to forget I was returning to prison, but once the metal gate clanked behind Onassis and me, the cloud of gloom settled over my head. I undressed, lay down in bed and pulled the blanket over my head to stifle the antiseptic smell of the infirmary.

The next day I waited nervously, expecting someone to free me. Another day and my hopes had already begun to fade, but in the late afternoon a guard came for me. I dressed hurriedly in my ragged slacks and shirt, said goodbye to Onassis, who was reading the newspaper and humming to a tune on his radio. He wished me luck, but his eyes showed concern.

The guard took me downstairs and led me out the door toward a van at the curb. Another long ride ended at basement of the Calle Moreno police headquarters. It was a cruel blow after my taste of freedom. I felt that I would be forever shuffled from prison to prison, never charged with a crime, never sentenced to a definite term, just lost in a never-ending maze of look-alike cells. My spirit finally was broken. It had been three months since my arrest, and I knew I had been abandoned.

I decided I had to do something, something that would command the attention of the authorities. Analyzing my situation, I realized that I must still have some power, no matter how helpless I felt. They had not shot me, nor tortured me. Someone had had me moved to the infirmary. They didn't want me to die.

So, I reasoned in desperation, I would die. I would fake a suicide. Perhaps that would shake somebody up and force them to do something with me. The problem was how to attempt suicide without succeeding. I weighed the risk, and decided I had to take it. At this point, I would rather have died than spend another month in jail. I mentally listed all the methods of suicide, deciding that hanging was the only means available to me. The only place I could possibly carry it out was the urinal, the only place I was ever alone.

I began to hoard scraps of cloth—using what was left

of my torn underwear, part of a sheet that a prisoner had left behind when he was taken away, some rags left near the showers. Twisting these scraps together as I lay on my side, my back to the guards, I made a makeshift rope, about six feet long. It took me almost a week. When I went to the bathroom, I hid it by running it down the insides of my pant legs.

The first morning it was completed, I called the guard to ask to go to the bathroom. He answered my call and led me down the hallway, his gun drawn as usual. The urinal was behind a swinging wood door, similar to the kind in a Western saloon. The guards could see your feet underneath. I had been watching their behavior the past week and noted that they usually stood with their backs to the door, waiting until they heard the flush of the water. If someone was slow, they shouted at them to hurry up, and if a prisoner took too long, the guard would go in after him.

I went into the urinal and squatted over the hole in the tile floor, in case the guard looked under the door. Overhead there ran a pipe, with a faucet that could be turned on to wash out the urinal. Instead of dropping my trousers, I took out the rope, slipped it over the pipe, knotted it, and made a noose at the other end, position- ing it so it hung directly over the hole. Then, having carefully gauged the guard's probable reaction, I waited . . . five . . . six . . . seven minutes.

He started to get nervous. "Hey, what's the matter, you ever going to finish in there?"

I didn't answer. He waited a few minutes, and called out again. I was waiting for the exact moment when he would come to see what had happened to me. If I acted too soon, I could be dead of a broken neck by the time he reached me. If I waited too long, he'd stop me before I could get my head in the noose and jump into the hole. If

64

I wasn't injured the guard might not report the incident to avoid being reprimanded.

I stood perfectly still, watching the guard's scuffed brown boots, with their mud-caked soles. I sensed his feet begin to move and knew he was coming to the door. I put my head into the noose and stepped into the black hole.

5

I saw a blur of gray as the guard burst into the urinal, dropped his revolver, grabbed me around the waist, and lifted me up out of the hole. Then I blacked out. When I came to I was lying on the floor. Someone was shouting for an ambulance and several guards were standing over me, staring down. My body began to shake as I realized that, had the guard been a second slower, I might have broken my neck. Despite my cold-blooded planning, I hadn't been prepared for the reality of death.

Two guards lifted me onto a stretcher and ran to the ambulance, shoved the stretcher in, and climbed in after me. My heart was beating hard against my chest as the ambulance sped through the streets, siren screaming. In the hospital emergency room, I rose up on one elbow and asked one of the guards for his gun. "Let me finish the job," I asked him. A white-coated doctor bent over me. I saw the long needle, felt it prick my arm, and went under.

When I awoke, it was the afternoon of the next day. A guard was sitting near the door, watching me. When I stirred, he stood up, stuck his head out the door, and called to someone. A few minutes later a doctor came in and asked me if I felt strong enough to get dressed. Colonel Ramirez, the chief of police, wanted to see me.

I said I could make it; this was the confrontation I had wanted. I dressed slowly, with trembling hands. I looked into the mirror at a ghostly face. It didn't look like mine, and I stared in amazement for a moment. When I was dressed, two policemen accompanied me to a police van that returned us to police headquarters in Calle Moreno. Inside we were directed to a wooden bench in the waiting room.

After almost two hours, I was led into an elegantly-furnished office that seemed more suited to a government minister than a mere chief of police. Colonel Ramirez sat behind a wide expanse of desk, eyeing me closely. He waved me to a seat near his desk, then leaned forward. A neon light above my head buzzed angrily. Speaking in a warm voice that wasn't reflected in his eyes, he gently scolded me for attempting suicide. "Why did you do that, Erico?" he asked in an injured tone.

I decided to play along and assumed my most open manner. "Colonel, I don't believe you realize what's going on in the detention centers, what your police are doing. I figured I would be better off dead than alive. It's unbearable."

The colonel's brow knotted with concern, and he stared at a marble paperweight on his desktop as he pondered my fate. When he looked up again, he nodded as if agreeing with me. "All right. You can have your choice. You can go the Neuquén camp or you can leave the country. Which do you prefer?"

I didn't have to think about that choice. I had heard of Neuquén, a concentration camp in southernmost Argentina, a cold, harsh place where political undesirables were stashed and forgotten. I said I would prefer to leave the country.

Ramirez set his telephone at the edge of the desk near me. "You have family here, don't you? Call them

67

and tell them you'll be leaving on the eight o'clock boat for Montevideo tonight."

I asked for a telephone book, found my sister's number, and dialed it. When Gerty answered, I told her that I was being released. She began to cry and asked if she could come to get me. I cupped my hand over the speaker and asked Ramirez if my family could pick me up at headquarters.

"No. You will be escorted to the boat. They can see you at the dock if they wish."

I relayed the message and said goodbye. When I hung up, Ramirez asked me if I had any luggage. I suppressed a retort; I hadn't seen my suitcase since I had arrived at Calle Moreno three months ago. I said no, nothing.

The two policemen were called back and told to accompany me to a waiting room, where I was fed a hearty meal of meat, sausage, potatoes, vegetables, and coffee. I wondered as I devoured it if Ramirez wanted me to look slightly healthier when I arrived in Uruguay. Right now I wasn't a good advertisement for Argentine jails.

The second hand inched around the face of the clock, until, finally, about seven o'clock we left for the boat in an unmarked police car. At the parking lot near the dock, I saw Gertrude and her husband get out of a car. They started toward me, then hesitated and looked at the guards. I asked if I could say goodbye to my family, pointing to the couple. They said yes, but only for a minute. I hugged my sister, shook hands with her husband, and wished them well, asking them to give my love to my parents.

The ferry whistle blew, and the policemen gestured me toward the gangplank. They stood guard until the boat was underway. As I watched the Argentine coastline fade into the distance, I realized I was free. It was

January 6, 1944, and my three months and twenty-two days of imprisonment were ended. Because I had no cabin for the overnight voyage and was far too excited to sleep, I spent the night in the lounge, joining a card game with several other insomniac passengers.

As we neared the harbor of Montevideo the next morning, I moved to the prow of the ship, leaning against the railing as if I could hurry the boat. The morning sky was pale pink, and the rising sun silhouetted the peaceful city. I stared at the familiar dockside, the empty beaches, and the lighthouse on the Cerro. My throat felt tight.

On the pier, I could recognize Carlos Nogues, Batlle Pacheco, and the other members of the Senate Committee. I had to fight back tears of gratitude. As I walked down the gangplank, they rushed over to greet me and officially welcomed me back to Uruguay.

Pacheco was shocked at my physical condition and insisted on sending me to Punta del Este for two weeks of vacation. The Committee paid for my room and meals at a small oceanside hotel nestled among towering pine trees. A few weeks in this peaceful resort and I felt like my old self, discovering I could still make small talk, laugh, and enjoy more than ever the simple pleasures of day to day living.

When I returned to Montevideo, I was reassigned to the Senate Committee but, with the end of the war in sight, I was retired from active duty. My new job was to assess intelligence gathered from other agents and to help formulate national security policies, serving once again as an unofficial liaison between Uruguay and Allied intelligence.

The war in Europe reached its bloody conclusion, and I felt grim satisfaction in the complete defeat of Hitler and the other Nazi powers. I was an angry man and I wanted vengeance. Not only had my life been disrupted by the war but through the intelligence network I learned of the millions murdered in Nazi concentration camps.

Hitler's Final Solution, as the campaign to exterminate all Jews and other "inferior peoples" was euphemistically called, had been developed in 1941, when it looked as if Germany would rule Europe. Proceeding methodically, the Nazis set up special death camps where prisoners were murdered in huge gas chambers, thousands at a time. The largest was Auschwitz, where between one million and three million people lost their lives. No one has been able to determine the total number exterminated. Most estimates range from four to seven million. As if the statistics alone weren't staggering enough, the reports of sadism and brutality in the camps were even more appalling. From survivors came stories of trips to the camps packed like cattle in locked railroad freight cars, ingenious methods used to separate those who could work at hard labor from those who would die, agonizing scenes as families were wrenched from each other's arms, the sweet lies that the gas chambers were really only showers, the sadistic medical experiments conducted by quack doctors on human guinea pigs.

In 1945, I was willing to go to Berlin and kill Nazis with my bare hands, if necessary. I was in favor of the war crime trials and read with approval the reports of the 5,000 convictions and 800 death sentences handed down by the Nuremburg Court.

Only years later was I to learn that many high-level Nazis had managed to escape justice. I did not know that, in 1944, when the Nazis saw that defeat was inevitable, they laid the groundwork to ensure the Party's survival in the post-war world.

The SS and Gestapo leadership had false identity papers prepared and distributed to top Nazi leaders and

70

salted away a huge part of the Nazi fortune in bank accounts outside Germany to finance the resettling of the fugitive Germans and the building of the Fourth Reich. In 1946, the U.S. Treasury reported that the Germans had set up 750 companies overseas. These firms were often channels for Nazi funds into other countries and employers for Nazis who had to leave Germany after the war.

Near the end of the war, thousands of Nazis converged on SS intelligence headquarters at Aussee in the Austrian Alps. In one year, from 1944 to 1945, the population there mushroomed from 18,000 to 80,000 as Nazi fugitives swarmed in with private hoards of confiscated wealth—gold jewelry, counterfeit money, and art treasures plundered from thoughout Europe. Although the Allies tried to round up soldiers and suspected SS and Gestapo members, the chaos in war-torn Europe made escape easy. Many Nazi leaders escaped from the loosely-guarded POW camps, changed their names, and submerged into the civilian population.

Later, as the Allies became more organized and the war crime trials began, many Nazis decided they would be safer out of Germany. Ex-SS members formed associations to aid their escape. Best known of these underground organizations is ODESSA, which furnished papers to those who needed them and set up a network of couriers to escort them over the border into Switzerland or Spain.

Ironically, many Nazis enlisted the help of the Vatican, copying the methods and routes used by British intelligence in rescuing Jews during the war. Disguised as priests and carrying Vatican passports, Nazis slipped out of Germany and Italy with ease. Some Catholic officials were motivated by humanitarian concerns, considering it their duty to save human lives, regardless of the person's

71

character or crimes. Others, like the notorious Bishop Hudal of Rome, were avowedly pro-Nazi.

From Italy and Switzerland, the fugitives escaped to countries that had no extradition treaty with Germany or where there was a government friendly to Nazis. Some went to Spain, some to the Mideast, and great numbers headed for Argentina where dictator Juan Perón gave them refuge, often in exchange for healthy amounts of cash.

Argentina, like most other South American countries, had one other advantage. Because of its turbulent political history, the government in power was usually reluctant to extradite criminals, especially when the crime was in any way political. They were afraid that such a move might be used as a precedent to extradite them some day when they were forced to flee their country in the wake of a coup d'état.

In 1960, faced with the reluctance of the Argentine government to extradite Adolph Eichmann, the Israelis abducted the war-criminal from Buenos Aires and flew him to Israel to stand trial. Eichmann, who had risen from his lowly post in Austria to become head of the Jewish office of the Gestapo, subsequently revealed the story of his escape from Germany. It was typical of the methods used by so many Nazi leaders, most of whom would never be apprehended.

In the spring of 1945, Eichmann burned his office records and fled to the SS headquarters in the Austrian Alps. With forged papers identifying him as Adolph Karl Barth, Luftwaffe airman, he tried to cross through Germany to Italy, hoping to escape in the confusion of the immediate postwar period. He was captured by an American Army unit near Ulm, but escaped the loosely guarded camp when the Americans started to check prisoners for the tattooed blood-group marks identifying SS members. Arrested a second time, he claimed his papers had been destroyed; this time he was interned in *Oberdachstetten*, another prisoner of war camp.

Eichmann remained *incognito* in the camp during the Nuremberg Trials. When his name was mentioned frequently at the trials, he became frightened, went to the senior German officer in the prison camp and requested permission to escape, revealing his true identity. The officer not only approved his escape, but furnished him with forged papers.

With his new identity, Eichmann managed to live quietly in Kohlenbach, Germany, for four years. In 1950, still afraid he would be found, he made contact with *Die Spinne* (The Spider), one of the ex-Nazi groups that had been established to smuggle suspected war criminals out of Germany.

Eichmann and four other refugees were sent to a monestary in Genoa, Italy, where they were provided with new identity papers. Now he was Ricardo Klement, and under this name he obtained an Argentine visa and entered the country in 1950. Before Israeli agents kidnapped him ten years later, he had become so secure that he had used his own name in obtaining a job with Mercedes-Benz and was writing a book espousing his rabid anti-Semitic views.

The Nazi immigrants to South America did not arrive penniless as had so many of their victims. They smuggled fat bankrolls out of Germany and drew on the Argentine and numbered Swiss bank accounts set up by the Gestapo toward the end of the war. Part of the Nazi fortune was in jewelry, money, and gold fillings taken from concentration camp victims. Some of it was in forged foreign currencies supplied by the Gestapo's chief forger, Friedrich Schwend, another Nazi who sought refuge in South America after the war. The money was channeled through selected banks and German-owned businesses in South America and was used to finance the organization of Nazi groups throughout the continent, as well as to purchase land and businesses for the immigrants.

I heard rumors and read magazine articles about Nazi war criminals starting new lives in South America, but at this time I didn't spend much time worrying about it. To me, Hitler was dead, the Nazis had been defeated, and it was time to turn to other matters. I was more worried during this period about a threat closer to my doorstep—the *Peronistas*.

Juan Domingo Perón had been elected president of Argentina in 1946 and moved quickly to crush political opposition. Consequently, many politicians and intellectuals fled to neighboring Uruguay. Although Uruguay gladly gave them asylum, their presence made the country a target for Perón. Throughout his rule, he tried to infiltrate the Uruguayan government and the exiled Argentine political groups who were plotting to overthrow him. Many Uruguayans believed Perón would have invaded Uruguay if he had felt strong enough to get away with it. The threat to Uruguayan democracy and independence prompted its government leaders to reorganize their intelligence operations. Because of my wartime experience, I was involved in the reorganization and in maintaining contacts with the Argentine exile groups.

By September of 1955, Perón's own excesses and financial mismanagement led to his downfall. When the military, who had never forgiven him his alliance with labor, moved against him he surrendered his office and fled with millions of dollars from the national treasury. Jubilant, the Argentine politicians exiled in Uruguay boarded the ferry to Buenos Aires, while on the other side of the River Plate, Perón's followers fled to Uruguay. True to its democratic ideals and determined to retain its

74

neutrality, Uruguay gave refuge to the *Peronistas* despite its distaste for them.

The decade after the war was a carefree one for me, giving me a chance for the first time in almost ten years to relax and enjoy life. Montevideo was a city made for enjoyment, with its lively city-owned casinos on the Rambla, a beautiful oceanfront avenue, fine restaurants, free public beaches and nearby resorts, and the extraordinarily friendly people.

In addition to my security assignment, I became involved in Uruguayan politics, working for the election in 1947 of Luis Batlle Berres, a volatile but liberal politician. I helped organize neighborhood political clubs to support Berres' candidacy and formed another group of intellectuals that was called The Friends of the President. After Berres won, I served as one of his personal aides. During this period, some not altogether friendly wits in Montevideo nicknamed me "Perejil," Spanish for parsley, because they said I was in every soup, just like a sprig of parsley. It was true; I seemed to get involved in everything.

One of my assignments in the early fifties was to handle arrangements for Brazil's Labor Minister João Goulart when he arrived with his sick mother to consult Montevideo doctors.

I took an immediate liking to "Jango," as almost everyone called this amiable politician, and we became good friends during his frequent visits to Uruguay. Political heir to the benevolent Brazilian dictator Getulio Vargas, Jango was a champion of the workers, although he himself was a wealthy lawyer and landowner.

In 1955, he was elected vice-president and two years later he asked me if I would come to Brazil to work for him. Embroiled in a turbulent political atmosphere, he was concerned about his political security. He was aware

75

of my experience in Uruguayan politics and security and thought I could help him.

My work in Uruguay was complete. The Peronist threat was now over, the national security operations were running smoothly, and the presidency had been abolished democratically in favor of a nine-man executive council. I had recovered my health and my spirit of adventure and was willing to give up what I saw as a secure and boring middle age in Uruguay.

It didn't take longer than a few weeks in Rio de Janeiro to discover that my new life would be anything but boring or secure. Brazil in 1957 had seventeen political parties. Four or five were dominant, but none could claim a majority in any election. Consequently there were constant political intrigues among the various factions, who formed temporary alliances that soon dissolved into conflict. Extremist groups on both the far right and the far left threatened the country's fragile democracy.

Almost from the day of my arrival I was on the run, investigating coups by military commanders, political intrigues, and revolutionary movements. I traveled frequently, sometimes with Jango, talking to political leaders, cementing political alliances, making speeches, writing newspaper editorials, trying to hold together enough disparate elements to keep the government in power. I was like a mad volunteer fireman, rushing around trying to stamp out sparks before they could become raging, uncontrollable fires. It was not an easy task in a country larger than the continental United States and divided by social and economic class. Each state had its power brokers, including the independent state governors and various Army commanders stationed throughout the country.

As harried as my life was in Brazil, I fell in love with Rio de Janeiro, one of the world's most beautiful cities, with cool green mountains, tall graceful palms, aqua sea,

76

and white buildings with red tile roofs. Like all Brazilians, the people of Rio di Janeiro are easy-going; they live for the day and enjoy it from early morning to the last wild samba at dawn. I easily made the transition from Spanish to Portuguese, which is a mixture of Latin and Spanish with a handful of Arabic thrown in for good measure. Although Rio is like a European city in many ways, the people come in every possible shade and Brazilians are totally color blind. The separation is not between races, but between rich and poor. Downtown in the wealthy sections richly-fed, beautifully-dressed Brazilians live in splendid high-rise apartments, while not far away nestled into the mountains are the *favelas*, the tumbledown slum shacks where people live in squalor and ignorance.

In 1960, the liberal but eccentric Janio Quadros was elected president, with voters splitting their ballots to elect Jango vice-president, although he was of a different party. Quadros was immediately besieged by military critics and was unable to cope with the volatile political situation. In August 1961, only seven months after taking office, he submitted his resignation to Congress. If he hoped it would not be accepted, he miscalculated. It was, despite the fact that Goulart, who was next in line of succession, was in the People's Republic of China on a state visit.

The country waited nervously, most people expecting a military coup. The reactionary military ministers, unhappy with Goulart's ties to labor and his praise of the Red Chinese, issued a declaration stating that they considered the vice president's return inadvisable "for reasons of national security."

Goulart was unsure of what to do. If he returned to Brazil, he might be shot or arrested. He flew to Singapore, then to Paris, and from there called his security staff to ask what our opinion was. We met to analyze the situation, having checked with as many key political figures as we could, and then called him to tell him we thought the military did not have enough power to stage a coup, and said if he returned, he should fly to his home state of Rio Grande do Sul where the governor, Lionel Brizzola (Goulart's brother-in-law) and the commander of the Third Army, General Machado Lopes, had declared their support for Goulart.

In an act of great personal courage, Goulart returned to Pôrto Alegre, to a Governor's Palace ringed by General Lopes' soldiers. From there, he negotiated a compromise with the military ministers and Congress. After several tense days, he was allowed to take office, but only after Congress had stripped him of many of the president's traditional powers.

In 1963, Goulart won a plebiscite that restored most of his power, but his term was rocked by controversy and deepening political unrest. In a little more than two years, there were forty-four cabinet changes, a rash of crippling strikes, and soaring inflation. The cost of living rose three hundred percent.

The United States, fearful of what it saw as Communist influence in Goulart's government, severely reduced their aid. In my attempts to block military coups and amateur revolutions, I often encountered American CIA agents advising and training subversive groups. I wondered if the U.S. was worried more about Communism or the possible threat to large American corporations because of Goulart's efforts to make basic agrarian reforms and nationalize some industries. As I knew from working with Goulart, he was not a Communist, although some of his supporters were. Like most South American politicians, Jango put loyalty to his personal friends above all else, refusing to criticize or reprimand his more radical supporters. In the same way, he refused to admonish government officials caught with their hands in the public till. It was not a new problem. Brazil, a country rich in natural resources, was often bled by corrupt government officials. There is a popular saying that what Brazil grows at night, she steals in the daytime.

Now that Goulart was president, he assigned me to work with the National Security Council, an agency that combined the functions of a national police force, an intelligence organization, and an internal political watchdog. Because I was still an Austrian citizen, I could not receive an official position, but was hired as an expert in criminal investigation, police procedure, and intelligence evaluation.

As democratic processes broke down, my work became increasingly more difficult. No sooner was one coup thwarted than another would arise. A typical example of what we were up against was an investigation of disruptions in the state of Minas Gerais, shortly before Quadros resigned. There had been numerous right-wing demonstrations in the capital city, Belo Horizonte, with rumors of plots against the government. Jango asked me to investigate.

I arrived in Belo Horizonte on one of the streamlined modern trains that connected Rio de Janeiro with the state capitals and checked into the Hotel San Domingo. I was impressed by the city's obvious prosperity. When I commented on it to the cabdriver, he told me the numerous skyscrapers had been financed by the state's wealthy cattle breeders and bankers.

I made the rounds of popular social clubs, restaurants, and night spots—all the places I could hope to make some valuable contacts. A few days after I arrived, I went to a local club, where I joined a group of men who were gathered around the television set. They were listening to a speech given by a priest in one of the largest Catholic Churches in Belo Horizonte. The priest, Father

Ramirez, was denouncing Goulart, Quadros, and the other members of the government, warning of the "Red menace that was threatening to take over Brazil from within." The next day I paid a call on Father Ramirez, telling him I was just a visitor here, I was really an Austrian citizen, but I was impressed by what he had to say. I was well aware of the dangers of Communism. Was anybody doing anything about it, or were they just talking?

Father Ramirez took me with him to a meeting of a right-wing organization. Soon I was working with the members of this group to help organize anti-Communist clubs and demonstrations. I gave speeches, passed out pamphlets, and attacked the government viciously. I was a very popular convert, appreciated for my ardor and energy.

I was soon trusted enough to be introduced to Father Ramires' boss, a man named Josafat Macedo, who was president of a national rural association whose members were rich cattle breeders and ranchers. From Macedo and his friends, I heard of armed groups of farmers who could be mobilized to overthrow the government.

Within a month, I was a trusted part of the group, but heard very little in the way of hard facts that would provide an excuse for the national security police to move. One day, I was invited to a meeting at Macedo's house to meet the local fascist hero, a Colonel Bley, who with a group of other Army officers had led a raid on a pro-government newspaper. Angered at an editorial that had attacked the Army, Bley and his friends smashed the presses and assaulted the editor. The city's democrats were outraged and there were a number of violent demonstrations, for and against Bley.

Bley's language was even more extreme than I had heard from the group, but the audience loved it. For a few minutes I wondered if I were back in the forties; the language and attitudes of these people were no different from the Nazis that had met in the *Viejo Berlin* in Montevideo during the war. I had considered the Nazi menace defeated, but was beginning to realize now that it just took on new forms. Peronists, right-wing facsists, Nazis—the name didn't matter.

I joined in the discussion, shouting that if I had my way we would arm all the people on our side and move against these Communists. Macedo assured me they already had plans, and they would succeed. After the meeting, he confided to me that they even had the chief of police, Pedro Ferreira, on their side. And they had arms, although unfortunately, not enough. Weapons were hard to come by.

I pretended to be excited and said I could help obtain weapons if he wanted me to. What I wanted to know, but couldn't ask, was where their store of guns was held. Macedo took the bait and told me someone would get in touch with me to talk about this.

A few days later there was a knock on my hotel room door. A short stocky man introduced himself as Alfredo Hernandes. I knew better, having taken the precaution of locating Police Chief Ferreira's home address and watching him as he left for work one morning. I played along with his disguise and let him tell me that Macedo had sent him. Then I pretended to get nervous and took him into the hallway, peering both ways. I couldn't talk to him here; I was afraid my room was bugged, I told him. We agreed to meet at the bridge in front of the railroad station in an hour.

When we met again, he asked me how I was getting the arms. I said that they were Argentine weapons, smuggled through Paraguay, and would be brought in by airplane. I refused to say more. How much money did I want? Oh, I wouldn't take money. It was for the cause. I only wanted to be first in the battle lines. Ferreira smiled at my selflessness.

81

Every day I met with Ferreira with a new bit of information and new assurances that the shipment was on its way, hoping that he might let slip where they stored the guns. Finally, I said the airplanes were scheduled to arrive in two days. I needed to know where they could land safely.

Ferreira smiled slyly. "They can land at Pampulha Airport," he told me. Pampulha, the city's main airport? How was that possible?

Ferreira asked me if I had been to the airport. Once or twice, I said. Well, perhaps I had noticed right along the boundary of the airfield, not more than a hundred yards away, a Jesuit retreat. That was where they were stockpiling the weapons.

I told him I would contact my source with the instructions and let him know the time. Now I had to decide how to communicate the news to the National Security Council, who could authorize a raid on the cache. I was afraid if I disappeared without reason, I would arouse suspicion. I was reluctant to use the telephone. I stalled a few more days, going to the social club to play *pif-paf*, a popular Brazilian card game similar to gin rummy, and returned to my hotel about two in the morning.

As I walked toward the entrance, I was jumped by four men, who shoved me into a yellow Jeep parked in front of the hotel. They delivered me to DOPS, the state political police. I couldn't afford to tell them I was working for the National Security Council, since I could only assume Ferreira must have become suspicious and tipped them off. I didn't want him to discover my true identity. In the present political climate, I couldn't trust the police department, either. So I played dumb, said I was just a tourist, and was taken to a cell in their modern jail. I knew their state police files wouldn't have my fingerprints and I doubted that they could prove any charge against me. They questioned me about my offer to sell guns, but I assured them I had just been trying to act like a big shot. I didn't have access to any guns.

Since I had not tried to buy guns, there was no evidence against me. After five days, the DOPS decided the easiest thing to do would be to get rid of me, so they released me. Now I had a good reason to leave town, so I picked up my luggage at the hotel and boarded the train to Rio. I picked up a tail as soon as I left the jail and when I reached my seat in the train, there were two DOPS detectives sitting opposite me. Despite their nondescript clothes, they stuck out like sore thumbs. When I started a conversation with the porter, they stopped talking and looked fixedly out the window, ears cocked to hear what I was saying.

When I debarked from the train, my shadows still followed me. I was secure enough in my home territory to play a little joke on them. I hailed a cab and told the driver my destination, cautioning him that I was extremely tired from my long trip and would prefer that he drive slowly. The two plainclothesmen jumped into a cab behind me, and we cruised through the streets of Rio de Janeiro. We pulled up at my stop, the National Security Council. I paid the cabdriver, removed my suitcase, and watched the other cab out of the corner of my eye as the guard in front of the building greeted me familiarly and took my bag. As the second cab shot away, I saw the open-mouthed stares of two astounded policemen.

Not wanting to waste time, I took the steps two at a time and reported to the head of the Council. A meeting was hastily called and within a half hour a contingent of federal police were on their way to Belo Horizonte. In the basement of the Jesuit retreat they found hundreds of guns and a supply of ammunition. The plot was broken wide open, and the principal leaders were arrested. When the full dimensions were uncovered, it was discovered that the group had organized thousands of farm workers and city white collar workers as guerilla cadres, ready to march when the order was given.

The frustrating side of the investigation was that the destruction of this one conspiracy did not halt subversive activities in Minas Gerais. It was here that the coup that drove Goulart from power started.

When the final blow came, it was swift and bloodless. On March 30, 1964, Governor Magalháes-Pintos pledged that the state of Minas Gerais would restore "the constitutional order, which is now compromised." As if on cue, General Filho mobilized his troops in Minas Gerais and ordered a march on Rio de Janeiro to overthrow the government.

The generals Goulart had been depending on remained silent. His political enemy, Carlos Lacerda, the governor of the state of Rio de Janeiro, barricaded himself in the Governor's Palace, using state garbage trucks to block the streets leading to the palace. Armed with two submachine guns and a pistol, he telephoned police posts around the city to confirm that the coup was proceeding.

Goulart ordered the First Army to intercept Filho's troops, but they seemed unable to locate the enemy. Realizing that the army had deserted him, Jango fled to Brasilia, then to Pôrto Algre. That same night the president of the Senate declared the Presidency vacant and swore in an acting president.

Once again, Jango and his supporters were barricaded in the governor's palace in Pôrto Alegre. Goulart's brother-in-law, Lionel Brizzola, wanted Goulart to make a last-ditch stand, as I did. Goulart refused, telling me that he loved Brazil too much to shed her blood. Instead he left for Montevideo and the bull-necked General Castelo Blanco, the behind the scenes coordinator of the coup, became the new president. Within hours after the coup, United States President

Johnson sent a message expressing his country's "warmest wishes" to the new government.

The military moved quickly to consolidate its power, arresting 7,000 people immediately and forcing through Congress an Institutional Act that suspended for ten years the political rights of 378 citizens, including the most prominent politicians—Quadros, Goulart, Kubitchsek, six state governors, and 55 members of Congress. Although 1500 political prisoners were awaiting trial a year later, I was not arrested or harrassed, my only crime being loyalty to Goulart. This could be forgiven.

I could see, however, that I would find no place in the new government. The National Security Council was transformed into the dreaded SNI, a military security agency responsible to the dictatorship. Fortunately, many of the individual Brazilian states retained their independence for some time after the coup, and in one of these I found a new home.

6

On a visit to Paraná, a state in southern Brazil, I was introduced to Paulo Pimentel, a 38-year old liberal politician who was running for governor. Pimentel was a lawyer and was married to a wealthy sugar plantation owner's daughter. Although he was vain, he had a genuine concern for the problems of the people. Still retaining some hope for keeping democracy alive in Brazil and impressed by Pimentel's platform, I joined his campaign. As I had in Uruguay, I helped organize meetings and rallies throughout the state. Pimentel was a charismatic campaigner whose campaign symbol was the gaucho hat he wore at a jaunty angle as he waded through crowds of enthusiastic supporters. He was elected with a large majority.

Once in office, Pimentel assigned me to the Directory of Civil Police, under a special contract with the government. Because of the opposition of the military junta ruling the country, he could not immediately appoint me to an official position. The military could not yet halt free elections, but it tried to apply pressure on the state governments. Pimentel was clever enough to appoint friends he could trust to critical positions like the Justice Ministry and the police departments. Letting them deal with interference from the federal government, he devoted himself to helping the Paraná farmers and raising social standards.

Pimentel was quickly maneuvering himself into a position that would allow him to run for national office if and when democracy returned to Brazil. More confident after several months in office, he appointed me to my first official position: chief of investigation in the civil police, with responsibility for homicide, narcotics, vice, and DOPS (the political police). The chief of investigation was the working head of the civil police; chief of police was a political and honorary position.

Police headquarters was in Curitiba, the state capital, just down the street from the modern Civic Center, a cluster of government buildings which included the governor's palace, the state secretariats, the House of Assembly, the Treasury and the law courts. Curitiba is an attractive, prosperous city of close to one million inhabitants. Set on a high plateau not far from the sea, it has a brisk climate, but close access to seaside resorts.

The position gave me the independence I preferred. Although I was responsible for overseeing the various police departments, they generally ran smoothly. I met each morning with department heads and sifted through the inevitable paperwork connected with the job. When there was a vacancy in one of the top posts or a special case that required my help, I stepped in temporarily.

Police chiefs were generally lawyers and were addressed as "Doctor." Although I had begun law courses in Austria and had completed a course in criminal law while I was in Buenos Aires, I had never received a law degree. But I, too, was called "Doctor Erico," in a typically Brazilian mix of formality and friendliness.

The title is one indication of the power granted to a Brazilian law officer. I had much more latitude in pursuing criminals and a stronger hand in their punishment than any American or European policeman. When someone was convicted, usually in a trial before a judge, the sentence would be decided jointly by the police, prosecuting attorney, defense counsel, and the judge. If I needed to let an underling go in exchange for information about his superiors, I had the discretion. Although this system has its benefits in curbing crime, it also leads to abuses by dishonest or brutal policemen. Their discretion gives them power over citizens and leeway to torture prisoners that would never be allowed in a more rigid law enforcement system.

My experience up to now in South America had been in the unusual circumstance of war or in the political arena. In Paraná, I found that many of the same skills I used as an Allied agent during the war came in useful as a policeman. My investigatory skills made it possible for me to ferret out burglary, smuggling, and dope rings that required undercover work. My political experience made me instantly aware of terrorist and right-wing organizations that threatened the democratic stability of Paraná. The national military government might not like me, but they had to admit that I was a tough and honest cop.

One investigation that intrigued me during this period was a drug smuggling case that involved an old friend.

In the spring of 1965, I received a report from the São Paulo state police that a woman had been arrested there with a large amount of heroin which she had reportedly smuggled into Paraná from Paraguay. I had been in touch with my counterpart in São Paulo on a drug case, so he asked if I wanted to question this woman. I was certain that she wouldn't be working alone, not with such a large quantity of drugs, and asked that she be brought to Curitiba.

When she was brought in, she recognized me immediately. I looked at her more closely and, despite her bedraggled condition and the passage of years, I recognized Noemi, the woman Vice-President Chavez of Paraguay had loved so much during the war. She was still very beautiful, although she looked older than her thirty-four years. I dismissed the guard who had brought her to my office, told her to sit down, and asked her how she happened to be in this predicament.

In a quavering voice, she told me that she was guilty, that she had become mixed up in this dreadful business because she needed the money, that she couldn't tell me anything about it. She'd take the fall.

My temper flared, but died just as quickly. I realized she was simply afraid of telling me the truth. I had to get her to open up if I was going to find out anything. I told her that she left me no choice but to throw the book at her. She could get from fifteen to twenty years, and by the time she saw the light of day again she'd be an old woman. She still refused to tell me, so I had her returned to her cell. The next day I questioned her again and again she refused to talk. Finally after four days, the tears broke loose, and she started to talk, haltingly, between sobs. Despite her obvious fear, I sensed a relief to have the secret off her shoulders.

She said she was just a small cog in a huge machine that operated not only in Paraná, not only in Brazil, but over the entire world. She had been in contact with Arabs, Asians, Germans, Russians, Belgians, and Greeks as well as South Americans. These couriers and smugglers carried false passports from a wide variety of nations. She was acquainted with only one branch of the total organization, but she had heard enough information to be terrified. She had been told by her superiors that much money used to buy drugs was counterfeit, and she had heard that some of it was Nazi money brought into South America after the war. Drugs was only one of the organization's activities; they also provided coffee, whiskey, cigarettes, diamonds, chemicals—whatever someone would pay for.

I told Noemi I would see what I could do to help her. After a long conversation with Paulo Pimentel, I was given *carte blanche* to do what I felt necessary to pursue the investigation. My first act was to release Noemi, but with a warning to get in touch with me if she had any more information or if she needed help. I was worried that if her compatriots heard of her arrest and release they would know that she had talked. I knew she was terrified of her employers.

Sure enough, two days later Noemi was back at my headquarters, asking to see me. She felt her life was in danger; word had leaked out that she had talked to Paraná police. I gave her the keys to my apartment and had my chief aide, a sinister-looking detective named Angelo Silvera, take her there.

Noemi was to stay with me for two years. It was a strange relationship. Although we were very close, she was a lesbian and hated most men. She often brought her women friends to my apartment. Sometimes I ended up with them. In 1966, Noemi decided she wanted a child and announced to me that I was the only man she would consider for the father. I was taken aback, but I agreed, and within a few months she was pregnant, giving birth to a baby girl she named Claudia. Soon after the baby was born, she told me she now had what she wanted, she wasn't afraid any more, and she didn't want to destroy my life. She was going to return to Argentina where her family was living. I found it hard to let her go, even though I knew she was right. I never saw her again, although a year or so later I heard from friends in the São Paulo police department that someone using her name had tried to find me.

90

Meanwhile, the leads I received from Noemi started me on an investigation into the drug ring. Starting with the list of names she supplied, I got in touch with all the police departments that might have information—other state police departments, the federal police, and Interpol. Beginning with the underlings like Noemi, I worked my way up to the top level operatives in Brazil, freeing the small-time drug addicts and dealers in exchange for information about the higher-ups. It took more than a year of tedious probing, but when the investigation was complete and the indictments drawn up, I had driven most of the drug dealers out of Paraná.

Just as the drug investigation was coming to an end, I received a call from Senator Steinbruch in São Paulo, a friend from my years with Jango. Steinbruch told me that the São Paulo state government had received a tip from Simon Wiesenthal, the well-known Nazi hunter, that former Treblinka commandant Franz Paul Stangl was living in São Paulo.

Between 1942 and 1943 Stangl had been in charge of 700,000 inmates at the Polish extermination camp. Only forty were known to have survived. By 1943, the Jews in Poland had been eradicated, and Stangl was sent to an almost certain death at the Yugoslav front, a "reward" often given SS men who knew too much about the camps.

Stangl survived the war, however, and returned to Austria. There, in 1946, he was arrested and held for routine investigation in an American prisoner of war camp. He escaped in 1948 and fled to Damascus, Syria, with the help of ODESSA.

In 1964, Simon Wiesenthal, who had searched unsuccessfully for Stangl in Syria, received new information about his whereabouts. First a woman whose cousin had married Stangl told Wiesenthal that the former commandant was living in Brazil. Next, an ex-Gestapo agent offered to sell the secret of Stangl's location. He would make Wiesenthal a deal, he said. He'd settle for $7,000, a penny for each of Stangl's victims. Wiesenthal's eagerness to find Stangl overcame his disgust with the Gestapo agent, and he accepted the deal, learning that Stangl was working at a Volkswagen plant in São Paulo. Now that he had the information, Wiesenthal didn't know how to get Stangl. South American countries were still reluctant to extradite war criminals; Brazil had no extradition treaty with Austria in any case; and the Israelis had given up kidnapping war criminals after the furor that followed their abduction of Adolph Eichmann.

Three years later, however, São Paulo state elected a new governor who was a liberal, an avowed anti-Nazi, and a close friend of Brazil's most influential Jewish family. Wiesenthal alerted the new governor that Stangl was thought to be living in the state capital. Shocked at the news, the governor ordered the state DOPS to locate and arrest Stangl.

Senator Steinbruch knew about the order and was worried that DOPS would muff the case, given their unfamiliarity with the German community and language. He was aware of my work during the war and asked if I would lend a hand in locating the man.

I quickly agreed and left that same week for São Paulo. Not surprisingly, I learned that DOPS had already checked employee lists at all the German firms in São Paulo and discovered that Stangl's name was not on any of them. I took the less direct approach, the same one I had used with success during the war. I made the rounds of restaurants, bars, and clubs frequented by Germans, struck up an acquaintance with employees of the Volkswagen plant, and within a few days had learned that Stangl was still working at the plant as a mechanic. He lived in the affluent suburb of Brooklin, in a style much grander than his salary would indicate.

I turned the information over to DOPS, who on February 28 arrested Stangl as he returned from work in his red Volkswagen. He submitted calmly, telling the policemen, "I knew I would be captured."

Meanwhile, I had checked on Stangl's other acquaintances to see if perhaps he had been in contact with other Nazi war criminals living in Brazil. I discovered a German friend of Stangl's who spent almost every night at a São Paulo nightclub, where he had fallen in love with a bargirl. When I questioned her, she admitted that her admirer was a painter who was spending fifty or sixty dollars a night on her. This seemed an extravagant sum for an unknown painter, so I started to investigate his background. I learned that he was an East German, who mailed letters to his girlfriend back home every week. I brought in DOPS, who intercepted his mail. Among the letters from overseas was one from East Germany outlining information he was to obtain in São Paulo.

Deciding to check his outgoing mail, we followed him one morning to the corner mailbox and, after he left, opened it and retrieved a letter to his girlfriend. The message was innocuous, but when we steamed off the stamp we found a microdot underneath. It contained information about American firms in Brazil, including how much they exported from the country, how many people they employed, and their annual output.

The agent was arrested and confessed to being an East German spy. Ironically, he had lifted the so-called secret information he had sent his government from a pamphlet published by the United States Chamber of Commerce. It could be purchased in Chamber headquarters in São Paulo for 30 cruzeiros, about ten cents. For this espionage, the agent received a twelve-year prison sentence.

The Communist spy was the only other suspect I uncovered in my investigation, carried on in the midst of a fierce battle being waged over Franz Stangl. When the arrest was imminent, Wiesenthal had alerted the Austrian government, who carried Stangl on their list of wanted war criminals. They sent an arrest warrant to their representative in São Paulo to cover for the governor. Now began a four-month battle to extradite Stangl. Because there was no extradition treaty with Austria, the government had to apply to the Brazil Supreme Court within sixty days of the arrest for a special order of extradition.

Because Austria had little evidence against Stangl, two more arrest warrants were obtained, one from Germany and one from Poland. The German warrant was vaguely worded and failed to include the overwhelming evidence available in the Berlin Document Center or the war crime files at Ludwigsburg. Not that they lacked the evidence. In Berlin, for example, was one document, an order of transmittal from Treblinka to Berlin signed by Stangl. Among the items he sent from the camp by rail were 25 freight cars of women's hair, 248 freight cars of clothing, and 400,000 gold watches. The Polish were more thorough, sending to Brazil a three-man delegation of jurists with a well-documented case against Stangl. Faced with this evidence, the Supreme Court extradited Stangl to Germany on June 22. He was sentenced to life imprisonment, but died in 1968 at the age of sixty. Stangl was the first Nazi war criminal to be extradited from Brazil.

No sooner had I returned from São Paulo in February than I was drawn into a new case involving Nazis, a case that demonstrated that National Socialism had not died with the collapse of the Third Reich.

7

Like so many investigations, this last and most deadly of my career in South America began by chance, as a search motivated by my own guilt, a search that was to lead me into a maze that grew slowly more complex, more treacherous, more intriguing, until there was no turning back.

It started routinely, on an oppressive summer day in 1967, when my chief aide Angelo broke in on my half-hearted attempt to clear away some of the police reports that were threatening to engulf my desk top.

He apologized for disturbing me, smiling slightly at my obvious relief at the interruption. I waved him over to the massive, lumpy brown leather couch that squatted in the corner. He perched lightly on the edge. A man of few words, Angelo had won my confidence through his sound judgment and stubborn loyalty. He was my most trusted subordinate; I knew that whatever he had to report would be worth hearing.

"It's that foreigner. Remember, the one you ordered us to tail."

I remembered. The reports of this stranger's unusual behavior had sparked my curiosity. Since arriving in Curitiba almost a month ago, he had changed hotels as often as three times a week. Managers of the last two hotels complained that he had departed without paying his bill. In Brazil, that's not a crime; it is up to the hotel to ask for advance payment. But it was enough to arouse suspicion. Detectives investigating the charges found that the foreigner had checked in with no luggage, yet hotel clerks reported that he frequently left the hotel and came back with clean clothes or other belongings. He spoke Portuguese poorly, with a heavy German accent, and almost everyone who had come in contact with him described his behavior as "strange." He seemed to have no legitimate business in the city; nor was he looking for a job. My instincts had warned me that something was wrong, so a week before I had ordered a tail put on him.

Angelo continued his report. The detective assigned to the case had just called him to tell him the foreigner was in Hans's place, in Rua Riachuelo, last night asking everybody in the place to buy him a beer because he was broke. Then Heinrich Mueller, the executive secretary of the German-Brazilian Cultural Alliance, had come in. He took the man aside, and whispered angrily, something like "get out quickly, or . . ." The detective could only catch part of it. Then Mueller handed the guy a lot of money. The foreigner immediately ordered a round for the house, and Mueller got very red in the face and stalked out.

I had been right to put a tail on him. Mueller, a former Lutheran pastor, had been tossed out of his church in a little town in Santa Catarina during the war for his fascist views and for storing firearms in the church basement. The war should have taken care of Nazis like Mueller, but lots of them were still around and prospering. I'd had complaints from teachers at the private school run by the Alliance that students were being instructed only in the German language and culture, and not in Portuguese at all. From all accounts, Mueller's views had not mellowed with the years.

"I think we had better find out more about this man, Angelo. Bring him in."

As my aide headed for the door, I stopped him and told him to take the man to the Expresso, a restaurant and bar popular with off-duty policemen, and wait for me there. In that atmosphere I thought the stranger might be more likely to open up to me. My office was too intimidating.

I glanced at a few more reports from police sections under my command, but my mind was wandering. What was going on? Why the money? Maybe the foreigner was blackmailing Mueller? Or doing some dirty work for him?

Muffled voices wafted up from the courtyard through the open window behind my desk. A few rays of sun slipped through the heavy brown curtains, seeking out and exposing a layer of dust on the legs of the handsome, well-stuffed leather side chair I reserved for important visitors. I glanced up at the portrait of Governor Pimentel, who seemed to be peering down at me sympathetically. Alongside the oil painting was a light rectangle that betrayed the gradual darkening of the once-white walls. Not too long ago a painting of Jango had hung there, and I had delayed replacing it with a portrait of General Branco, the country's right-wing military leader. I liked the empty space; it symbolized my own patient wait for change. The ceiling fan whirred monotonously, sending periodic murmurs of complaint through the neglected papers. I swore softly and reached for another report.

About seven o'clock the telephone rang. It was the bartender at the Expresso telling me that my aide was waiting for me there. I hadn't expected that Angelo would have any trouble. In Brazil you are not surprised if you are accosted by a burly man in street clothes who orders you to accompany him. Few men will risk asking for a badge, especially if the man has a face like Angelo's.

I pushed the papers back into some semblance of order, checked that my .38 was loaded and tucked it securely in my belt, and headed down the stairs, past the military guards, to the Expresso.

The cool of evening had brought the city alive, waking it from the stupor of the long, hot afternoon. People moved easily through the crowded streets; nobody seemed in a hurry. A group of teenagers laughed and shouted at friends across the street. Roselmira, one of the prettier bargirls, called my name softly from the door of La Fazenda as I passed.

I turned off Rua Rio Branco, a major street lined with government and older office buildings, into a narrow side street jammed with many small shops and bars. The painted wood sign—"Expresso-Restaurant-Bar"—creaked in the evening breeze as I opened the door leading into the restaurant section, a clean, utilitarian room with about thirty tables set in straight rows on a shiny black tile floor. Angelo and his prisoner sat at the last table in the row next to the latticework grille separating the restaurant from the bar. Angelo faced the door, listening impassively to the foreigner, whose back was to me.

With a slight nod to Angelo, I crossed the restaurant, passed the two men, and walked into the bar. I greeted the bartender and several policemen from the station house across the street while I studied Angelo's friend. He was close to six feet tall, rather fleshy, with pallid skin, about sixty, I guessed. His suit was well cut, obviously expensive, but rumpled like his blue-striped shirt. A half-finished beer sat in front of him, and as he talked, he stroked the handle of the stein nervously. His face was intelligent, I thought, although marred by a weak chin.

98

He looked down and out, but something about his bearing suggested that he once had been accustomed to respect.

My eyes glanced over the rest of the diners. About half the tables were filled, some with persons eating alone, others with couples or groups of friends. Nobody seemed to be paying any attention to Angelo and his man.

I walked slowly to the table, pulled out a chair, and sat down. I turned to the foreigner and asked to see his papers. He showed no surprise, but fumbled slightly as he reached into his left breast pocket and pulled out a slim passport-sized booklet. He glanced at me warily. Sizing up my features, he addressed me in German: "Here you are . . . your name, please?"

So Angelo would understand our conversation and to keep the man off guard, I answered in Portuguese. "I ask the questions. You answer."

I took the booklet and leafed quickly through it. Eugene Parries, a citizen of Luxembourg. A work permit showed that he had arrived in Brazil in 1952 and that he had worked in the Banco Holandés Unido in São Paulo from the time of his arrival until 1954. There were no more entries, but I had guessed correctly; he had been important. Only through the intervention of someone influential could any foreigner get a working permit in Brazil with less than two years' residence. The Hollandshē Bank also registered. It belonged to an international trust managed by La Societé General Belgique, a very powerful European complex that was rumored to have been one of the corporations that had absorbed enormous fortunes from the fallen Third Reich. Parries had either lost his position there, or he still held it and for some reason was trying to hide it.

I nodded to Angelo, who muttered a curt goodbye to Parries, got up and walked over to the bar and ordered a *cachaça*, the powerful Brazilian national drink, an evil-smelling, colorless liquor made from sugar cane. With his back to the dining room Angelo kept an eye on the table through the mirror. Parries appeared to relax now that he was out from under Angelo's shadow. He straightened up in his chair, adjusted his suit jacket, and took a swig of beer.

I took the offensive. I told him I would be frank with him, and hoped he would be smart enough to take advantage of it. I told him who I was, and that he could consider himself under arrest. I let him know we were aware of his movements since he had arrived in Curitiba. "You know as well as I do that I have lots of reasons to have you booked. But . . ." I hesitated, acting on instinct, operating on the popular Brazilian advice: "Throw green, fetch ripe." By making it appear that I knew much more than I did, I hoped to get him to open up, to tell me more to avoid jail if he could. The strategy worked. The air almost visibly seeped out of him. His shoulders drooped, and his hands shook as they traced a pattern on the beer stein.

I lowered my voice confidentially, and told him that if he was willing to talk, I'd leave him alone. I wasn't after him. But, if he lied, I'd make sure he was in a cell for as long as it took to investigate his life, beginning with the day he was born. It was up to him.

The words came rushing out in a torrent of strongly accented Portuguese. "I come from a small town in Luxembourg . . . the war made me homeless . . . I came to Brazil, I'm broke . . . my brother-in-law, the bastard, stole me blind . . . cheated me . . . my wife, she . . ."

"Quel etait votre situation en Luxembourg?" I interrupted, to see if Parries spoke French as a Luxembourger would.

Parries frowned. In German, he asked, "Pardon, sir?"

I rose from my chair. Angelo glided around the partition and clamped a firm hand on Parries' arm. I told Angelo to take him in.

Parries rose and leaned toward me. Speaking haltingly, he pleaded that he was an old and almost broken man, tired of living, tired of running. He swore he was not lying now. "I'll tell you what you want to know . . . more than you want to hear," he assured me. He asked only that he be allowed to stay in his hotel, not in jail. He gave his word of honor that tomorrow morning he would come to my office, but he was too old for Brazilian jails.

I am a sucker for a straight offer. Parries was obviously not a common criminal, only a very weak old man. I could understand his reluctance to spend the night in our ancient jail. I could put a guard at the door of his hotel room; he couldn't get very far in Paraná anyway without me tracking him down. Then, too, I still knew very little, and I figured that if he had tangible proof that I trusted him and was grateful for a small favor, he might tell me what he knew. Something told me the story would be worth hearing.

I spoke German now, slowly, "All right. I'll do that for you. But don't try anything . . . you'll be sorry."

Parries's face relaxed, the panic receding. With a nod from me, Angelo guided the prisoner quickly through the room and out the door. I tossed down a Scotch at the bar. By eleven o'clock I was back at the Expresso for a nightcap, and my mind turned back to Parries. What did he know? I figured he was a German, not a Luxembourger, by his use of high German and ignorance of French. His age was right for him to have held a position in Nazi Germany, perhaps stationed in Luxembourg. He had Nazi contacts here, and he was clearly eager to avoid an investigation into his background. His words came back to me, "I'll tell you more than you want to hear."

101

The next morning I dressed quickly, washed down a stale roll with a cup of strong coffee, and hurried to my office. There the stacks of unfinished reports reproached me. I plunged into them, hoping to finish them before Parries arrived. At the back of my mind, I mulled over the best tack to take with him.

About half a hour later, Angelo came in; he was clearly unhappy. Our man had not shown. Angelo had talked to the guard, Miranda. Parries hadn't answered the knock.

"Tell Miranda to get him out. Get a key from the hotel. Break down the door if he has to. I want Parries here in fifteen minutes."

I shuffled through the papers, annoyed at the man. I didn't plan to go easy on him. I found myself planning my line of questioning instead of concentrating on the reports.

The telephone jangled. I reached for it, scattering papers onto the floor. "Parries. He's dead, sir. . . . Strangled." Usually cool and impassive, Angelo sounded shaken; his voice was muffled. After checking the hotel room number, I told him not to do anything. I'd be right over. I dropped the receiver, then slammed my palm down on the top of the phone. Close behind the anger rising in my chest was guilt. If I'd taken him in last night . . . Anyway, what did he know that was so important that he had to be killed?

The Hotel Martín wasn't far. I decided to walk, wending my way through the narrow side streets to the rundown neighborhood where Parries had stayed. I looked up at the whitewashed building, noting several large brown stains across the front. A shabbily dressed woman was listlessly scrubbing the front lobby. The clerk looked up with a frown, recognized me, and nodded curtly. His lips were pursed in disapproval—of the dead body above?

I returned his greeting, then walked quickly up the stairway before he could register a complaint. To the left, down the dim hallway, I saw Angelo leaning against a doorway, smoking a cigarette.

Homicide had been notified, reported Angelo. Miranda, the guard, knew nothing. He was told to see that the man didn't leave the hotel; that's just what he did. Angelo thought he probably went down to talk to the night clerk to pass the time . . . or out for a beer. Nobody would say.

The door to Parries's room was open and the wood along the door jamb was splintered; no wonder the clerk had been unhappy. I walked inside. Parries was directly ahead of me, propped up against the cheap iron-frame bed. He still wore the same suit pants and striped shirt that he had had on at the restaurant. A necktie was wound around his neck. It was tied to one end of his belt, the other end was wrapped around the bedpost. His neck hung slackly; I thought it might be broken.

I commented to Angelo that whoever did this was trying to make it look like a suicide, but if that was the case, it was the first man I ever knew who hanged himself from a bed frame three feet off the ground.

We agreed that they must have strangled him with the tie, then knotted it to the belt. "Look, the belt isn't even pulled tight. Amateurs!" While I said it, the voice in the back of my head chided me. Amateurs, sure, but they outsmarted you, cop.

I forced down the anger and looked around the room. It was sparsely furnished. Parries's suit coat was lying on the bed. A wooden chair with a cracked leg, a dresser painted a sickly green, a night table, and lamp were the only other pieces of furniture.

I asked Angelo if Parries had had any other belongings, and he said there was nothing. He had sent a man over to the bus station locker where Detective Kulick had

103

seen him go to get clothing. The contents would be sent over to homicide.

I picked up Parries's coat and searched the pockets, finding his identity papers and a roll of bills as thick as my fist. There were over 1,000 cruizeiros (about $50). The booklet felt thinner. Sure enough, several pages had been torn out, leaving only the working permit. I noticed something else that I had not noticed last night. On the cover was some writing in blue ink. "Pharmacist . . . Santa Catarina." Above the words was a crudely drawn map, showing the common borders of Germany, Belgium and Luxembourg, with Belgium and Luxembourg transposed. I tucked the booklet in my back pocket.

Angelo told me that Senhor Delago, the night clerk he had sent for, was here. Outside the door stood a sleepy-looking, short, dumpy man, leaning toward the room, hesitant to come any closer than the center of the hallway. His shirt was stuffed carelessly into his pants. I asked him to come in and tell us what had happened last night.

Delago edged slightly closer to the door, just barely in the room, ready to bolt. Stuttering, he reported that two men had checked in about midnight, said they were friends of Senhor Parries. They were German. The clerk told them Senhor Parries had retired for the night. They said, fine, they'd catch him in the morning. Could they have rooms next to his? "I saw nothing wrong in that," the clerk pleaded, his eyes darting to my face then to Angelo's for confirmation. Seeing none, he stammered, talking faster. He had assigned them to rooms thirty-five and thirty-one. He knew nothing about any guard, any trouble with the police, he assured us.

The room clerk was staring at the dead man now, having finally screwed up his courage. Tonight, he would recount the details to his friends at the bar, reserving a heroic role for himself, no doubt. He hesitated.

Angelo nodded in dismissal, and the clerk scurried noiselessly down the hall.

I noticed there were no doors connecting Parries's room to the adjoining rooms. I asked Angelo if the door had been locked when he had arrived that morning.

"Yes, sir. From the inside." I walked over and picked up the large room key. I turned it over in my hand. I could see the two men closing in on Parries, the struggle, the swift, brutal twist of the necktie, and the sharp crack as Parries's neck snapped. My hand gripped the key tighter, until it cut into my hand. The key . . . Angelo said the door was locked from the inside.

They must have used a common burglar's trick. With a large keyhole like this, it was easy to tie a string to the throat of the key, thread the string through the keyhole from the inside of the room, step outside and close the door, then pull the string until the key slipped up into place, making it look as if Parries had locked himself in before hanging himself from the bed.

We tried the key in another door and it opened easily; all the room keys were interchangeable. We walked over to room 35. My eye caught something on the floor. I bent over and picked up a six-inch piece of white string. The previous night's tenant, if he had even been in the room, had left no traces. Room 31 was equally bare.

"Let's go. There's nothing more to be done." These murderers were third rate. I was sure we would catch up with them very quickly. We would leave it to homicide, I told Angelo.

Angelo glanced at me skeptically. I avoided his gaze. I knew I wouldn't drop the case. I owed that dead man something . . . and he died owing me something. I intended to collect.

8

It was late the next morning. I looked down at Parries's body, laid out in the heavy metal drawer of the morgue's refrigerated vault, his skin waxy and blue in the harsh neon light.

The morgue attendant handed me the autopsy report I had asked for as he entered the room. I took the file and skimmed it quickly. There were no surprises: death by stangulation, presumably the tie. Broken neck. No unusual marks on the rest of the body to indicate a struggle.

I asked the attendant for an ink pad and some paper. He opened the center drawer of his desk, then the right, pushing the contents from one side to the other. He found some order forms for supplies and a stamp for the official seal, and asked if they would do.

I took a few pieces of paper and the ink pad, opened it, and pressed it against Parries's rigid right thumb, then carefully placed the thumb against a piece of paper.

While the ink dried, I stood and stared at the print, one of the few clues to the mystery of Eugene Parries. No autopsy could reveal the answers to my questions. The story I wanted to hear was permanently locked inside his nude corpse, impervious to any surgeon's scalpel.

I folded the paper in half, tucked it in my shirt pocket, and walked slowly back through the almost empty streets to my office. Most of Curitiba's residents had been driven inside by the searing midday sun, but after the dank, tomblike atmosphere of the morgue, I welcomed the penetrating heat.

Entering the building courtyard, I spotted Angelo leaning against the wall in the shadow of the building and chatting with another detective. I signalled, and he crossed the courtyard to meet me. In my office, I sank into my desk chair, leaned back so the faint breeze from the ceiling fan would cool my face, and pulled the paper out of my pocket. Giving it to Angelo, I asked him to send it to the fingerprint bank, Policia Tecnica. Perhaps we could discover something more about Eugene Parries, if that was even his real name.

I told Angelo to keep an eye out for anybody that turned up to claim the body. I had released the story as a suicide, so the murderers would think we bought their clumsy suicide cover-up, and so friends or relatives wouldn't be scared away. If anybody showed up, I wanted to see them.

Angelo nodded. "Any word on who did it?"

I shook my head. Homicide had put out a wanted bulletin with their names and descriptions. I had a feeling it wouldn't take long to catch those two; their methods hadn't been very subtle.

*   *   *

It didn't take long for Parries's mourner to appear. Two days later, Angelo poked his head into my office, to tell me a man had shown up asking for Parries's body, and was waiting outside. I told him to bring him in.

The stocky, blond man accompanying Angelo bowed slightly as I greeted him. He wore a stiff smile.

I greeted him, introduced myself, and asked if he was a relative of Parries.

He wasn't. His name was Edgar Renner, and he owned a shoe store in Rio do Sul, Santa Catarina. Parries's brother-in-law had asked him to come and identify the body.

"And Parries's family? They're not coming?" I asked.

"No, Senhor. The man's wife died several years ago. Senhor Parries did not get along with his family. They wanted nothing to do with him when he was alive." What could be a sneer crossed Renner's face as he mentioned Parries; it seemed he had no use for the dead man either.

I asked what his family's problem was that no one even planned to show up at his funeral.

Renner shrugged. He didn't know anything about it. There were business disputes, family troubles. He leaned over to flick away a tiny piece of lint that had caught on his expensive silk suit.

"And does the family at least wish to pay for the man's burial?" I asked, with some sarcasm.

"No, Senhor." replied Renner, meeting my gaze with a bland stare.

"Very well, Senhor Renner. "It's a pauper's grave, then. Thank you for your trouble." I rose to my feet, and Angelo escorted Renner out of my office.

I sank back into my chair. An attractive fellow this Parries was turning out to be. Not that I could say much for his friends or family. There was one other possibility for a decent burial, however.

I picked up the telephone and dialed Mr. Andréas, the Belgian consul, explaining that the murdered man had been a citizen of Luxembourg. The Belgian consulate also represented Luxembourg here in Curitiba, and I wanted to inform them in case there were relatives in Luxembourg who would be willing to pay for his burial

108

expenses or in case Belgium would be willing to pick up the tab.

"No, thank you, Dr. Erdstein. Not that man!" He was vehement.

Surprised that Andréas knew anything about Parries, I asked him what he meant. He told me Parries had come to see him a couple of weeks ago, saying he was in financial trouble. Andréas told him he'd get back to him, but thought he was a strange, irrational man. His papers showed he used to work at the Hollandshē Bank in São Paulo. Andréas knew a general manager of the bank, and called him to ask about Parries. Don't trust that guy, he was told. He's a thief. Evidently, the manager had caught Parries stealing and fired him on the spot. That was some years ago, about 1955. The bank manager also told Andréas that Parries's family was in Brazil, somewhere in Santa Catarina, he thought. He suggested I try there.

I thanked Andréas for the information, and hung up. If Parries had been in trouble in São Paulo, the police there might have more information on him. I called a friend in the department and asked him to check on Parries to see if the bank had reported the theft and if any action had been taken. Meanwhile, I decided to have a chat with Heinrich Mueller.

I found him at the Brazilian-German Alliance headquarters, in a small, elegantly furnished office. His slight body seemed dwarfed by his large leather swivel chair and richly ornamented walnut desk. He squinted at me, smiling with his usual oily charm, and asked what he could do for me.

"I've come to see what you can tell me about Eugene Parries," I said, settling into a comfortable velvet armchair next to his desk.

"Ach, poor man. Such a tragic death. I read about it in the papers, of course..." Mueller drifted off helplessly, as if he were at a loss to know how to help me.

I decided to try to shake him, telling him that I knew that he had given Parries quite a sum of money on the day of the murder, and wondered why.

Mueller's eyes narrowed slightly, but the smile remained. He told me Parries had come up to him at the *bier stube* and said friends of his in Rio do Sul had told him to look Mueller up. Mueller had had a few drinks with Parries, who was buying drinks for everybody. Mueller said he seemed like a nice enough fellow, but strange, and a bit down and out. Parries had been in Hans's place a lot the past few weeks, and Mueller talked with him several times. Then a few nights ago, he showed up again, and he was broke. So, Mueller had helped him out a little, a guy from the old home town, you know, he said as he shrugged modestly.

"Over 1,000 cruzeiros . . . you're a very generous man, Heinrich."

Mueller merely smiled. He was a slick customer who wouldn't be panicked into revealing any information, and I didn't know enough to bluff him. I thanked him curtly, told him he'd undoubtedly be hearing from me again, and left, more convinced than ever that he knew something about Parries's murder.

When I got back to the office, there was a message from my friend in São Paulo. No report had been made to the police about the theft at the Hollandshē Bank. He had taken the liberty of checking with the bank, who assured him there must have been a misunderstanding. Senhor Parries had left voluntarily.

*   *   *

Regular duties occupied me during the next few weeks, and I put the Parries file aside, knowing that the fingerprint bureau moved with something less than com-

110

puter-like efficiency and that it would take time for homicide to track down the murderers. One morning about three weeks later, I sat down at my desk and started to push aside the paperwork, when my eye caught a glimpse of the letterhead of the Policia Tecnica. I picked up the report and ran through it quickly.

The fingerprints I had sent had been in the federal file and matched those of Eugene Parries. His file contained an Interpol report that said he had been a minister in the Nazi occupation government of Luxembourg during World War II, had been tried, and condemned to death as a collaborator and for embezzling funds. Luckily for Parries, the Nazi collapse and the chaos at the end of the war gave him an opportunity to escape before the sentence could be carried out. There was no record of criminal activity in Brazil and no record of a legal entry permit into this country.

As I finished the report, Angelo came in, holding a paper in his hand. "I thought you'd want to see this right away," he said. "They caught up with Parries's murderers in Santa Catarina."

I wanted him to see the fingerprint report, so I traded papers. The report from Santa Catarina state police said that a local police *delegado* had recognized the names of our suspects as those of two men who had reported their work permits stolen close to a month ago. State police questioned the two, who were working in a factory in Santa Catarina; both had solid alibis. After checking the plant's records, however, it was determined that two Germans fitting the descriptions of the suspects worked at the plant and had skipped work the week of the murder. They were taken in for questioning, and promptly confessed but refused to say why they had killed Parries.

We discussed the report. Before he left, Angelo said he wasn't surprised that the men confessed. "All it took was a little talk of the *pão de arara*, and they sang a pretty tune, I imagine."

Translated roughly as "the parrot's stick," the dreaded *pão de arara* torture consists of stripping a man naked, running a pole under his knees, drawing his hands up between his legs, and tying them to the pole. The victim is then suspended over a tub of water. Uncooperative prisoners are hosed with cold water, beaten on the soles of the feet and held underwater by the hair. By taping the knees and wrists beforehand, such a victim can be hauled up before a judge an hour after being tortured and not show a mark. I agreed with Angelo; the threat alone undoubtedly had been enough to elicit a willing confession. It didn't help me much. It made a tight murder case for the Santa Catarina police, and that's all they were interested in, but I still didn't know what Parries was going to tell me.

I stared at the wall, seeing Parries's desperate face that night in the Expresso, Heinrich Mueller's smug grin, and myself, looking down at Parries's corpse in the morgue and feeling the same guilt I had felt in the hotel room the morning after he was murdered. In the back of my mind some instinct kept prodding me to see this through.

*   *   *

I worked doggedly during the next several weeks to catch up on my regular duties. When I felt that things were in order, I wrote a report on Parries's case and sent it to Paulo Pimentel. At the same time, I called and made an appointment with his secretary for the next morning at ten o'clock.

I showed up a few minutes early at the government house and stood outside while I finished a cigarette. Then I ground the cigarette out under my heel and

112

walked up the well-worn staircase with its smooth, carved banister.

Paulo's secretary showed me into the large, Spartan office. Modern, utilitarian office furniture was combined with a few handsome antique Spanish chairs and tables, reflecting the mixture of old and new that typified the governor.

Motioning me to a side chair next to the desk, Paulo smiled broadly. His beige linen suit looked crisp and neat even on this scorching afternoon. He reached for a wooden box on the corner of his desk and, opening it, offered me a slim Cuban cigar.

He told me he had read my report and sensed that I wasn't satisfied with the outcome of the Parries's case.

Smiling at his perceptiveness, I told him he was right. I was convinced that there was more to it and that the Nazis were mixed up in it, at least Heinrich Mueller was. Seeing my opportunity, I confessed I couldn't do much more here, but would like to go to Rio do Sul, take a leave of absence just for a short while to see what I could find. I outlined for him briefly the tracks that kept leading to Santa Catarina, to Rio do Sul—the note on Parries's papers, the conversation with Andréas, the tie-in with Mueller, and the unsatisfactory visit from Renner.

"Erico, you're getting restless. You weren't meant to be a bureaucrat, chained to your desk. You're happier out there with your nose to the ground, not in some stuffy office."

I had the feeling from his wistful tone that Paulo wasn't only talking about me, but about himself. He too was happiest out in the streets, wading through a crowd of people, his gaucho hat tipped at a jaunty angle.

I laughed and admitted he was right, but that I also thought there was something in this case that should be pursued. The state police in Santa Catarina weren't going to follow it up. They considered the case closed now

113

that they had caught the murderers. I wanted to know the rest of the story. And I thought the tracks led to Rio do Sul.

"Once in the middle of it, you may wish you'd left well enough alone," he cautioned. But he gave his permission, recommending that I start by contacting Rio do Sul's public prosecutor, Priamo Amaral, who had worked in Pimentel's campaign, and the local police chief, or *delegado*, Hector von Schee. He buzzed for his secretary and asked her to draft letters to the two officials, asking them to give me all the help they could in my investigation. He also loaned me his department's Jeep station wagon for the trip.

When his secretary left, I thanked him.

"Oh, I've learned to trust your hunches, Erico," Paulo said as he rose from his chair and extended his hand. "Good luck to you, and keep me informed of your progress."

I stopped at the garage on my way out of the government house to check on the car. It would come in handy, since I would be unable to rely on paved roads once I was out of the city. Only a Jeep could handle the potholes, ruts, and intermittent lengths of washed-out road that I was likely to encounter in the interior of Paraná.

I arranged with Rodriguez to pick up the car the next morning, went back and finished up some last-minute details, and set my office in order. Then I returned to the government house to pick up the letters of introduction and went out for some supper. Later in the evening, I ran into my favorite girl, a singer named Maria. When I told her I'd be out of town for a few days, she was eager to give me a proper send-off, so we strolled back to my apartment. My short leave seemed to appeal to her melodramatic nature, and she threw herself into our lovemaking with abandon.

9

The alarm's persistent buzz at five o'clock the next morning bored into my brain. I reached out and hit the button; Maria sighed and rolled over on her stomach. While I packed, she slept soundly. Across the dark room I could see her long hair spread out on the pillow like a pool of black ink against the sheets. Leaving her a note, I slipped out and hiked over to the government house where the car was parked with the key under the floor mat.

The city was just beginning to stir with delivery trucks making early morning rounds and storekeepers sweeping their front steps and setting up displays in front of their shops. I rolled down the window, lit a cigarette, and turned on the radio for the morning news. Leaving Curitiba behind, I headed south down the coastal highway, which sliced through tropical forests.

Cutting inland to Rio do Sul, the road became rougher, and the landscape gradually lost its tropical flavor, changing to rolling hills covered with pine forests and laced with small rivers. I could see why the area had attracted so many German immigrants; it resembled the Black Forest. I passed small European-style farm cottages with ruffled curtains swaying in the breeze against the predictable windowbox of flowers. In the yard there

115

was often a blond, red-cheeked *hausfrau* with a blousey starched white apron, scattering feed for chickens. It was easy to forget that I was in South America at all.

Late that afternoon I drove into Rio do Sul in a cloud of dust thrown up by a rusty jalopy in front of me. Like the countryside I had just passed through, the town was German in appearance, small and peaceful, with one major unpaved street that contained most of the stores and offices, the police station, and the only hotel. Deciding I had better get a room first, I parked the jeep in front of the hotel, walked in, and introduced myself to the desk clerk, a pale elderly man who rolled his eyes with pleasure at the prospect of sheltering "such an eminent official." He escorted me to a sunny, plain second-story room at the front of the hotel, overlooking the main street.

"The best room in the house, Senhor," he assured me. I thanked him and handed him a substantial tip, which seemed merited by my newly exalted position. I deposited my suitcase on the luggage rack and washed the dust from my hands and face.

Leaving the bag unpacked, I walked over to the police station, which I had spotted on the way into town, and introduced myself to the roly-poly policeman at the front desk, then asked to see Dr. von Schee.

With effort, he heaved himself out of his chair and led me to a small corner office.

"Dr. von Schee, this man asked to see you," the sergeant offered before turning and waddling back to his station.

The young man, whom I noticed had an unusually long face and a classic Roman nose, stood and extended his hand. I introduced myself and handed him Pimentel's letter of introduction. He read it quickly, and looked up with a smile, saying he would be glad to do what he could to help me.

116

I summarized the Parries case and explained my reasons for coming to Rio do Sul. The *delegado* leaned forward intently, his eyes evaluating me as he listened to my story. When I finished, he told me he was familiar with Parries. The dead man had been accused of forgery last year by his brother-in-law, the man I had mentioned, Dr. Gemballa. Gemballa was a wealthy man who owned a pharmacy with a laboratory above it. Von Schee interrupted his story to ask me if I wouldn't prefer discussing this over a drink. I must be thirsty after my long, hot drive.

We walked over to a nearby bar, where I ordered a stein of the local beer and a sandwich while von Schee continued. I learned that Gemballa was the leader of the Nazi movement in Rio do Sul, the local Führer, according to von Schee. He had received his pharmaceutical training in Germany in the 1930s and returned a convert to Hitler. He organized the Nazi party here during the war, along with my old friend Heinrich Mueller. Mueller and Gemballa were arrested in 1943 for storing guns and were interned for a short while. The scandal resulted in Mueller's being thrown out of his church and forced to leave town, but because of his business Gemballa stayed, and his influence and wealth had grown since the war. A lot of townspeople were afraid of him.

The Nazis were still active here then? Von Schee said yes, they were a strong and fanatical group. They still worshipped Adolph Hitler and dreamed of resurrecting the German Reich.

He told me that Rio do Sul was almost exclusively German, at least ninety percent. He himself was German on one side. But only a small minority, maybe ten percent, of the population was Nazi. Most of the Germans clung to the old country's customs, however, maintaining their own clubs, newspapers, and schools. The Nazis

117

exploited these nationalistic feelings to control local politics. They were the people with money, positions of authority, good education . . . and they were more ruthless than the rest of the people.

The organization through which the Nazis exerted their control was the German/Brazilian Cultural Alliance, which "welcomed contributions," as von Schee sarcastically put it. Actually, many times it was little more than protection money.

I asked him why the police hadn't been able to curb the Alliance. Von Schee said people were just too scared to fight back, afraid of what would happen to them if they dared to challenge the Nazis.

I turned the conversation back to Parries. Von Schee said he wouldn't be surprised to find Gemballa behind the murder. There had been bad blood between the in-laws. Parries had been Gemballa's errand boy for years, but was never trusted with any real responsibility. Nobody trusted Parries, although he was always trying to ingratiate himself with the Alliance members.

Last year, Gemballa had sworn out a complaint against Parries, accusing him of forging the pharmacist's name on some promissory notes and cashing them at the local bank. Gemballa couldn't prove the charge and finally dropped it. There were rumors in town that Parries was blackmailing his brother-in-law, but both men denied it. Not long after the incident, Gemballa had had two psychiatrists testify that Parries was insane and had him committed to a mental institution. Evidently, he had escaped from there and had fled to Curitiba.

Von Schee didn't think Parries had forged the notes, although he personally thought Parries was shifty and spineless. He thought the dead man had been blackmailing his brother-in-law and Gemballa had tired of paying. That gave Gemballa a strong motive for murder, but he could give me other names to check out later if I wanted them. If I needed any assistance, he was available and he would be glad to put his right-hand man, Oscar Cordeiro, at my disposal.

I took von Schee up on his offer, and the next morning after meeting Cordeiro, I took him with me to Dr. Gemballa's pharmacy. Cordeiro waited outside while I went into the store. Behind the counter next to the cash register stood a square-faced, bull-necked young man, his burly arms crossed in front of him. He looked more like a guard than a sales clerk.

"Good morning," I greeted him. "I'm here to see Dr. Gemballa."

"What about?" he asked.

"Police business."

"Police?" he echoed, less confidently. "Uh, wait a minute. I, uh, I'll tell him you're here . . ."

He hesitated. "Tell him? Where?" I interrupted.

He motioned toward the door in the back of the room and opened his mouth to speak again. I walked quickly to the door and up the stairs before he could collect himself. He shouted after me, but didn't follow.

At the top of the stairs was an open area with a reception desk. Down the hall I could see a laboratory. A secretary was walking out of an office on the right. She stopped and peered over her glasses at me.

"Do you have an appointment?" She glanced back over her shoulder nervously.

"Yes, thank you," I said, walking past her into the office.

A balding, blond man in a white lab coat sat behind the desk, writing. He looked up, clearly annoyed, and asked me what I wanted. He spoke in Portuguese, marred by a strong German accent.

"Dr. Gemballa, I'm here because I believe you murdered your brother-in-law, Eugene Parries."

119

Gemballa shot to his feet. "I-I-I don't know what you're talking about! Get out of here."

"Take it easy. If you want to answer my questions, sit down. If not, just let me know, and I'll take you down to headquarters." I flashed my badge.

Gemballa sank slowly back into his chair, eyeing me warily. "What do you want to know?"

Although he was trying to regain his composure, he was clearly frightened. Before I could answer, he started to talk. In short bursts and incomplete sentences, he told me he had had nothing to do with his brother-in-law's death. He had understood the death was a suicide. His brother-in-law was a thief, a blackmailer, a crazy man, and he had been forced to have him committed. He paused for breath and asked if he could speak in German.

I agreed, since I was having trouble following his mangled Portuguese. Gemballa told me that Parries treated his sister like dirt, ran around with other women, and drank too much. According to Gemballa, Parries murdered his sister with his brutal treatment of her. Gemballa had finally had him put away. He admitted that he had never tried to hide his contempt for Parries, but kill him. . . . He spread his arms, as if to point out his respectable, professional surroundings.

I ignored the gesture, and asked why he hadn't allowed Parries's daughters to go to the funeral. He insisted they were grown girls; they hadn't wanted to go. Parries didn't treat them any better than his wife.

I asked why Parries was blackmailing him. He shook his head violently. It wasn't blackmail; Parries just put pressure on Gemballa to bail him out of the troubles he got himself into, abusing the family connection.

I smiled thinly and shook my head. No, I didn't think so, I said. From what I had heard, I thought it more likely that Parries knew about his illegal activities, about the money he extorted from frightened citizens for the German/Brazilian Alliance, and to shut him up, Gemballa had Parries committed. And when he escaped, killed.

The blow had struck home. Gemballa started sputtering about halfway through my speech. "No . . . no . . . no. Nothing like that," he shouted, his face darkened with rage.

I had accomplished my purpose. He was frightened and angry. I'd see that Cordeiro tailed him for a while, to see where he would lead us. I turned on my heel and left him sitting at his desk staring at me, walked past the secretary, down the stairs, and out past the officious sales clerk.

Cordeiro was leaning against the building smoking a cigarette when I came out. I told him to have someone keep an eye on Gemballa for a few days, to see where he went and whom he saw.

When I returned to von Schee's office, he was with a lanky young man. "Bom dia, Erico," von Schee greeted me, falling naturally into a first-name basis. I wasn't surprised since we had immediately taken a liking to one another. He introduced me to the young man, Priamo Amaral, the public prosecutor.

I shook his hand, surprised at his youth. I had called him the night before to let him know I was here and to pass on Paulo's regards. I told him I would be here this morning, and would appreciate hearing his opinions, too. Von Schee asked me what I'd learned from Gemballa.

I repeated my conversation. Amaral laughed. "It seems you dropped a lighted match on his *cola de palha*." I laughed at the sight of the pompous pharmacist dancing around with a blazing "straw tail" (Brazil's colorful term for a bad conscience).

"I have, if you'll pardon the pun, put a tail on him" I

said, relaying my instructions to Cordeiro. I asked if they could provide any other leads.

It was almost noon when I left the police station, my notebook filled with names of people who might have information about Gemballa, Parries, and the Nazi party in Rio do Sul. It took me several days to track down everyone on the list, and what I discovered completely changed the focus of my investigation. Probing the people of Rio do Sul, I unwittingly tapped a geyser of hostility that had been seething underneath the surface for years. From a torrent of whispered rumors and accusations, I was able to piece together an ugly picture of fear and oppression.

The president of the local Rotary group confirmed a rumor I had heard that Gemballa had been forced out of the organization after his unsuccessful attempt to transform it into a neo-Nazi front group. The principal of the local high school invited me to her home to talk with some of her friends. She told me about two doctors at the local hospital who had recently fled town after one of them—a Dr. Oetzer—had stabbed a young folk singer who had called him a Nazi. According to the rumors, this Dr. Oetzer and a Dr. Schraft were former SS physicians, who were in the country illegally. I took down the names of the doctors and made a note to check with von Schee about the case. Later that night, I received a call at the hotel from a man who had attended the meeting at the school principal's house. He had been afraid to mention it in front of the group, but he had witnessed the stabbing. Yes, he would be willing to testify.

Another story I heard at the meeting and elsewhere concerned a young man called Lothar Paul. He was the son of a prominent merchant in Rio do Sul who had been forced out of the Brazilian Air Force during World War II for his Nazi sympathies. Shortly after his return home his father died under mysterious circumstances and

122

Lothar inherited the family business and joined the local Nazi party. Most of the group insisted that the young man had killed his father. True or not, the accusation was an indication of the hatred and suspicion among the townspeople.

Recently, Lothar Paul had been reinstated in the military, with the rank of Colonel and was assigned to the SNI, the federal military political police.

On Friday I visited a bartender named Klaus Wemmer, a former SS officer who had soured on the Nazis. Wemmer was a heavy set, genial man who would have looked more at home as a tuba player in a Munich beer hall than as a Nazi thug. He was eager to talk to me when I explained my purpose here, telling me he had come to Rio do Sul after the war ended to begin a new life. He had become disillusioned with the Nazis and just wanted to live a simple, decent life.

But the Nazis, who knew about his past, assumed Wemmer would join eagerly in their Nazi revival here. He attended a few meetings, saw their "shrine," a secret room in the Alliance headquarters filled with Nazi banners, swastikas, and pictures of Hitler and other Nazi leaders. They tried to get Wemmer to contribute to the cause, using subtle pressure, saying they could blacken his reputation, but he refused. "Everybody knows about me; I'm not the only one around here who can't boast about his war record."

But Wemmer insisted that many others had succumbed and now paid monthly "social dues", as the Alliance called it. Only a fraction of it ever went for social activities, according to Wemmer. He was convinced most of it went right into Gemballa's pocket and from there who knew where. "I know some of that money goes to help the war criminals," he said.

"War criminals . . . how?" I asked, startled at this new information.

Wemmer seemed surprised that this was news to me. He said the money helped pay for false identity papers, shelter, and living expenses for ex-Nazis who had escaped after the war. The local group was not just a local organization, but part of a network throughout this part of South America. It included prominent Nazi leaders, wanted by Germany or Israel, who stay in a country until a friendly government falls or someone uncovers their true identity. Then they have to move on, utilizing the network of Nazi groups. The top officials travel all the time, checking on Nazi groups throughout the region. I asked Wemmer if he knew who had come through here.

"Oh, some big fish . . . Dr. Joseph Mengele, the Auschwitz doctor, the one they called the 'Angel of Death,' for example. He comes often. You've heard of him, I suppose."

I had of course read horror storeis of the notorious doctor of Auschwitz, who had been singled out by concentration camp survivors for his sadism, his cruel medical experiments upon prisoners, and the incongruous, angelic smile he wore as he performed his duties. Most of the other names, too, I recalled from Interpol reports and newspaper articles, names like Rolf Meissner, nephew of the German State Secretary Otto von Meissner, who assisted Hitler in his takeover of the Weimar Republic; Heinrich Mueller, the head of the Gestapo; and, of course, Martin Bormann, Hitler's secretary and deputy Führer.

Had Wemmer actually seen any of these men, I asked. He hadn't, but friends of his had. One of them was a man who had seen Dr. Mengele before and recognized him. He trusted the man, and he had heard the story from enough people to convince him it was true.

Wemmer did know where they usually stayed. It was a villa outside town in the country, called Dona Ema, and

124

it belonged to a Dr. Alexander Lenard. Did I know about him?

The name sounded familiar, but I didn't remember where I had heard it. Wemmer refreshed my memory. Lenard was an expert on Bach, the man who had won all the money on the TV quiz show in Brazil a few years ago. He was a remarkable man, a Hungarian refugee, although his name didn't sound Hungarian to me. Alexander in Hungarian is Sandor. And Lenard hardly sounds Hungarian. The man was a painter, a linguist who translated *Winnie the Pooh* into Latin. Supposedly he was just a gentleman farmer now, but he had been known to treat patients in the area and prescribe medicine. Most significantly, he had very mysterious visitors.

I left Hans Wemmer, dazed by these new allegations. Later, as I picked halfheartedly at my dinner, I pondered the rumors and accusations that seemed to spew forth from Rio do Sul like lava from a volcano. They were assuming more serious proportions than I had imagined, especially if what Wemmer said was true. Not only was a town dominated by a movement I thought had been discredited and buried twenty years ago, but the same old enemies now appeared to be springing from the dead. I remembered the magazine articles I had scoffed at when I read them. Who could believe that twenty years later Martin Bormann and Joseph Mengele were still plotting a Nazi revolution?

Eugene Parries now seemed insignificant, only a minor character in a complex plot. I felt that I was close to uncovering the story he had planned to tell me. If it was what I thought it was, it was worth tracking down. It was the kind of mystery and challenge no cop could resist . . . *if*, I kept reminding myself, it was true.

*   *   *

Later that evening I talked again to several of my informants. Once I indicated that I knew all about the visiting Nazi war criminals, they were eager to tell me what they knew, often filling in new details. The same names kept cropping up—Mengele, Meissner, Mueller, Lenard, now and then Bormann. Mengele was the one most often mentioned in connection with Dr. Lenard; it was said that he visited the villa frequently, driving a yellow Simca. Almost everyone seemed very sure of their facts, but no one I talked to had actually seen any of the criminals.

Next I telephoned a bank manager, Helio Westphalen, whom Priamo Amaral had told me might be willing to give me information about Nazi funds. Westphalen was cautious but he seemed willing to help. He suggested I meet him at the bank Sunday morning, when it was closed and I could have access to the files.

I found the portly, balding man standing near the side door of the bank as agreed. We shook hands and I waited while he fumbled nervously with the door key. He sighed with relief once we were safely inside. Once I explained in more detail the kind of information I was after, Westphalen pulled a thick manila file folder from the cabinet in his office, marked with the account number and Gemballa's name. He explained that the pharmacist had two accounts with the bank, his personal account and a second one for German/Brazilian Alliance funds. This exhausted his store of conversation and he fell silent, sitting quietly with his hands clasped in his lap until I asked a question or requested another file. Gemballa's Alliance account was substantial, containing at that time more than 200,000 cruzeiros ($10,000). I flipped through the record of transactions, then checked them against the bank account of several other men associated with the Nazi group. From the files, I began to get a clearer picture of the local Nazi network.

126

One transaction caught my eye. Lothar Paul had withdrawn from his account almost 10,000 cruzeiros one day last month. Checking back with Gemballa's account, I found that the pharmacist had deposited that exact amount in his Alliance account the very next day. Once alerted, I noted regular transactions of this nature. Evidently Paul acted as a Nazi "fund raiser." Gemballa, too, made periodic withdrawals of large sums, but I was not able to determine their destination. I was disappointed to learn that Dr. Lenard did not have an account with the bank.

When I had completed my notes, Westphalen told me a friend, a good client of the bank, wanted to talk to me. Sensing his secretive, almost amused tone, I followed him without a word down the street to a Catholic church. A priest? But Westphalen walked past the front door and down a pathway to a small building that had been grafted onto the rear wall of the church. We walked inside the one-room adobe hut, stopping to let our eyes adjust to the dim light. About fifteen people sat on stools and chairs arranged in a circle on the dirt floor. At the front was a small altar with a throne-like chair. In this place of honor sat a handsome black man, with fine, almost delicate features and liquid brown eyes, wearing a sports shirt, slacks, and sandals.

We picked chairs near the door and as people drifted into the room, Westphalen leaned toward me, smiling as he whispered, "Do you believe in voodoo, Dr. Erdstein?"

I raised my eyebrows. Keeping his voice low, Westphalen told me that Poquo, the man in the front, had asked him to bring me to this seance. He wanted to pass along some information second-hand. Poquo had told Westphalen that he had heard that I was asking questions about Nazi war criminals. He had some answers, or rather it seemed that his medium would have some answers this morning. That way it came from the spirit world, and nobody could blame Poquo for telling tales. Westphalen broke off, pointing toward the front of the room. Poquo stood up, raised his arms, greeted his flock, and then selected several people from the audience, asking them if they would object to being put into a trance so that the spirits could reveal themselves. The mediums selected came to the front of the room and sat on chairs. With a few mumbled words from Poquo, they became rigid, their eyes unseeing. Poquo turned to the audience, inviting questions. Several people asked about relatives who had died, requested cures for illnesses, or sought assistance with a difficult love affair. When there was a pause, I asked my question, feeling more than a bit foolish.

"Are Nazi war criminals hiding out in this region?"

"Yes, such men are here . . . nearby . . . I can feel their presence." I forced back a chuckle; a medium who had been speaking unaccented Portuguese now spoke with a heavy German accent, slowly as if from a dream. "They come . . . and go. I see a man named Joseph, Joseph Mengele, a German doctor, I believe . . . and a man called Alexander . . . also a doctor . . . I see them in a hospital, in an operating room. They travel secretly by night, to a house in the forest. I see a yellow car; I see a woman, a housekeeper. I sense evil, danger."

The medium continued, mentioning many of the names I had already heard, many of the rumors about Nazi criminals. I wanted to take notes, but when I reached for my notepad, Westphalen nudged me and shook his head.

The medium trailed off, his vision apparently at an end. After a pause, someone else asked a question, and he returned to his regular unaccented Portuguese. Westphalen nodded his head toward the door, and we rose and left quietly.

Once we were on the main street headed back toward my hotel, I asked Westphalen if this Poquo was reliable. He said he thought so. The session today had been a set-up, of course. Poquo was an uneducated man, afraid of rich men like Lenard and Gemballa, but he was honest and highly respected for his supernatural powers. "You know," Westphalen confided, "when you live in Brazil, you begin to wonder about this voodoo. I've seen some amazing things. Who's to say?"

I recalled the time I had a severe back pain and a friend had talked me into going to see an old woman who could cure with voodoo. I scoffed, but went along for the fun of it. She chanted over me, asked me to stand up, and my backache had gone. Ever since then, I hesitated to laugh at the Brazilian black magic. Voodoo or not, Poquo's story fit in with what I had been hearing from other people. This Dr. Lenard intrigued me. I asked Westphalen if he knew the doctor. He had met him once, he said, and found him strange, arrogant, and not at all likable. He had talked a little about his past, he remembered, and said he had gone to school in Vienna, in Klosterneuburg. He remembered that because Wesphalen had a relative from there.

I couldn't believe the coincidence. That was the neighborhood where I had gone to school. How old did he think this Lenard was? Westphalen guessed he must be about my age, in his forties. Now I was even more interested in the mysterious gentleman farmer, and decided I would pay him a visit. When we reached my hotel, I asked Westphalen to draw me a map to the villa.

The bank manager's carefully drawn map was easy to follow, and about forty-five minutes later I drove up in front of the imposing wooden gates of Dona Ema. The main house was set on a curving, unpaved road and was surrounded by a dense forest.

I drove past the house and stopped at several neighboring houses, identifying myself as a newspaper reporter and asking about Dr. Lenard. To a man, the neighbors expressed hostility toward the doctor. He was an arrogant, cold man, they said. "Oh, him, he thinks he's lord of the manor. He walks around here barefoot, doesn't lower himself to speak to us poor peasants. I don't know who he thinks he is," one said.

A sunburned farmer told me that Lenard kept to himself, although sometimes the people in the neighborhood went to him for medicine when they were sick. He was a good doctor. Whom did he associate with? He had friends who came to visit often.

I stopped at a small grocery store at the next crossroads and bought a Coke from the storekeeper. While I leaned against the counter, she filled me in on Dr. Lenard. She knew his housekeeper, a woman named Natalie Klein, who bragged about the important company the doctor entertained.

"She's a brute, that woman," the storekeeper spit out, warming to her subject. Looking around, she leaned across the counter toward me, and in a low voice, told me that Natalie Klein was born in Rio do Sul, but went to Germany during the war and worked for the Nazis in the concentration camps. That's where she had met Dr. Lenard and the people who visit at Dona Ema. The storekeeper didn't know the visitors' names. Frau Klein was very secretive about them, but openly broadcast her Nazi views. The storekeeper was German, and thought Natalie Klein assumed that therefore she was a Nazi. "I could care who her Nazi friends are, could be Hitler himself for all I care," she muttered. Before I left, she told me if I was planning to go up there, I wouldn't find Lenard at home. He was gone this week.

I nodded, paid for my Coke, and left, deciding to get a look at the house. I parked my Jeep outside the gate, which was open, and walked up the driveway to the main house, a typical German suburban mansion of wood and brick with fortress-like turrets and small, narrow windows. Off to the side was a small one or two room cottage. As I waited for an answer to my knock, I saw a huge, muscle-bound man walk around the side of the cottage and pause, watching me.

The door opened a crack, and an ugly woman with stringy brown hair and dull, gray eyes poked her head out.

"Yes, what do you want?" she asked, in a harsh, low voice.

I addressed her in German, introducing myself as Dr. Martin, from Vienna, saying that I had heard in Rio do Sul that Dr. Lenard lived here. He was an old school friend of mine, from Klosterneuburg. I hadn't seen him since high school. I told her I had had to leave Austria after the war, hinting that I had been an SS member and had come to South America via Spain.

The woman brightened as I talked, until she was almost smiling. She apologized. Dr. Lenard was away at the present time and would be so sorry he missed me. She ran into the hallway to get a pencil to write down my name.

"Dr. Martin, Friedrich Martin. What a shame. I'd like to talk over old times . . . the good old days, no?" I said, smiling significantly.

She took the bait and launched into a monologue about her illustrious part in the war working at the Herman Goering Werke and at Belsen and Auschwitz. She stated this proudly. After the war, she continued, she had returned to Brazil and was fortunate enough to work for Dr. Lenard, a remarkable man who hadn't forgotten what it was like under the Führer. Neither had I, I thought bitterly.

I told her I understood that Dr. Lenard, in addition to his other accomplishments, spoke thirteen languages.

131

Yes, she bragged. All the European ones including Scandinavian.

Scandinavian, I repeated, as if duly impressed. Natalie revealed that she was sure about that because Lenard had told her that he spoke Norwegian with the captain of the boat when he came over after the war. His Norwegian friends had even come to visit him. She assured me the good doctor would want to talk with me. Could I come back when he returned next week? I said, unfortunately, I was leaving the area tomorrow but perhaps would be able to see him on a return visit.

As I drove back to the hotel, I sorted out the tangle of facts, accusations, and rumors. I had promised Paulo I would be gone only a week, and my time had run out. Tomorrow I would have to leave Rio do Sul. From my hotel room I called von Schee and told him I would like to meet the next morning with him, Amaral, and the local judge, Dr. Ruy Olimpio de Olveira, who would have jurisdiction over any cases arising from my investigation.

The meeting was arranged for nine o'clock at the prosecutor's office. When we were all there, I summarized the results of my week's work, concluding that I did not have enough evidence to arrest Dr. Gemballa. He had contacted other Nazi leaders immediately after I talked with him, but our surveillance hadn't uncovered any evidence linking him to Parries' murder. I recommended that von Schee keep an eye on Gemballa and the other Nazi leaders, however. If they could prove that any of the Alliance contributions were gained through extortion, blackmail or fraud, they could put Gemballa away for some time and might be able to break up this group. I realized that police resources were limited. It would require close surveillance, maybe even someone who could infiltrate their ranks. I had only scratched the surface of the problem.

Besides, right now I was more interested in the ac-

132

tivities at Dr. Lenard's villa, and in the identity of his mysterious visitors. From what I had heard in Rio do Sul, Dr. Joseph Mengele visited often, about once a month. I asked von Schee if he could stake out the place until the next visit? I thought we should pay Dr. Lenard a call.

Von Schee assured me it was no problem. He thought the activity at the villa was closely connected with the Nazi problem in town. I told the men that I'd be back in a couple of weeks after I had had a chance to check out some of the information I'd uncovered. Meanwhile, I would appreciate it if they would let me know if anybody showed up. I also would be looking for this Dr. Oetzer, the man who stabbed the folksinger. I had located a witness who would be willing to testify, and I hoped to find out where the doctor had gone.

I shook hands, wished the men luck, and left for Curitiba. On the long drive back I couldn't help comparing my feelings now with those on the trip down to Rio do Sul. Then, if anyone had asked me, I would have scoffed at the idea of Nazi war criminals hiding out in South American jungles, plotting revenge and the rise of a Fourth Reich. Now that I had seen the fear in this small town, I began to see the problem as a real one—real at least to these Brazilians. I felt again as I had twenty years before when I dug up the coffins of the *Graf Spee* crewmen and found them filled not with corpses but with guns. Once again the enemy I had thought was vanquished had mocked death. Victory had seemed complete in 1945, but had it been?

My instincts as a policeman made me want to pursue the tantalizing clues further, and, I had to admit, I had a personal stake in all this.

10

In Curitiba I was able to check the list of names I had compiled in Rio do Sul against my own police files, federal police files, and Interpol. My main target, of course, was Dr. Mengele. Interpol informed me that there was a warrant for his arrest outstanding from the Land Court in Dusseldorf, Germany. Mengele had been tried *in absentia* and had been sentenced to death if and when he was apprehended.

Not knowing much about the Auschwitz doctor, I checked further and discovered that he had earned his title as the "Angel of Death." Only one of many doctors at the Austrian extermination camp who decided which prisoners would live or die, Mengele was the one the survivors remembered.

They recalled the short, swarthy physician's spotless white gloves, the monocle through which he fixed a piercing gaze on his victims, his detached smile, and his brutality. At Nuremberg, witnesses told how he threw an infant into a fire in front of its mother, killed a teenage girl by splitting her head open with a meat cleaver, and experimented upon prisoners without benefit of anesthesia.

Mengele was evidently not tortured by his job in the

camp as so many other workers were. He considered it his duty to kill "biologically inferior specimens." The cold-blooded statement demonstrated not only his anti-Semitism but his belief that he was a scientist rather than a sadist. He worked in the research laboratories at Auschwitz, trying to discover how twins could be produced, knowing that Germany would need a high post-war birthrate to replace its war dead. His other interest was in altering pigmentation, probably a reflection of his own dissatisfaction with his dark, non-Aryan complexion.

Mengele never let emotion interfere with efficiency. Once, during a typhus epidemic, he ordered a complete barracks of sick women to the gas chambers. Then he disinfected the barracks they had occupied, so it could be filled with another group of prisoners, who were stripped, disinfected and deloused before being allowed into the barracks. This created another empty barracks that could be disinfected and filled with another group of women. So it went until the disease was eradicated. When Mengele was asked why he hadn't merely built a new barracks instead of murdering the first group of women, he maintained the camp administrators would never have given him approval.

Mengele, like so many other Nazis, escaped from Germany in the post-war confusion. He was unknown to Allied authorities at the time. Even today, of the 6,000 SS men that worked at Auschwitz, only 900 are known by name. Mengele, the son of a wealthy industrialist, fled to Beunos Aires where his family conveniently acquired half interest in a farm equipment company. Mengele managed the family firm's local office. In July of 1959, the Germans issued a warrant for Mengele's arrest and asked that he be apprehended and extradited to Germany to stand trial. Before the SS physician could be found, Mengele fled to Paraguay, where he was made a naturalized citizen, thanks to the beneficence of President Alfredo Stroessner, son of a Bavarian merchant and an ardent pro-Nazi.

In 1959, Mengele is reported to have attended his father's funeral in his home town of Günzberg, Germany. His family was the most important in town, and Mengele was hidden by the townspeople. When it was later discovered that he had been in Günzberg, there was an outcry in the German press. By then, however, Mengele was back in South America.

In 1960, an Israeli named Nora Eldoc spotted Dr. Mengele in Bariloche, a resort town in the Argentine Andes. She had been sterilized by Mengele while an inmate in Auschwitz and when she saw the doctor in a hotel ballroom, she could only stare in horror. According to the girl's mother, Mengele did not seem to recognize his former prisoner, but he did notice the tatooed number on her arm that marked her forever as a concentration camp survivor. A few days later, Miss Eldoc was found dead at the bottom of a cliff, the victim of a mountain-climbing accident according to the official police report.

When Eichmann was kidnapped in Argentina, Dr. Mengele fled to Paraguay once again, where he was reported to be living in 1967. Some accounts said he lived in Asunción; others said he lived in one of the German settlements near the Alto Paraná River, not far from the Brazilian border. There were still other reports that he lived on an estate near Encarnación, or that he owned a hospital outside Hohenau, where he continued to conduct his medical experiments. He was said to play an active part in organizing the rebirth of the Fourth Reich in South America, traveling frequently to visit local Nazi organizations.

It no longer seemed so unlikely that Dr. Lenard's visitor had been Joseph Mengele. I was determined to be

136

on hand next time the mysterious visitor turned up at Dona Ema.

About three weeks after my trip to Rio do Sul, I received word from one of my detectives that he had traced Dr. Oetzer, the man who stabbed the folk singer. Oetzer had set up practice in a small town about an hour west of Rio do Sul. I decided to pay him a visit and check on events in Rio do Sul at the same time. There were some more people I wanted to question now that I was armed with more information.

During this trip, I had company: Francisco Camargo, an enthusiastic reporter from the *Tribuna do Estado*, Curitiba's liberal newspaper. He had interviewed me after my return from Rio do Sul to find out the reason for my leave of absence and immediately became convinced that this was his chance to get an exclusive eyewitness account of the capture of Nazi war criminals.

I was happy to have him. I didn't mind the company and felt that a little publicity might help in turning up more information and maybe even some funds to help pay for this investigation. So far my efforts had been strictly free-lance, with some support from von Schee's office. I was running low on money and was counting on Dr. Lenard's visitors to break this case.

Bouncing up and down in the bucking Jeep, Camargo took advantage of his captive audience, chatting merrily, smoking a foul-smelling cigar, and peppering me with questions. By the time we drove up in front of the Rio do Sul police station, I was exhausted. Inside, von Schee greeted me warmly, but offered little encouragement. There had been no sign of visitors at Dona Ema since my last visit.

The next day I went to find Dr. Oetzer, convincing Camargo that he should stay and talk to von Schee about the Nazi situation in Rio do Sul. I felt slightly guilty and sorry for von Schee, but I was relieved to be alone in the car during the drive.

The town in which Dr. Oetzer now lived was similar to Rio do Sul, small and European in appearance. I asked a few storekeepers about the doctor and found out where his office was located. I also learned that Dr. Schraft, who had left Rio do Sul with Oetzer, had settled on a ranch only a few miles outside town. He had died recently, however, according to the pharmacist, and the cause of death had not been determined. It was a strange coincidence, and I wondered if perhaps Dr. Oetzer had decided his colleague knew too much.

After lunch, I walked into Dr. Oetzer's office, complaining loudly of a bad back, and asked the nurse if I could possibly get in to see the doctor. She assured me it wouldn't be long, and I sat stiffly in one of the straight-back chairs until she called my name.

Dr. Oetzer was a silver-haired man with opaque brown eyes. His starched white jacket gave him a formal, cold appearance. He nodded at me and took the card the nurse had left on his desk. "What seems to be the trouble?"

"The trouble is the matter you left behind in Rio do Sul, doctor," I held out my police identification; he took it from me and studied it closely.

"Yes?" he asked coolly.

I repeated the story of the murder as I had heard it in Rio do Sul, emphasizing that I had a witness who was willing to testify in court.

Oetzer, still calm, commented that I was a little outside my territory. "What will it take to send you home, Dr. Erdstein? Say 10,000 *cruzeiros*?" He spoke as calmly as if he were prescribing medicine.

I stood up, and told him that I just wanted to be sure I had the right man. I would turn my information over to

138

the local authorities. I was sure they would be interested in what I knew.

Oetzer laughed harshly and called me a fool. The local authorities would laugh in my face, and I'd be out some money, he said.

"We'll see who laughs," I snapped as I turned and walked out. Fifteen minutes later, I stood before the local *delegado* presenting my evidence. I expected surprise, even outrage, but the *delegado*, a smug, beer-bellied blond named Schultz, merely shrugged. He knew Oetzer. He was a good doctor and they needed good doctors. He wasn't interested in any folksinger who got himself killed. The bum probably asked for it.

I walked out, seething with anger and frustration. I had no jurisdiction here, and by the time I notified the state police, Dr. Oetzer would be long gone. It was an ominous sign of things to come, but I didn't worry about it too long, for as I was filing a report with the state police from the police station in Rio do Sul, von Schee walked in to tell me there had been a lot of activity at the villa, and the housekeeper had bought a large supply of groceries that morning. According to the storekeeper, that was usually a sign that visitors were coming. Von Schee had posted a couple of additional lookouts in the vicinity to make sure we didn't miss anything.

This was it. The gamble looked as if it might pay off, but all I could do now was wait. For the next two days, I marked time, hanging around the police station reviewing plans for the raid, sitting for hours in the café next to the hotel nursing a beer and listening to Camargo's interminable stories. My nerves were stretched, and as I sat watching the steady rain late Wednesday afternoon, my initial excitement started to turn to pessimism.

I was trying to decide how many more days I could afford to sit around here when Priamo Amaral burst in the front door. The visitors had arrived, in a yellow Simca.

Camargo and I threw some change on the table, grabbed our jackets, and ran out behind Amaral. Outside police headquarters, von Schee had gathered ten policemen in four cars. Amaral was to stay behind to wait for our report. Camargo and I jumped into the closest car, and we raced for the villa, glancing through the left rear window at the sinking sun which was barely visible through the clouds. We had to get to the villa before sundown; after that we could not legally enter the house. From sundown to sunup, a man's home is inviolate, protected from police search.

The rains had made the dirt road as slick as soap, and the cars slid from one side to another on the curves. We stopped just a few yards short of the villa and leaped out of the cars, but von Schee halted us with a motion of his arm. It was too late. I walked over to von Schee.

"What do you think?" he asked me.

I said I thought we should stay right where we were and wait for dawn. Whoever was in the house couldn't go anywhere; we had all the roads blocked.

Von Schee nodded, and I returned to the car to settle myself in for the night, only to find Camargo in a panic.

"What if they have guns? They probably heard us drive up. They'll be ready for us. They may even sneak up on us. We could all get killed!" he chattered on, grabbing my coat sleeve.

I told him to calm down and stay in the car if he was scared. I suggested he get some sleep; we had a long night ahead.

I decided my night would be less nerve-wracking if I ignored the reporter, so I went back to von Schee's car and sat in silence. Time dragged as I sat watching the rain stream steadily down the windshield. Through the gloom I could see an occasional glow of a cigarette in one of the other cars.

About midnight, a truck drove up and stopped alongside our caravan. After a muffled conversation, a policeman came over to the car to tell me the driver of the truck wanted to see me.

It was the farmer I had talked to about Dr. Lenard on my first visit to Rio do Sul. He said he wanted to warn me. Last night his son had come home very late and, as he drove by Dona Ema, he saw some men stringing wire from the high voltage lines down to the fence in front of the villa.

I thanked him for the tip, and he wished us luck. As he started the balky motor and lurched off into the night, I turned back to the car, and saw several of the policemen running along the ground by the fence with flashlights. One wore leather gloves and carried a huge wire cutter. The flashlight beams danced in the black mist. I ran over to ask them to shield the lights, but before I reached them they had located the main wire and cut it.

If anyone was watching from the house, he probably had spotted us by now, but I wasn't too worried. Where could they go, after all? We had the only road blockaded at both ends and were guarding the front gate.

About a half hour before dawn, the rain ended and a fog settled over the forest, obscuring the tops of the giant pines. I gathered all the policemen in a ring, and crouched near the ground to draw in the mud with a stick the exact positions everyone should take during the raid. Camargo, who I was sure had not slept all night, beamed a quivering flashlight over my shoulder.

As the first tentative rays of sun tried to pierce the fog, I gave the signal to proceed. The men scaled the fence and ran up the hill toward the darkened villa, fanning out to encircle the two houses. The men farthest from me were mere gray shapes in the fog, hunched

141

down near the ground and running silently through the slick, wet grass. Camargo ran close at my back, like an independent-minded shadow who kept bobbing up and down behind me, out of rhythm. He saw me head for the front door of the main house, and fell back to a safer position behind the most formidable-looking cop.

I banged on the door and shouted: "Police! Come on out! Hands on your heads."

Almost immediately the door swung open. In the dim hallway stood a defiant Natalie Klein, a sneer on her lips.

"You're too late," she gloated. "There's nobody here but me. You want to arrest an old lady with all these cops? You need all these men to bring me in?"

Before I could answer, I heard von Schee shout my name from behind the house. Instructing two men to search the house and another to watch Natalie Klein, I ran to von Schee. He pointed to the hill directly behind the house. Peering through the mist, I saw a stone staircase built into the hillside, disappearing among the pine trees. Cleverly concealed, it could be seen only from a certain angle.

Without a word, von Schee and I ran up the slippery steps, two at a time. At the top was a small frame house that was completely dark. I walked up to the flimsy front door, kicked it open with the heel of my shoe, and ran into the front door, gun drawn. From a back room a short stocky man in a nightshirt stumbled out, yawning. From behind him peered a woman and three small children, staring wide-eyed at this wild man standing in their doorway. In answer to my question, the man said they were the Koenig's, caretakers of Dr. Lenard's villa. The visitors? Oh, they were staying in the big house . . . their car was up at the top of the hill, under the trees.

My heart dropped into my stomach. I turned without a word and ran out the door and up the embankment. There was a dirt road, not much wider than a path, but there was no yellow Simca. I wanted to hit somebody. Von Schee stood beside me. His eyes mirrored my own despair.

His voice low, he said he didn't understand it. There had never been a road here. His police had checked with all the neighbors and with the former owners of the villa. I told him to have his men radio ahead to the roadblocks to see if they had seen the car. We might still intercept them.

I walked around the tree. In the fresh mud I could see tire tracks, and men's footprints leading out onto the road. It looked as if several men had pushed the car part way down the road, to a point where it was possible to coast down the hill and start the motor without being heard.

I walked back to the caretaker's house to find the Koenig family sitting in a row on a large, overstuffed sofa. I apologized for our forced entry and returned to the main house to use the phone. I called Amaral and reported our failure, asking him to check neighboring towns to see if anybody had spotted the Simca.

Searching the house, I found nothing on the main floor. It was merely a comfortable, cluttered German country house, with a bust of Bach, a large record collection, and a wealth of bric-a-brac.

Downstairs my search proved more rewarding. Here there was a conference room of sorts, filled with Nazi memorabilia, including a photograph of Adolph Hitler's death mask. I took it off the wall, and turned it over. On the back was written. "Sculpture by Fielder, 1946, Rome." The date puzzled me, since it indicated the mask was made the year after the Führer had committed suicide in a Berlin bunker.

In the desk I found a collection of snapshots, most of them identified on the back. There were photographs of

Dr. Mengele with a young, pretty blond named Karen Fiedler (a relation to the sculptor?), Natalie Klein and Mengele, and Dr. Lenard with Mengele and another man who wasn't identified. Dr. Mengele looked like the other photos I had seen of him, although in this snapshot he sported a trim beard.

A post card in the top desk drawer intrigued me. It was addressed to Natalie Klein and read: "From the voyage which should bring us plants and seeds, heartfelt greetings." It was signed by Dr. Alexander Lenard.

The rest of the basement had been converted into an operating room. Here I found medical records, bills for injections, a complete set of surgical instruments, a fully stocked medicine chest, and a kilo of cocaine.

Pocketing the photographs and the post card, I walked back upstairs to question Frau Klein.

She sat in the front room glaring at a policeman who stood in the doorway. The hate on her face gave her a half-crazed look. She refused to give me any information about the house guests, sitting smugly, ignoring my questions.

I reminded her that her "service" in Germany during the war meant she was probably wanted in that country, and we would be only too happy to oblige a request for her extradition.

"I never did anything wrong. I never harmed any Jews. They were going to die anyway. I just did what they told me to do."

And Lenard and Mengele, I asked, were they just following orders, too? She jumped eagerly to the defense of the two men, without thinking to deny that the visitor had been Dr. Mengele. She told me Joseph Mengele was a great man, a physician who had advanced the cause of science.

I could tell she was beginning on a familiar harangue. I told the policeman to bring her into the station until we could check on her, and walked back to the car where von Schee was waiting.

During the drive back we sat in silence. The sun was beginning to burn off the early morning fog, but sunshine couldn't raise the mantle of gloom in the car. I retraced the entire operation in my mind, considering all the measures we should have taken, castigating myself for not making a thorough search of the entire estate, feeling like a fool for having waited outside in the rain all night.

There was no good news to greet us at the police headquarters. Amaral said the car hadn't passed the roadblocks; the road came out to the main road on the other side of our roadblock.

Camargo only reinforced my depression. On the trip back to Curitiba, he slumped glumly against the doorjamb.

"Cheer up, Camargo. You still have a dramatic story, about the big one that got away. That'll sell some papers for you."

I was the one who was left empty-handed, with no real answer to Parries's murder, no Dr. Oetzer in custody, no closer to the truth about the mysterious Dr. Lenard, with the dubious distinction of having let the notorious Angel of Death, Dr. Mengele, slip through my fingers.

11

On my return to Curitiba, I reported to Paulo Pimentel. Pointing to the newspaper on his desk that carried Camargo's lead story, he said I seemed to have stirred up a hornet's nest.

I started to catalog my mistakes, but Paulo shrugged them off. He was more interested in what I had heard since the raid.

I told him what I knew. The yellow Simca had been spotted at several small towns past the roadblocks. The driver had lost his way and asked directions. Then, the car had vanished. They must have stashed the car someplace, probably at a friendly villa. The housekeeper, Natalie Klein, had been taken in for questioning, but there was no reason to hold her. She hadn't committed any crime in Brazil and her jobs in Germany had been pretty menial. She wouldn't be worth trying to extradite. As soon as she was released, she and the Koenigs had packed everything at the villa and left.

Gemballa was still in Rio do Sul, but I thought he might tread a little more softly from now on. We had shaken the local Nazis.

As for the men who had escaped, I didn't have much hope of locating them. The Santa Catarina state police except for von Schee hadn't been very cooperative. They had refused to allow me to interrogate Parries's murderers. They didn't appear very interested in Dr. Oetzer, and they were lackadaisical about tracking the Simca. Paulo frowned and reminded me that the federal government wasn't very interested in right-wing extremists; after all, they were right-wingers themselves. That attitude was bound to seep down to the state levels. But he thought I might hear of Mengele and Lenard again. All the publicity should turn up some new leads.

Smiling, he held up the two Curitiba newspapers and asked if I had enjoyed the stories. The conservative paper screamed about the interference by Paraná police in the civil rights of honest, decent, German citizens. The *Tribuna do Estado* carried Camargo's melodramatic account of the dawn raid on the Nazi nest of vipers and editorialized about the disgraceful Nazi domination in Santa Catarina.

For the first time that day I smiled and agreed that Paulo was right about the publicity. I had already had requests for information from all over Brazil and calls from people with similar stories of neo-Nazi organizations and tips about fugitive war criminals. I'd had official requests for information from the U.S. and German embassies in Brasilia and Rio, from the federal police, and from the São Paulo state police. The cultural attaché at the German embassy wanted me to go to see him. Frankly, I'd been surprised at the reaction. Dona Ema seemed to have been the tip of an iceberg.

The Nazis seemed well-organized in this part of South America and obviously people were taking them seriously—not just in places like Rio do Sul, but in Rio de Janeiro, and not just local officials like Hector von Schee, but federal police officials and politicians. Everyone seemed to be suddenly interested in what I knew, wanting to compare it with their information. I didn't un-

147

derstand how I had suddenly become a Nazi-hunter.

Paulo encouraged me to pursue the case. Now that I had them on the run, why not keep them running, right out of Brazil?

* * *

My curiosity was aroused, and I hated to end with a failure. So, a few weeks later, I found myself accepting the invitation of Dr. Uwe Koestner, the German cultural attaché in Rio, to come and discuss this matter of the Nazi organizations. He was not surprised at my story. I gave him some of the photographs I had found at Dr. Lenard's villa, including the ones of Mengele and Lenard. In return, Koestner told me what he knew about Nazi activity elsewhere in Brazil, confirming my suspicions that there was a central Nazi organization operating throughout South America.

He gave me the name of a man who might have some connection with the men I was looking for: Franz Rybka, the chief forger for Brazilian Nazis. Rybka, who was headquartered in São Paulo but was presently thought to be in Pôrto Alegre, was in charge of providing false identities for his fellow Nazis. Koestner had given Brazilian federal police this information, but nobody else seemed interested in tracking the man down or arresting him. Perhaps I would be.

He was right. I was interested in this aspect of the case. Here was a man who had committed his crimes in Brazil and had contacts with Nazi organizations. He might lead to higher officials in the Nazi network. I doubted that the federal government or other state police departments would search very actively for these Nazis. But confronted with Rybka, the government might be forced to take action.

148

As soon as I had some free time, I took the bus down to Pôrto Alegre, a large, modern city in Rio Grande do Sul, the southernmost province of Brazil. I knew the area well and had several old friends there from my days with Jango. I liked the brazen *gauchos* of the south, who were convinced that they were the brightest, most congenial, and most cultured of all Brazilians.

Posing as an Austrian immigrant, I wandered from one German bar to another, striking up conversations with the bartenders and other patrons, hinting that I needed papers that would allow me to stay in Brazil. The third evening, I walked into a *confiteria* called "Old Vienna." I had been told that this elegant restaurant and lounge on the second floor of a deluxe high-rise building was a congenial place for Germans. I took a seat at the bar and watched the gypsy violinist wend his way among the tables, where flickering candles enclosed the diners in intimate circles of light. I ordered a Scotch and water, in German, from the bartender, a small blond fox, who darted back and forth between the bar and tables. When he served me a second drink, I introduced myself as Erich Straussner from Vienna and said I had heard that this was a good German place. The bartender flashed a smile.

"Franz Rybka, glad to meet you," he said.

He scurried around the lounge, rarely remaining in one spot for more than a few minutes; even when he stood still, his eyes kept moving, watching. The man next to me was getting drunk and started a conversation with Rybka and anyone else within earshot. He began discussing a man both he and Rybka knew, but soon swerved off into a monologue on the superiority of Germans. I had the feeling this wasn't the first time for the discourse; it sounded well rehearsed. Rybka seconded the customer's views, and I nodded agreement. The man finally ran out of steam, and settled his bill. Rybka short-changed him, but he didn't notice. He stuffed the change in his pocket and walked slowly out, weaving slightly.

By midnight, a small, friendly group was left at the bar. Rybka introduced me to Adolph Wohlmacher, a burly, barrel-chested blond with a red face and a loud laugh. Wohlmacher took a liking to me; he was from Vienna, too, he said, from a working class neighborhood that I remembered as even poorer than the neighborhood that I was claiming as my home. When I left, I told them I'd come back, that I liked the *gemütliche* atmosphere.

Over the next two weeks I became increasingly friendly with the manager and bartender of Old Vienna, chatting with them a little longer each time. I hinted at troubles from which I had escaped, spouted Nazi views that inevitably found a ready audience, groused at not having proper papers so I could get a job. When he heard this, Rybka stopped wiping the bar glass he was holding and listened closely, but there were several other people at the bar and he didn't pursue it.

When I wasn't at the Old Vienna, I looked up my old friends, whom I usually found at a nightclub called Monica's. It was run by a middle-aged, retired prostitute and was the scene of many an important business transaction and political deal. One of the hottest topics during my visit, however, was Monica herself, who had taken up with a young man half her age. Everyone was convinced that he would steal her blind, since he had a reputation as a hotshot gambler.

I slept late most mornings, recuperating from the night life, but in the afternoon I often wandered up and down the hilly streets of Pôrto Alegre, enjoying the gleaming white buildings, gardens, and the other pedestrians. Rio Grande do Sul's people are the most handsome in Brazil, and they were a joy to watch. One day I passed by the governor's palace on my way to the Old

Vienna. The last time I had seen it was when Jango was deposed. Then it had been ringed by soldiers with machine guns, and the atmosphere had been tense. This day it was peaceful, surrounded by lovers and old people on park benches.

*   *   *

One morning a few days later, I returned to the Old Vienna. My eyes squinted to adjust to the dim light as Rybka corralled me. Soon he was gossiping about Wohlmacher, whom he said had had to leave his used car lot in Germany in the late fifties rather than face prosecution for theft. In Pôrto Alegre, he had been befriended by a man named Richard Eichler, the Chevrolet representative in town and the owner of the building that housed the Old Vienna.

"You see this fancy place," Rybka muttered. "Well you don't think Wohlmacher, the stupid bastard, could get a good deal like this on his own? It's not Wohlmacher that Eichler is impressed with. It's his wife Leni. Wait until you see her. She has the old man doing cartwheels. Wohlmacher, he's just a pimp."

I had a chance to see Leni that afternoon, while I played cards with Wohlmacher, Rybka, and several other regulars. Conversation stopped as everyone watched her entrance. She was fully conscious of the impact she made as she strolled across the room, hips swaying, bracelets tinkling, and her pointed high-heeled sandals clicking on the tile floor.

She pulled up a chair behind Wohlmacher and smiled in response to the eager greetings from the gamblers. While we played, she sat and smoked American cigarettes, looking around the room absentmindedly. I good-naturedly lost hand after hand, playing the fool. I had noticed several days before that Rybka dealt off the

151

bottom of the deck, but I didn't mind playing the sucker.

After a while, the game broke up, and the players scattered. Wohlmacher saw Eichler come in through the back door, and excused himself. Leni talked with an attentive Rybka in a low, silky voice that disguised the mundane nature of her conversation. Rybka hung on every word, jumping to light her cigarette. She leaned close to him and smiled.

Wohlmacher came bouncing back to tell Leni that old man Eichler was grumbling, and she had better go butter him up.

Leni twisted out of her chair and sauntered over to Eichler, setting a chair close to his and chucking him under the chin. Rybka's eyes reluctantly left Leni and turned to me. He said I seemed preoccupied. Was anything wrong? I told him I was getting restless with nothing to do. If I could only get some papers, I could get a job and buy some land.

Rybka looked around, then leaned forward and spoke in a low voice. He hadn't wanted to mention it before, but he could fix me up. He had a small press in São Paulo. If I was willing to pay for his trip there, he could make me some identity papers that the President himself wouldn't question.

I heaved a sigh of relief, and agreed that I could use his help. I told him I was scheduled to meet some friends in São Paulo next month. Could he have the papers ready by then?

He assured me it was no problem, and we agreed to meet in a month to the day at two o'clock at the *confiteria* Vienna. Having gained the information I needed, I invented an excuse to leave Pôrto Alegre a few days later and returned to Curitiba.

About a week before I was to leave for São Paulo, I had a telephone call from one of my informants, a small-time smuggler and perfume manufacturer named

Wilhelm Langen. Langen was one of thousands of Brazilian smugglers who profited from the reluctance of the citizens to pay high import duties imposed on foreign goods. Langen's specialty was to mix up batches of mediocre perfume and bottle it as the expensive French variety. In return for my tacit consent to his illegal activities, he provided me with a steady stream of information from the underworld. This time he had information about a forger from São Paulo named Franz Rybka.

Amazed at the coincidence, I told Langen I had just been investigating Rybka. Langen told me what he knew, including Rybka's São Paulo address. That might be useful, especially if Rybka didn't show for our appointment.

Two days later, I caught the streamlined bus to São Paulo. Curitiba seemed a village in comparison with this vibrant, boisterous city. On almost every block they were tearing down an old building or erecting a new one. I stopped off at police headquarters and asked for my friend, an official named Raoul Lamos. I told him about Rybka, and since I didn't have jurisdiction in this state, I asked him if he could arrange for two detectives to follow me and make the arrest after Rybka handed over the papers. He was glad to cooperate, and called in two detectives to talk with me. I filled them in on the details and made plans to meet them at the *confiteria* Vienna the next afternoon.

When I arrived, the two detectives were already sitting in a navy blue sedan parked at the curb. I bought a newspaper at a corner stand and walked past the car to a table on the outside terrace. Rybka wasn't there, so I ordered coffee and read the newspaper. All of a sudden my eyes riveted on a small item and photograph on the back page of the paper.

"Man tortured, dumped in Guanabara Bay," read the headline. The story continued, "The body of

153

Wilhelm Langen, perfume manufacturer, was found Tuesday in Guanabara Bay, Rio de Janeiro. According to police, he had been tortured and shot through the head before being dumped in the bay, with four sledgehammers strapped to his body. Police have no suspects in the killing."

I wondered if the murder had any connection to Langen's phone call to me. I couldn't imagine why anyone would kill this inoffensive man. Surely not for his perfume fraud or smuggling activities; they were common enough. On the way over to the Vienna, I had seen in one cigar store window more cigarettes than legally were allowed into the country in an entire year.

I glanced at my watch nervously. It was twenty after two. Had Rybka been tipped off? I signalled the waiter for another cup of coffee. As the waiter poured it, I heard my name called. Turning, I saw Rybka bobbing up and down in the crowd on the sidewalk.

We exchanged greetings and he filled me in on Adolph's and Leni's activities. I interrupted to ask about my papers. He smiled and told me not to worry. They were ready, and we could go out to his house and pick them up now if I wished.

We paid the bill and hailed a cab. I glanced over my shoulder to see if the two detectives were still at the curb and saw them pull out behind us. The cab driver weaved through the knots of snarled traffic, but the sedan stayed with us. We left the congestion of the city and drove to a tree-shaded suburb of modest houses. Rybka instructed the driver to pull over in front of a yellow stucco house. As I climbed out of the back seat, I saw the blue sedan slow down, then pass us, turning at the next corner.

The shop was down in the cellar. As we walked up the sidewalk, Rybka cackled that this was a Jewish suburb. Who would look for a Nazi here?

We walked down several steps at the side of the house, and Rybka unlocked the door. The cellar was dark, but I could see what looked like a small printing press in the corner, partially covered by a canvas tarpaulin. There was no furniture except a desk and chair. Rybka took another, smaller key and opened the top drawer of his desk. He snapped on a goose-neck lamp on the desk and handed me a manila envelope. Inside was a landed immigrant permit, official permission from the Brazilian government to make a home in the country. As I held them under the light, Rybka explained that he had obtained the blanks from a government clerk. The forgery was excellent, complete with signatures and official seal. Even with my training, I wouldn't have spotted them as fake.

I looked up at Rybka, who stood smiling over my shoulder at his work, waiting for my congratulations and thanks.

"I'm afraid you're under arrest, Franzl. I'm with the police . . ."

Rybka's quickness took me by surprise. He leapt for my throat, yelling, punching, and scratching like an enraged housecat. I pushed him against the desk, knocking the metal wastebasket across the floor. The door burst open, and the two detectives ran in, guns drawn.

Rybka sat on the floor against the desk, looking up through narrowed eyes. "You dirty cop bastard!" He continued with a spate of German obscenities. I walked over to the detectives and handed them the false papers. One of the detectives searched the room. In a corner, wrapped in an old piece of canvas he found two printing plates, for U.S. ten and one hundred dollar bills. I pulled open the desk drawers. There were a few file folders and four U.S. ten dollar bills inside. I tucked one in my pocket so I could examine it later, and handed the other three to the detectives, along with Rybka's records.

* * *

The next day I visited a sullen Rybka in his cell. I apologized for arresting him, but I was a cop, I reminded him. He'd have done the same thing in my shoes. I complimented him on his craftmanship. The papers were unbelievable and if the money I had found in his desk was a forgery, I couldn't tell it.

Rybka sneered at me. "It's mine, and it's good all right . . . better than the U. S. Mint makes." He asked me to give it to him for a minute.

He pulled out a corner of his wrinkled white shirt and rubbed the bill against it. There was no smudge of ink. Try that with the real thing, Rybka confided, and you'll get green ink on your shirt. That's how good his forgeries were. Of course, he wasn't in that game any more. But in Germany during the war he'd worked with Friedrich Schwend and they'd made millions in forged currencies. They even were able to get the same Turkish paper the British used.

I was amazed that he would keep the plates as a souvenir. It still surprised me to find, time and time again, a criminal clinging to the evidence of his crime—a murderer still carrying around the gun that would prove his guilt, Rybka hanging onto the tools of his trade.

After I left the forger, I stopped in to see the CIA agent in São Paulo, a man I had met before. His office oddly enough was in state police headquarters. I passed along the information about the money, gave him the sample, and we tested it against an American bill he had in his wallet. Sure enough, the green ink rubbed off on the authentic bill.

I returned to Curitiba in a better frame of mind.

This time I'd been successful, and my man hadn't escaped. The São Paulo state police should be able to probe further into Rybka's contacts with the Nazi groups. They'd promised me a full report. I'd done all I could do. Now maybe I could concentrate on my normal duties and forget about this Nazi business for a while.

12

It was Monday morning, and I was having trouble concentrating on the work in front of me. I downed another cup of steaming hot coffee. As it burned its way down my throat, the telephone rang.

It was Raoul, my friend from the São Paulo police department. He hemmed and hawed, then said he was afraid he had some bad news for me. He asked if I had seen the new issue of *Manchete*, a liberal magazine with a reputation for exposing political corruption. I said I hadn't, and Raoul paused, then muttered, "Your friend Franz Rybka escaped."

The São Paulo police was the most efficient in Brazil. It was hard to believe they'd let a prisoner slip through their fingers, but according to the police, Rybka had forged a writ of *habeus corpus* in his cell, signed by no less than the President of the Supreme Court, and had walked out.

Raoul insisted that that was the official story, fantastic as it seemed. *Manchete*'s editor had been as skeptical as I was, and Raoul himself thought there had been pressure from high up in the government.

I thanked him for calling and hung up in disgust. So much for Rybka. He probably was on his way to join his friends the Wohlmachers by now. I had heard from police contacts in Rio that the couple left Pôrto Alegre after Rybka's arrest, absconding with all the money from the Old Vienna. Evidently, they figured that Eichler would be so humiliated at being taken for a fool that he wouldn't report them. They underestimated the old man, however. He did go to the police, who located Adolph and Leni running a cafe in Rio that they had foolishly named Old Vienna. With typical lassitude, the Rio police didn't arrest them; they just issued a citation, closing the place. The Wohlmachers fled, reportedly to Peru.

At the time I had other problems. I had recently been asked to assist in a murder investigation in Ponta Grossa, a city of about 75,000, an hour north of Curitiba. A well-known Brazilian politician and retired Army officer named Humberto Molinaro had been shot and killed in his home by an intruder. The local police had been unable to solve the crime and the local *delegado* asked me to lend a hand. Because of Molinaro's background, I was reluctant to let the case die.

In 1956, Colonel Molinaro had been commander of the Brazilian Expeditionary Corps that was part of the United Nations' peacekeeping force in the Suez. He was arrested for allegedly smuggling a suitcase full of drugs into Brazil from Egypt. Molinaro maintained that he had been framed by an Army sergeant who was paid by military leaders opposed to Molinaro's democratic politics. He instituted a lawsuit but was never able to prove he had been framed. The public believed the Colonel's version, however, and in the early sixties he was elected to Congress from his hometown of Ponta Grossa.

Molinaro was on the floor of Congress when he received information that Carlos Lacerda, the right-wing governor of Rio de Janeiro, was behind the plot to frame him. He pulled a pistol from his coat and threatened to murder Lacerda. Several other Congressmen wrestled

159

the gun from Molinaro, but the public furor over the incident forced Molinaro to resign his seat and retire in Ponta Grossa. Here he began work on his memoirs, still seeking to clear his name.

When I arrived in Ponta Grossa I could see that this was not a matter that could be settled within a few days. The local police were obviously afraid of digging too deeply into the murder. Ponta Grossa was the headquarters for the Third Army, which had always dominated the town and the local police, even more so now that the military was in control of the federal government. One officer in particular was known to be an enemy of Molinaro's, a Major Romualdo Castaneda, whose nickname was *O Indio*, "The Indian," because of his swarthy complexion and features.

I obtained the basic facts about the murder from the local *delegado* and talked with Molinaro's widow, who was recuperating in the hospital from bullet wounds she received the night of the murder. According to her, Molinaro had stayed up late to work on his memoirs. About midnight he went to bed, joining his wife in their bedroom in the basement. At one o'clock, the couple heard footsteps on the living room floor above. Molinaro grabbed a small caliber pistol from the nightstand and went upstairs to investigate. His frightened wife waited a few minutes, then followed him.

At the top of the stairs, Molinaro foolishly turned on the hall light, putting himself in a spotlight. As his wife came up the stairs, the intruder shot Molinaro several times. One of the bullets hit the politician's wife, who was a few steps behind him on the stairway. Molinaro dragged himself to the bathroom where he died in a pool of blood. His wife ran to the kitchen, bleeding from the neck, and shouted for help.

Her father, who lived in an adjoining house, heard her screams, raced over in his pajamas, and called the police and an ambulance. Immediately afterwards there was a knock on the door. It was a security guard who had been hired to patrol the neighborhood after a series of local robberies. He said he had heard the shots and come running.

Significantly, the police report showed that no property was missing from the house except the manuscript for Molinaro's memoirs. It seemed that the object of the break-in had been to steal the manuscript.

I returned from the hospital to my hotel room. As I turned the key in the lock, I heard the telephone ringing. I picked up the phone and said hello. There was a pause. Then a low, rough voice said, "If you're smart, cop, you'll lay off the Molinaro case." The telephone line went dead. It was the first of three calls I received that week.

I ignored the threats, having become used to such calls during my work on drug cases. I went the next day to question the guard who had been patrolling the street the night of the murder. His story was suspicious. He seemed to remember very little of what had happened that night. I determined his route and checkpoints and retraced his path. Starting from his last checkpoint, where he had recorded the time on a logbook, I walked around the block. I didn't see how he could have known from which house the shots came, since he should have been around the corner from the Molinaro house when the shots were fired.

Investigating his background, I learned that he had been a soldier and was an ardent admirer of Major Castaneda. His political views were conservative, and he had been heard accusing Molinaro of being a Communist and an enemy of the military.

The finger seemed to point toward the military rightwing, which was involved in a struggle with more democratically-inclined factions for control of the government. I assumed that the Army would not relish

161

Molinaro's revelations of corruption and intrigue within the military. From talking with his wife and friends, I knew that Molinaro believed the fascist elements in the Army were the greatest threat to Brazilian democracy.

My version was just a theory; I had to prove it. With the local police afraid to move, my only assistance came from a friend, Stanislav Pasternak. He had been a member of the Free Polish Army in England during World War II and had been a British agent. After the war, he came to Paraná, where his relatives owned a farm equipment business. He joined the firm, commuting between Curitiba and Ponta Grossa. On one of his trips a mutual friend had introduced us, knowing that we both had been British agents and had a lot in common. Pasternak was suspicious of the military and was eager to assist me.

My first break was the discovery that there was a right-wing organization in Ponta Grossa that met in an abandoned house about eight miles out of town. According to my informant, Major Castaneda attended the meetings in civilian clothes. There were rumors that the group was stockpiling arms to overthrow Pimentel's government. I decided to drive out to the house to see what I could find.

I called Pasternak and asked him if he wanted to go along. He said he'd be glad to, so I told him to meet me at the police station the next morning. I told no one else of my plans, except the aide who had been assigned by the local police to assist me, a man named Edelmiro, whom I had asked to get me a Jeep from the police station.

Pasternak was waiting at nine o'clock sharp in front of the police garage. It was a hot day, and his ash blond hair was plastered against his forehead. As I walked up to him I admired his erect, military bearing.

We grabbed a cup of coffee at the local café while the Jeep was filled with gas, then left for the abandoned

162

house. The dirt road we took was no longer in use. Thick underbrush swept against the sides of the Jeep, branches snapping back as we passed.

By the time we left it was late morning, and the heat was already intense. The dust swirled up and through the open windows. The sun pounded on the roof of the Jeep, turning it into an oven. About fifteen minutes from town, I was suffocating. Near a meadow clearing, I opened the door and leaned out, hoping to catch a breeze.

I woke up in a hospital bed three days later, in excruciating pain, my head swathed in bandages. The police *delegado* was there and explained to me that just as I had leaned out, the Jeep had exploded. I had been thrown clear, but had been badly burned.

I tried to ask about Pasternak, but couldn't speak clearly; my mouth wouldn't move. The *delegado* knew what I was asking. Pasternak was dead, burned beyond recognition. I had been luckier. My injuries were serious, but would heal. Someone in a nearby farmhouse heard the explosion and saw the flames. They called the police, who arrived about half an hour after the accident. The Jeep was a hunk of smoldering metal. I lay unconscious about twenty feet from the wreck.

The artery to my nose had been severed and the blood was pumping over my head, which was swollen to twice its normal size from the burns. My hair and eyebrows had been burned off. The police raced me to the hospital, where doctors sawed off part of my nose and sewed my face back together. This was all done without anesthesia, but I didn't remember any of it.

The *delegado* also told me that my aide, Edelmiro, was missing and Major Castaneda had received a sudden transfer to the Second Army in São Paulo. I ordered the abandoned house searched, but as I suspected, any arms that had been stored there were gone.

It was almost two weeks before I was allowed to return to Curitiba and almost a month before the swelling went down and the burns healed. Never handsome, I was a sight to behold now, with fresh pink scars, one missing eyebrow, and dislodged teeth. I didn't mind my appearance or the frequent twinges of pain. I felt lucky to be alive and anguished that Pasternak had died because I had invited him to accompany me.

Paulo Pimentel visited me soon after I returned and told me that he had been ordered by the federal government to call me off the case. "It isn't worth it," he told me. "You'll just get yourself killed. The army is slugging it out among themselves, and anybody who gets in the way is just asking for trouble. Remember your motto, Erico: 'Live dangerously, but be careful.' Now's the time to be careful."

While I was still recuperating, violence exploded again. On a cool afternoon, I was sitting in the lobby of the Hotel Ambassador having a cocktail with a friend, when the hotel clerk signalled me from across the room. When I came over to the front desk he told me there was a call forwarded from my office, long distance from Rio. I took the telephone receiver from his outstretched hand. The caller introduced himself as Major von Westernhagen of the German Bundeswehr. He urgently wanted to meet with me at my earliest convenience.

Intrigued, I agreed immediately, and asked him if he could come to Curitiba. He said yes, he could fly down tomorrow if that was agreeable to me.

The rest of the day I thought about the call and wondered what message this German major was bringing. The next morning I woke earlier than usual. On the way to my office, I decided to stop for a cup of coffee. I passed the corner newsstand, reached in my pocket for change, and caught the bold headline out of the corner of my eye: "German army officer murdered!" I grabbed the newspaper and stared at the photograph of a man's body lying on the pavement against a rough stone wall, blood flowing from beneath him. The victim was identified as Major von Westernhagen, the man who had called me the day before.

Just past noon, only minutes after he had phoned me, he left his hotel. As he stepped off the curb, four men jumped from a black Volkswagen and opened fire, riddling his body with fifty machine gun bullets. According to witnesses, the occupants of the car were Europeans, probably Germans.

I stared at the photograph with dread. Parries. Langen. Pasternak. Von Westernhagen. All murdered to protect someone's secret. I felt as if I were walking through a mine field, explosives detonating around me. How long would I be able to side-step them?

13

Before I had a chance to think about returning to Ponta Grossa, Paulo Pimentel was clever enough to divert me temporarily with a new assignment, one that would prevent me from pursuing Molinaro's murder—or any other case.

The first week I was back in my office, a young man named Werner Wanderer came to police headquarters asking to see me. The slim, boyish lawyer was the mayor of Marechal Candido Rondon, a small town in western Paraná not far from the Paraguayan border.

Wanderer told me that his town had been taken over by a group of Nazis who were intimidating the native Brazilians. Many residents had complained to Wanderer, but he didn't know how to gain control of the situation. He was also concerned about men who were being smuggled over the border from Paraguay to some of the farms run by the Nazis leaders. The local *delegado* was a simple, lazy fellow whom the Nazis controlled with payoffs. Governor Pimentel had told Wanderer that I might be willing to look into it.

After questioning him further, I agreed to come for a few days to investigate the situation, talk to the local police, and see what could be done. I was especially interested in the border activity. Maybe I would have another chance to track down the Nazi fugitives who visited Rio do Sul. The next week I flew to the border town of Foz do Iguaçu, rented a car, and drove to Marechal Rondon.

This part of Brazil was still a frontier region, only recently settled. Many of the colonists were Europeans, some arriving in large groups and farming a variety of crops on small farms, just as they had in Europe. There were also scattered cattle ranches and isolated towns that served as marketplaces for the farmers. Marechal Rondon was a town that was too small to appear on most maps.

As I drove up in front of the dilapidated hotel, a bus pulled in next to me and disgorged ten or twelve passengers. The red dust swirled up, sifting into my nose, ears, eyes, and down my throat. I hurried inside the Hotel *La Amizade* (Friendship). A desk clerk sat on a stool, listening to a radio. As I checked in, a Wagnerian opera ended and the announcer broke in: *"Bom dia, Guten tag."* I was taken by surprise at the German greeting. The announcer continued in German and Portuguese, *"ZYS-91, Radio Marechal Rondon. Gib mir eine flashe bier. Una cerveja temque ser Golden Bier."*

That evening I ate dinner in the hotel restaurant, listening to the conversations at the tables near me, conducted in guttural German against a background of Bach, Wagner, Beethoven, and Brahms from the radio.

The next morning I went over to the police station, passing shops owned by Mueller, Rotman, Schwemmer, von Gaza, and the movie theater which featured a film called "Die Nacht." The police station was a one-room adobe hut, surrounded by a picket fence. Several chickens strutted among a few slumbering pigs. Inside, I saw a circle of four or five policemen, in faded tan military uniforms, with guns and knives stuck in their belts. I

167

felt as if I had stepped into a lair of Mexican bandits.

Nobody noticed me at first. A copper tea kettle on a hot plate in the corner started to whistle, and one of the men stood up and poured the boiling water into the *chimarrão*, a gourd filled with crumbled maté tea leaves. He waited a few minutes, stirring the mixture with a tin straw, took a sip, then sat down and passed the gourd to the next man.

I cleared my throat and asked for the *delegado*. A huge man whose belly strained against his uniform looked up at me and asked who I was.

"Erdstein, chief of investigation, state police."

The man passed the *chimarrão* quickly to the man on his right and heaved himself to his feet, dusting off the seat of his pants. "Oh, I didn't know . . . Delegado Marcio Sarraceno Lemos Pinto, Senhor. Come into my office."

His "office" was a wooden desk in the corner of the room, covered with papers and cigar ashes. Pinto waved me into his chair, and pulled up a stool for himself, sitting down warily, his eyes on me. A visit from headquarters wasn't good news.

I told him I was investigating complaints that there was a Nazi organization in Marechal Rondon that was suppressing the rights of native Brazilians and dominating the community. What did he know about it?

Pinto scratched the back of his neck, and looked at me blankly. There were a lot of Germans in this area. They controlled the aldermanic council and most of the important businesses. He stopped and glanced at me, as if hopeful he could stop there.

"Germans, only, or Nazis?," I asked.

"Well, yes, there is a Nazi party."

"Who are the leaders?" I asked, pulling out my notebook.

He gave me a few names, reluctantly—the leader Dr.

Seyboth, a physician, and his wife Ingrun; Herbert von Gaza, who runs the camera store; and Franz Wenzler.

Had he had complaints about the Nazi group? Yes, a couple, he admitted. The radio station manager, Senhor Caretta, an Italian. And Dr. Lima, a doctor who complained that the Nazis chased off his patients. His father, Colonel Lima, and Dr. Campos, a lawyer, had also complained.

"And what have you done about these complaints?"

"Oh, Senhor, somebody's always complaining," Pinto sighed. "I don't want to get involved in politics."

I extracted a few more facts from the *delegado* and then left for Werner Wanderer's office. Over lunch, he added to my list of Nazis and anti-Nazis.

I told him my opinion of Pinto's intelligence and that I wouldn't be surprised if he frequently let someone slip him a few cruzeiros to look the other way.

Wanderer agreed that Pinto's main interest was sitting around sipping from the *chimarrão* all day. The Nazis couldn't hope for a better *delegado*. He suggested I concentrate on some of the people who were upset about things, like Antonio Caretta, the radio station manager.

We walked to the radio station and found Caretta with one of his announcers and a soy bean merchant whose nickname was "Cabeza" (the Head). Wanderer explained why I was in Marechal Rondon, and introduced me to the other men.

I told Caretta that I had heard his broadcast from downstairs in the hotel the night before. I noticed his preference for German classics.

Caretta shook his head and said it wasn't his choice. He was told what to play and to broadcast in German. The Portuguese was an afterthought. The entire town was a replica of Germany, as perhaps I'd noticed—the homes, the movies, the newspapers, even the school. As he spoke, Carretta became agitated and his grayish face turned deep red. He began to sweat; I thought he must not be a well man. Caretta explained that the Germans settled this region when it was just uninhabited frontier, building their ranches and farms. The trouble started four or five years ago, when the first Brazilians moved in. The Nazis, a small minority of the townspeople, didn't like it, called the natives "niggers," and tried to keep them out of town, especially the educated, professional people. They pressured people to boycott Dr. Lima and Dr. Campos. They had influenced the school. Dr. Seyboth's wife, Ingrun, was a teacher at the high school and had led a protest recently against the law that requires the singing of Brazil's nation anthem. She had her students singing the *Horst Wessel Lied* and was filling their heads with "that Nazis nonsense." It wasn't bad enough that the older people still clung to such discredited ideas, but they were poisoning the minds of the young people, too.

I asked Caretta to tell me about the Seyboths. He said Seyboth had been in the SS Luftwaffe and fled to Paraguay after the war, arriving with quite a bit of money, or so rumor had it. Anyway, he went broke there, but several years ago he showed up in Marechal Rondon with enough money to build a hospital and buy a ranch and several thousand head of cattle. He was an alderman now. His wife, the schoolteacher, managed to talk Seyboth into bringing her lover over from Germany, a man named Herbert von Gaza. Seyboth signed a certificate stating that he needed von Gaza as an opthamologist at the hospital to get him entry into the country. Von Gaza wasn't an opthamologist at all, but was a very well-known physicist in Germany. Now he ran an optical and camera shop. He was good friends with Blüchner, another Nazi rancher.

Cabeza interrupted. "Blüchner . . . isn't he that old geezer with the young wife?"

It was the same man; he was in his eighties and his wife only about twenty five. He was another one who came from Germany, after the war, and was a fanatic.

I asked if Blüchner was the rancher who sheltered the fugitives. Wanderer said no, the main headquarters for the fugitives was a ranch owned by Friedrich Isenberg. A man named von Ammon, who was now in São Paulo, used to be their courier, the man who would bring people over the border.

Isenberg was a strange man, according to Caretta. He had fought in the Luftwaffe in World War II and was injured. He was a recluse, never leaving his ranch. He didn't farm or have any other occupation. But there was a lot of traffic through the ranch. There were rumors that Martin Bormann had stayed there, among others.

I said I thought Bormann was dead. Caretta shrugged.

Later in the afternoon I went with Wanderer to visit Dr. Lima at his hospital. We found him in a small laboratory, bent over a microscope. He was a handsome, muscular man whom Wanderer told me had been Brazil's swimming champion in 1954. Dr. Lima showed me around his almost deserted hospital, explaining that Dr. Seyboth had managed to empty his hospital and drive away his patients. The residents of Marechal Rondon were afraid to come to Dr. Lima, the "nigger" doctor. Dr. Lima's father, a retired Army Colonel, had been threatened for speaking out against the Nazis.

As we talked, a man walked in looking for Dr. Lima. Lima greeted him and introduced him as Dr. Campos, a Brazilian lawyer.

Campos shook hands with me and pulled up a chair to add his story. He told me that as white as he was, he would always be the "black" Campos because he was a native Brazilian, not a German. He had served in the Army and was proud of his country. But what was hap-

171

pening had shaken his faith. He had the same problem as Dr. Lima in attracting clients; people were afraid to come to him. The Nazis in Marechal Rondon lived in a dream world, always sure that the Fourth Reich was about to be established. When Campos had first come here he had overheard a conversation in the hotel restaurant about how the Nazis were going to gain power again; all over the world people would rise under the Nazi banner . . . that Martin Bormann and other powerful Nazi leaders were still alive, here in South America, and were organizing to overtake various governments. He had missed the next part; it was drowned out by a man talking loudly at another table. Then he heard one of the men say, "It all gets back to the Jewish problem. We should finish the job the next time!" Campos had never forgotten the venom in his voice.

I had heard enough to realize the extent of the problem in Marechal Rondon. I returned to Curitiba and assigned a special detail to work on the case, checking my list of names against every available file from our state police, the federal police, and Interpol sources. I wanted to discover whether these Nazis were in Brazil legally or illegally and whether they were wanted for any crimes in Brazil or in other countries.

I returned armed with more information, but still on shaky ground. Most of the Nazis were pretty clean, without criminal records here or abroad. Although many of them were in the country illegally, some had been here more than ten years and legally couldn't be deported. And though some, like the von Seyboths, theoretically could be deported, I wasn't sure that they really would be. I'd have to bluff my way through this one.

A young reporter named Moses Rabinowitz from the São Paulo newspaper, *Journal da Tarde*, learned about this new investigation when he called to interview me about the raid on Dona Ema. He was in Marechal

172

Rondon when I returned. I referred him to Caretta, the station manager, while I paid a visit on the von Seyboths. I questioned them about their political activities and membership in the Nazi party, which they didn't hesitate to confirm.

Seyboth stared at me through his thick, wire frame glasses, which magnified his eyes grotesquely. "You're German, aren't you . . . Austrian? . . . well, you should be on our side. I don't understand your concern. Your mother country is part of the GrossDeutschland. We're superior people, and we have a right to rule here."

Angered, I told him I was a Brazilian. I told him he had no right to dominate and subjugate these people, and I intended to put a stop to it. Von Seyboth was in this country illegally, I reminded him. He had been harboring fugitives who were entering this country illegally. I planned to draw up warrants for his arrest. Until then, I told him, I was putting him at the disposition of the government. Under the new federal régime, this general order meant a person could be arrested at any time and was forbidden to leave the city or the country. I could have detained Seyboth in jail, but I figured that he wouldn't leave town because of the hospital and the ranch.

I noticed that von Seyboth didn't bother to deny that fugitives had stayed at his home. To judge his reaction, I threw out another question.

"Where is Martin Bormann?"

Von Seyboth's wife answered before her husband could. "Do you think we would tell you?"

Her husband frowned at her, and I was sure they knew something. Von Seyboth and his wife were angry with me when I left, but even more, they seemed confused that I, as an Austrian, would be against them. Despite my hostile questions, they couldn't believe that once I knew about their plans, I too wouldn't be secretly

173

plotting for a return of the glorious German Reich.

I stopped on the way back to town at Isenberg's *fazenda* a few miles down the road. It was a warm, dry afternoon and a spume of dust billowed out behind me. The ranch was surrounded by a barbed wire fence and a wooden gate. There was no sign of anyone around, although a white Volkswagen van was parked near the house. I opened the heavy gate, got back into my car and drove in. Only a few yards inside the gate, a shot rang out, ricocheting off the hood of the car. There was a second retort as I jammed the car in reverse and shot out the gate. The wheels squealed as I executed a 180-degree turn, and took off down the road.

I recounted the story to Moses Rabinowitz that evening over dinner. "It seems Caretta was right when he said that Isenberg wasn't too social. He didn't seem to be receiving visitors today, for sure."

Rabinowitz didn't see the humor, and he looked nervous when I suggested that he go with me that evening to see another of the Nazi leaders, Franz Wenzler, a Yugoslav who had worked as an interpreter in the concentration camps during the war. As a young Jew, Moses told me, he had been raised on stories of Nazi atrocities, but he never thought that he himself would have to face the monsters.

After dinner, I drove the reporter around the small town, pointing out the local landmarks—the bust of one of the town's founders, a man named Willy Bartz; the cemetery with its rows of headstones inscribed in German; the movie theater that this week featured a German war film.

"You and I ought to catch a movie while we're here, Moses. Why there may be people in this town who think that the Germans won the war!"

We pulled up in front of Wenzler's home, which was only four or five blocks from the hotel. As we walked up

174

the sidewalk, it loomed out of the darkness like a medieval castle with fortress-like turrets and massive wooden door. I lifted a brass knocker that was shaped like a lion's head, and let it drop.

An elderly man answered the door. I identified myself and said I was here to speak to Herr Wenzler. The man shuffled off and returned a few minutes later, asking us to follow him into the living room. Wenzler rose, greeted us, and introduced his wife, who was sitting on the couch. The Wenzlers were dwarfed by the massive old-fashioned walnut furniture. Wenzler asked if we would like a drink and poured *cachaça* into a delicate crystal goblet. Rabinowitz caught my eye, and I smiled.

After the formalities, I accused them, as I had the von Seyboths, of interfering with the rights of the Brazilian citizens in the town. They, too, seemed surprised that I, obviously German myself, wouldn't understand.

I tried to explain in simple terms. "You're conspiring against the country that has given you refuge," I explained.

That was ridiculous, they said. They just wanted to be Germans. They weren't Brazilians. Didn't I feel the same? I was a German, wasn't I? Didn't I want to preserve my culture?

"Why don't you go back to Germany if you feel like that?" I asked.

Because Germany was run by the Communists now. They couldn't live there.

"Because you're Nazis?" I asked.

They didn't answer, but the mood darkened. A man walked silently into the room and took a chair in the corner. Nobody bothered to introduce him. I glanced at Moses; sweat beaded his upper lip. I turned back to Wenzler. I told him I'd checked into his background, of course. I knew about his work in the concentration camps. I knew he had entered this country illegally. I could have him deported.

Wenzler's jaw tightened, but he didn't answer. His wife turned on me. "You have your nerve, coming in here, threatening us. We haven't done anything illegal. You should help us, not threaten us. You're a fool."

I ignored her, and told Wenzler that I was putting them at the disposition of the government, and promised him he would hear from me again. I stood up, and Moses and I walked to the front door, followed by the man who had been sitting in the corner. He stood at the door, watching us walk down the path to the rented car. In the light from the doorway, I could see it was sagging toward the ground. I bent over; sure enough, the tires had been slashed. The door to the house closed with a solid thud.

Moses grabbed my arm. I told him not to worry; we were only about five blocks from the hotel. I had a gun, but I doubted that we would need it. This was just a warning. We walked quickly through the empty streets; clouds had obscured the moon. The town was deadly quiet. As we turned a corner, I heard a noise, and motioned Moses to stop. It was the whirr of bicycle wheels, and as I turned toward the sound, five cyclists appeared out of the darkness. Two of them speeded up to pass us, so that we were surrounded by them. The middle-aged men riding them were hulking shadows in the dark. They pedalled slowly, to keep abreast of us, and one of them called out. "You won't get out of here. We know how to handle Communists."

At an unseen signal, they began to close in on us. The two men in front dismounted and leaned their bicycles against a tree. They turned and started to walk back toward us. I drew my gun from my belt. "That's far enough. You're under arrest."

They kept walking. I aimed at their feet and shot into the dust several times. At the sound, the men whirled around and ran into the night, disappearing in seconds. I turned in time to see the other two cyclists pedalling away. Once again, we stood in the silent streets, straining to hear any sound.

I tugged at Moses, warning him that we would be smart to return to the hotel before our friends realized that they outnumbered us, gun or no gun.

Moses trotted alongside me, down the next street and around the corner, onto the main street. Once inside the hotel lobby, he threw me a mournful glance. His hands were shaking as he reached for the banister. He finally found his voice. "You're crazy, Erico. There were five of them. What if they had guns?"

I shrugged. "Well, we weren't in a very good spot to call for help, so I had to take a chance. I didn't think they'd fight back. They just wanted to scare us off. Let's call it a night."

It was a long night. Moses wouldn't be left alone, so I sat up all night in his room, in an uncomfortable chair, facing the door, while the reporter lay fully dressed and wide awake on the bed.

The next morning I described the men to Pinto as well as I could, considering the darkness. As I expected, he didn't seem to have any ideas on their identities, but he sent two men to take care of the car.

That afternoon I suggested that Moses drop off some of his photographs at Herbert von Gaza's photo shop, more to get a look at von Gaza than from necessity. I was interested to see von Gaza's reaction to the photos of the movie theater, the cemetery, Isenberg's ranch, the Seyboths sitting in their garden, and Dr. Lima's empty hospital. The handsome scientist-turned-shopkeeper was cordial and promised to have the prints ready later in the day.

When we came back late that afternoon, von Gaza explained that the negatives had all been ruined. "Just an

177

accident. Some chemicals splashed on them. Oh, well it couldn't be helped, but then you can take them again." He smiled blandly, but his stare was icy. I assured him Moses would be taking more photographs.

Outside Rabinowitz stared at me with sorrowful eyes. I tried to jolly him out of his foul mood, even offering to buy him dinner. With a few drinks, he cheered up a little. We were ordering coffee when Werner Wanderer came into the hotel restaurant. His smile was strained.

I asked why he wasn't home with his wife. Why was he looking for us?

There was a rumor that I was going to be killed tonight. Wanderer considered it his duty to stay with me this evening to make sure nothing happened.

Moses muttered to himself. To cut the tension, I suggested we drive around, and maybe the trouble would find us.

Moses looked at me like I was crazy, then shrugged resignedly. "Sure, why not."

We drove around town several times, without seeing anything suspicious. I suggested we go to the movies.

"You're a real joker, Erico," Moses retorted.

"Well, why not, it's as safe as any place and I've been dying to see these films."

We parked in front of the movie theater, walked in, and took seats near the back of the theater. After a few minutes the lights dimmed, and the credits began to roll. Tonight's short feature was an action-packed naval battle from a 1943 newsreel. Suddenly, the sound track warbled, and the screen went dark. The lights rose, and a man walked out on the stage, squinting into the audience. In German he announced:

"I regret to inform you, ladies and gentlemen, that our feature film for tonight cannot be shown. We have experienced some mechanical difficulty. I'm sorry. You can get a refund at the ticket office."

There was grumbling, as we shuffled out with the disappointed fans. Outside a small group of men was milling around, many of them having wandered out from the bar next door. There was a menacing undercurrent of tension. A space opened around us.

I elbowed through the crowd, and we hopped into Wanderer's car and drove over to the police station. Pinto and his friends were lounging around, drinking beer.

I told Pinto that there was likely to be some trouble. I wanted him and a couple of his men to make their presence felt.

Pinto protested that he couldn't leave the station unprotected. I told him to stay here, if he preferred, but to give me a couple of his men and his Jeep.

I ordered the men to patrol the main street for the rest of the night and arrest any troublemakers. Stationing one outside the hotel, I bid Wanderer good night. Rabinowitz and I went upstairs. I assured him the policemen could handle any trouble. I was exhausted, and I wasn't about to sit up for a second night. Moses followed my instructions meekly; he was worn down by the tension and lack of sleep, too. I left him at the top of the stairs. Before he left, he said softly, "Just think, Erico, if they act that way here in Brazil, think how they must have acted in Germany!"

The next day I reviewed the situation with Wanderer and told him that breaking the stranglehold these people had on Marechal Rondon was not going to be easy. I was returning to Curitiba, but I'd be back with warrants for the arrests of the von Seyboths, von Gaza, Wenzler, and Isenberg. I wasn't sure I could make them stick, but it was worth a try. They were under orders not to leave town and I doubted they'd try; they had too much to lose. But I wouldn't be disappointed if they did flee. Then we could track them down and arrest them. As it was now we could bring them in for questioning, but it was going to take a full-scale investigation to break up this ring. I planned to bring back a special detail of state police to clean up this mess and keep an eye out for fugitives.

*   *   *

Before I returned to Marechal Rondon, I traced the courier Caretta had mentioned, Fritz von Ammon, to São Paulo, and found him with two forged Arab passports in his pocket. Threatening him with arrest, I agreed to make a deal with him. For information about the Nazi organization in Marechal Rondon and its contacts with other Nazi groups, I'd leave him alone. He was eager to talk. He told me about the connections between the Nazi leaders in town, gave me names of Nazi members I hadn't known about before, and drew a clearer picture of the entire Nazi network.

According to von Ammon, Marechal Rondon was ideally located for an area headquarters. It was near the border, the Nazis were in control there, and it was out of the way so nobody noticed the constant movement of men. Surely I realized I wasn't dealing with just a local organization. The Nazis were well organized throughout South America, taking orders from higher up—all the way up to Martin Bormann, who still called the shots. Paraguay's government was friendly to them, and their main base of operations was there, but they had groups in Rio, São Paulo, all the big cities. They couldn't travel between countries legally, so they crossed secretly back and forth over the border, with money and orders for terrorist activities. They already had a sympathetic ruler

180

in Paraguay, and they wanted to see right-wing governments throughout South America. They had great hopes of manipulating the dictators of this country. And it was the same in Chile, Peru, and Venezuela. "We're getting stronger," von Ammon bragged. "We'll control the rest of the world too."

*   *   *

Two weeks later I was back in Marechal Rondon with the warrants and an order to close down Isenberg's ranch. I had been able to find an old state law designed to promote settlement of the frontier that gave the government power to close down a ranch that was not using the land productively.

Pinto, his sad face even longer and more mournful at seeing me again, greeted me with bad news. "They're all gone, Dr. Erico. Von Seyboth and his wife, von Gaza, Isenberg, Wenzler. They just left everything and fled."

He looked upset, as well as he should be. I had brought a state police delegation to take over the situation here, a hand-picked group that could be trusted to crack down on the Nazis; among them was a replacement for Pinto.

I berated him for allowing them to escape, but secretly, I was not at all displeased. Now I could track them down, if they were still in the country, and I would have a stronger case for prosecuting them. Simply residing in Brazil illegally wasn't considered much of a crime. Brazil needed colonists too badly, and what was the government going to do with them . . . throw them into the sea? And, if they had already fled over the border, at least they were gone. They'd be someone else's problem.

I installed the new police force and left Marechal Rondon. I had a feeling that with the Nazi hierarchy broken up, men like Lima, Caretta, Wanderer, and Cam-

181

pos could start to build a new community here, a Brazilian community.

I could do no more in Marechal Rondon, but I was already planning ahead. The border area was the center of action, and I had jurisdiction on the Brazilian side. I planned to pursue the fugitives from Marechal Rondon there, and I hoped to get closer to the heart of the Nazi organization, which everyone led me to believe was centered in this border area where Brazil, Argentina, and Paraguay meet. My main target was the traveling doctor, Joseph Mengele.

14

Paulo Pimentel, who was glad to see I had taken the bait, agreed to appoint me chief of investigation for the border region, with an indefinite leave of absence from my regular duties. This would give me the authority and the time to track down the Nazi operatives that I had dispersed from Marechal Rondon.

I selected Foz do Iguaçu as my base of operations. In this frontier region, it was one of the few towns with a modern airport and microwave communications with Curitiba. The town itself wasn't very large or impressive, but it was an attraction for tourists who came from all over the world to view the Iguaçu Falls, a series of thunderous cataracts along the Alto Paraná River. Although the falls were in Argentina they could be seen best from the Brazilian side of the river. The luxury hotel gave the tourists a view of the falls from their windows.

Foz do Iguaçu was a magnet for another type of traveler: smugglers, who were attracted by the brisk and illegal trade between Paraguay, Argentina, and Brazil. Paraguay, with no local industries to protect, tolerated smugglers and consequently was swarming with them. Wartime military transports flew into Asunción from Miami regularly with American cigarettes, cameras, nylons, perfume, and other goods. American cigarettes were cheaper in Asunción than in New York City. Brazil and Argentina had high import tariffs that their citizens were eager to circumvent by dealing with Paraguayan smugglers. In exchange the Paraguayans wanted Brazilian coffee and Argentine produce at a cheap price. The Brazilian smugglers were usually Arabs stationed in Foz do Iguaçu, who wheeled and dealed out of small, ramshackle wood stores that lined the town's dusty main street. Paraguayan smugglers plied their trade across the Alto Paraná River by night. If the Brazilian Army or police tried to pursue them, they were likely to be shot at by the Paraguayan border patrols who protected the smugglers.

My first priority here was to set up a network of informants who could provide me with information about Nazi organizations and who would report any unusual movement of people across the border. I used police *delegados* I knew to be trustworthy and Brazilians who were willing to keep me informed, either out of idealism, anti-German feelings, or for pay.

I was particularly interested in the situation in Paraguay, since I had heard from Fritz von Ammon and others that that country was the center of Nazism in South America. I began to frequent the hotel casino in Puerto Presidente Stroessner, a Paraguayan village across the Friendship Bridge from Foz do Iguaçu. It was packed every night with tourists, businessmen, Army officers, policemen, prostitutes, pimps, and smugglers since it was the only source of evening entertainment in the area. It was small, with one bacarrat table and four French roulette wheels run by Argentine croupiers.

I struck up an acquaintance with some Paraguayan army officers who were antagonistic to the dictator, President Alfredo Stroessner. The officers confirmed that many Nazi war criminals that had taken refuge in

Argentina in the fifties fled to Paraguay after Perón was deposed. Stroessner had welcomed them and given them protection. He allowed the Nazis to meet openly in Asunción, gave them identity papers, and sometimes even furnished them with military guards. According to one young officer, Martin Bormann was now living in a jungle fortress protected by the military.

One of the officers, a Major Acosta, was familiar with Joseph Mengele and his brother Alois, who owned a plywood factory in the small town of El Dorado along the Alto Paraná River. The Nazis used Alois's boat, named the *Viking V* after an SS patrol boat, to travel across the river to and from Argentina. Joseph Mengele was a close friend of Stroessner and the dictator had warned that if any harm came to Mengele, the Jews in Paraguay would pay. Acosta and the other officers said the top Nazis, many of them war criminals who still retained their grip on the South American organization, traveled continuously—sometimes overtly, using false identity papers, sometimes surreptitiously. This bore out what I had heard in Rio do Sul and Marechal Rondon, and what I was hearing from my informants in other towns.

For each grain of truth, however, I had to sift through hundreds of rumors and false bits of information, believing only what I heard from several different reliable sources or could personally substantiate. Gradually, I perceived the outline of what some journalists were now calling the Nazi "Fourth Reich," and I learned about the Nazi methods and techniques. Not finding support for a mass movement, the Nazis kept their ideals and organization alive in small, elite corps spotted throughout South America. The officers warned me that the Nazis were especially wary now that Eichmann and Franz Stangl had been captured. They were careful to throw pursuers off their trail. They acted like the cuckoo, Acosta told me, placing their eggs in one place, then

185

flying some distance away to raise a fuss, hoping to divert the enemy.

It took an encounter with the Nazi leadership for me to learn this lesson. I was going through paperwork in my office in the Foz do Iguaçu police headquarters one morning in June, 1968, when two German Jewish refugees whom I knew slightly, burst into my office. Moises Apfelbaum, a local shopkeeper, and Bruno Erntler, an accountant, were out of breath and extremely agitated.

"You've got to come with us, now, right now," Apfelbaum gasped, tugging at my arm, "We've just seen Martin Bormann at the bus station café!"

I stifled the urge to laugh out loud, but they caught my smirk, and protested that they were not crazy. It was Bormann; they were positive. One of them was from Berlin and had seen the Deputy Führer several times during the war. Both of them had seen photographs of Bormann and were sure this was the man.

This was not the first time I had heard stories from people who thought they had spotted Bormann. The furtive Deputy Führer had preferred to stay behind the scenes, making sure that Hitler's every order was carried out. A master of intrigue, he manipulated Hitler and others and was hated and mistrusted by most of the other Nazi leaders. He was closer to the Führer than any other man. When Hitler committed suicide in the underground Berlin bunker, Bormann, ever the pragmatist, decided to try to escape through Russian lines to reach the man Hitler had named as his successor, Admiral Doenitz.

Although several not altogether reliable witnesses later swore that they saw Bormann hit by Russian tank fire near the Reichs Chancellery while escaping on May 1, 1945, his body was never found. With the arch-enemy dead, Bormann became the number one target of those who wanted vengeance against the Nazis. Bormann came to symbolize all the Nazis who had eluded justice.

I could see that I would never hear the end of it if I refused to go with Apfelbaum and Erntler, so I let them drag me through the dusty street to the corner opposite the bus station. They pointed to a thick-set man sitting at one of the small tables with a glass and a half-empty bottle of beer in front of him. We had a clear view into the café, which was open on three sides, with poles at each corner supporting the tin roof.

The man was dressed in an old-fashioned dark brown wool suit, a white shirt and tie, and a hat. Four men were sitting at a table behind them; they too were dressed in heavy winter suits. This alone set them apart from the other customers, who like most people in this area were dressed in light-colored shirts and slacks, more suited to the hot climate and informal atmopshere.

"So this is Martin Bormann?" I asked, not about to volunteer to question the man. Already, I was being twitted for seeing Nazis under every bush because of all the newspaper publicity about Rio do Sul and Marechal Rondon. I was sure the two refugees were slightly paranoid because of their wartime experiences. Their imaginations had obviously run away with them.

They were not about to give up on me, however. They still insisted that the man was Martin Bormann. What was I going to do about it? Finally, after some argument, I agreed to check him out. I went into the grocery story opposite the café and asked the owner if I could use his phone. He agreed, and I called the bartender, who was leaning against the bar, wiping a glass. Through the store window, I saw him move toward the back wall to answer the telephone.

"Hello, Fredo. This is Dr. Erico, from the state police. Do me a favor will you? See that man in the dark suit sitting alone? Don't stare at him. Just act natural. Does he speak Portuguese?"

"Well, he said '*cerveza*,' when he ordered the beer," Fredo reported.

"Okay. This is what I'd like you to do. Take him a full bottle of beer and a glass and set them down, then pick up the ones on the table. Be careful not to smudge or wipe the fingerprints on the glass or bottle. Just put them down in the back room as if you were going to wash them, and save them for me. Play the fool. Don't act nervous or suspicious. I'll send someone over later. Thanks."

I watched from the grocery store window as Fredo waited a few minutes, then walked over to the table, picked up the glass and bottle, left another, and walked into the back room. I turned to Apfelbaum and Erntler and asked if they were satisfied.

They could see I'd done all I was going to do, and I assured them the man could easily be traced later, if it was necessary. I returned to my office to finish the morning reports. I had already dismissed the mysterious "Herr Bormann" when I came across a report from the border patrol, who were members of the state police. They reported that the Paraguayans had turned back five men who had tried to enter Paraguay last night at the control station on the Friendship Bridge. The men had no passports and were not known to Brazilian police, but they had obviously been Germans.

Now my interest was aroused. The descriptions of the five men fit the men in the bus station. On a hunch, I left my office and went back to the station. The men were gone. According to the ticket agent, they had bought tickets for Guairá and had boarded the bus, which had left about twenty minutes ago.

Assuming that the Germans were going to try to cross the border at Guairá, I decided to intercept them there. I picked up the Willys station wagon from headquarters and set out after the bus. I still didn't put any credence in the Bormann story, but thought the men might be Nazi leaders on a trip into Brazil.

The highway north along the river was a dirt road, riddled with potholes; it was barely winning a battle against the encroaching underbrush. It passed through several small towns like Pôrto Mendes and Marechal Rondon, past isolated farmhouses and an occasional store. It was a hot, dry morning and the dust was thick, but that was preferable to a rainy day, when the red clay roadbed would turn into an impassable river of mud.

I caught up to the bus about an hour outside Guairá, passed it, and drove into town, where I waited at the bus station. Before long, the antiquated bus rattled down the street, throwing up a cloud of red dust. I positioned myself so I could see the passengers disembark. There were about ten poorly dressed farmers. None were the men from the bus station. I met the driver as he descended and asked about the five men.

He remembered then and said they had gotten off the bus in Marechal Rondon. I winced; I'd been tricked by the cuckoo, stupidly thinking that they would go all the way to Guairá just because they had bought tickets to that city. I thanked the bus driver, jumped back in the Willys, and retraced my route.

By the time I arrived in Marechal Rondon there were only a few people sitting in the hotel café next to the bus station. I questioned the stationmaster and the few people standing around outside the hotel. Once again, the strangers' clothes had drawn attention to them. Several people remembered that they had been picked up by a white Volkswagen van. The ticket agent recognized it as the one Isenberg's farmhands drove into town each week when they bought supplies.

I walked over to the police station to ask Ricardo, the *delegado* I had appointed, to accompany me to the ranch.

I had not forgotten that I had been shot at once before when I visited the Isenberg ranch alone.

This time the main house was boarded up, evidently deserted since the owners had fled a few months ago. There were still several farmers living in small cottages on the land, however. The Germans were not with them, and they said they had not seen any strangers.

We found the van in the garage, just where they told us it was. It was dusty and empty. It was getting late; there was nothing to do but go back to Marechal Rondon. I returned to the hotel café adjoining the bus station and talked to two traveling salesmen who were eating an early dinner. They had arrived on the bus from Foz do Iguaçu that afternoon and were staying in town a few days.

I asked them about the five men who had taken the bus with them. Yes, they had noticed them. One of the salesmen said that the "boss" sat next to an old man in ragged clothes. The weatherbeaten old man, face shaded by a floppy straw hat, talked to the German as if he knew him. What had attracted the attention of the salesman, who was also German, was that the old man spoke *Hochdeutsch*, the pure German of the Rhine and of the educated classes. The salesman had thought it odd that such a poorly dressed man would speak such good German. The old man had also debarked in Marechal Rondon and had left in the white van with the five Germans.

I asked the *delegado* to keep a lookout for the Germans and for the old man in the straw hat and made arrangements with Werner Wanderer to borrow his private plane and his pilot the next day to look for the men.

The twin-engined Piper was kept at a small airport in Pôrto Mendes. When I met the pilot the next morning it was cloudy and threatening to rain. We flew low to the ground, searching for any suspicious hideouts, covering most of the territory between Foz do Iguaçu and Guaíra.

190

Returning to Pôrto Mendes, we flew over the Alto Paraná River, then circled over the Paraguayan jungles before making our approach to the airport. As we turned back toward Brazil, I caught a glimpse of a clearing in the jungle below. I asked the pilot to circle the area again. On the second pass, I could see a group of buildings, surrounded by a wood fence. There were a couple of stone blockhouses and several wood cabins. I noticed a path leading from the compound toward the river and wondered if this was a smugglers' camp. On the third pass we flew even lower, skimming the tree tops and hoping to see more details. This time, we saw several men run out of the buildings, accompanied by two German shepherd dogs. Four or five of the men were in civilian clothes, others wore some kind of uniform, with dark shirts, high boots, and caps. With a chill I was reminded of the SS uniform of World War II, but dismissed the notion. I noticed that the uniformed men ran stiffly, as if they were old.

Suddenly, we heard the staccato chatter of machine guns. The pilot swore and pulled the plane up sharply into a steep climb. I glanced back to see where the gunfire was coming from and saw two men in military uniforms shooting at us from the roof of the blockhouse. By this time a few of the men in the dark shirts were also firing at our plane with small handguns.

We called it quits for the day, but later in the week, we retraced our flight to the camp, plotting the location by time and direction. The compound was about eighteen miles inside the jungle, almost directly opposite Pôrto Mendes.

I spent three more weeks combing the countryside by Jeep, asking everyone I saw if they knew the old man in the straw hat. I had no luck, until one day on my way back to Foz do Iguaçu I stopped at a small grocery store along the road for a soft drink. Almost by habit, I asked

191

the storekeeper if she knew anyone fitting the old man's description.

"Why, that sounds like my father," she said. "Carl Kraft."

I asked if she could tell me where to find him. She was closing up the store soon and volunteered to show me the way. The rutted path to their house twisted in and out of the hills toward the river; I was glad I had a guide. When we arrived, two children ran out of a tumbledown shack to greet the woman. Grandfather wasn't there, they said. He was down at the lake.

"Is your father a fisherman?" I asked, a light beginning to dawn. She said her father owned a small boat that he kept at the river, and he bred carp at the pond over the hill. She pointed out the path to the pond.

I told her I'd go look for him. As I walked over the hill, I saw an old man coming toward me. He fit the description of the man on the bus perfectly, dressed in baggy overalls, with a battered straw hat pulled over one eye.

He looked at me closely as I approached him, his eyes fixing on the bulge under my shirt where my Taurus .38 was tucked into my slacks. I told him I was with the state police from Foz do Iguaçu, and I had information that he had been illegally ferrying people across the river to and from Paraguay. I was here to arrest him.

Kraft was frightened and immediately began to plead with me. He was an old man. Who would tend his fish if he were in jail? His daughter and her children depended on him.

I said he should have thought of that before he started smuggling foreigners into Brazil. That was a serious crime for which he would spend years in jail. He could be deported. Kraft had decided by now that I was a German and appealed to our common bond of nationality. Surely I wouldn't arrest a fellow German?

I said I was a law officer. I had no choice . . . unless he wanted to talk, tell me about his activities, about the men he had transported across the river. I wasn't interested in him. He was a nobody.

Slightly miffed at my condescension but greatly relieved, Kraft told me he was the "bridge" across the Alto Paraná for Germans who visited friends in Brazil. They provided an outboard motor, which they brought along for the trips. When someone wanted to cross they would send him word, usually by one of the ranch hands from Isenberg's farm. They paid him very little, but it was an honor. They were very important men, German leaders.

I said I understood that he had carried Martin Bormann across the river just the other week. Kraft couldn't help letting his pride show. He hadn't known the man, hadn't ever seen him before, but it was true, the other men with him called him "Herr Bormann."

Before I left Kraft, I gave him another dose of threats. I told him I wouldn't hesitate to toss him in jail if he breathed a word of our conversation. I had inside informants who had told me about Bormann and Kraft and who would tell me if Kraft ran back to his superiors with word that I had been there. Kraft swore that he wouldn't tell a soul. He didn't care. He was just an old man who wanted to fish and be left alone.

"Fine, then keep your mouth shut," I said. The next time he was asked to ferry someone across the river, I told him to go to Pôrto Mendes and tell Wanderer's pilot. I gave him the address and added a final warning. "If I find out you've been carrying any more men without telling me, the result will be the same. Into jail you'll go."

I left the house, with a goodbye and thank you to Kraft's daughter, who stared at me quizzically. As I drove away, I saw her run up the path to meet her father.

The next evening, I went to the casino and asked Major Acosta if he knew about the compound I had seen in the jungle, describing its location. He said he didn't know anything about it, but he would ask around and let me know what he learned.

About a week later, he took me aside in the casino and told me I had evidently discovered the hiding place of Martin Bormann. According to friends of his, a military patrol was sent to the fortress with supplies and a change of guard every twenty-one days. The camp was guarded not only by the Paraguayan army, but by Bormann's personal bodyguards, most of whom were old SS men who had come over after the war. There were approximately twenty Germans living there. He said he had also heard that Bormann was a sick old man, with bleeding ulcers. Maybe he had left his refuge to get medical attention in Brazil.

I didn't know what to believe now, but whoever the men had been, I was irritated that I had let them slip away. A week or so later, I had reason for more than mere irritation. The report on the fingerprints came back from Curitiba, after having been sent to the Federal Police in Rio do Janeiro for identification. The prints on the bottle and glass had been in their files. The man in the café was Martin Bormann.

15

Colonel Gralha, the chief of military intelligence for the frontier region, leaned forward in his chair, kneading his large hands together. I could tell the light conversation had come to an end. I stared at the drink in my hand, tilting it so it caught the light, and waited.

"Erico, I like you very much. You know that." Gralha hesitated, as if unsure of how to proceed. I smiled but didn't answer. There was an awkward pause, then he blurted, "This situation is intolerable, Erico. Why can't you stick to ordinary crime, like drugs or smuggling? That's what you're good at—why you're the best we have in Brazil. But you've got to lay off this Nazi hunt. It's just going to cause trouble. Go after subversives, if you must dabble in political matters."

"Subversives?" I asked. "I don't know anything about subversives, Colonel. I have a feeling that what the government calls subversives are my friends. I'm one of Jango's people; you know that. I'm too old to change my politics. And if I told you I had, you wouldn't believe me. You'd just lose any respect for me. And these Nazis . . . they're criminals. Don't you think they should be apprehended and punished?"

"It doesn't matter what I think," Gralha said, pleading with his eyes. I liked the Colonel and knew he had no choice. He had obviously been ordered to warn me. I told him I understood what he was saying. He looked relieved, and quickly switched to a safer topic.

As I drove back from his barracks to my hotel I thought about the conversation. I knew that if the military government insisted, they could have me yanked back to Curitiba and ordered off the case for good. The hardliners in the military were gaining the upper hand. They were exerting pressure on the government to force through repressive legislation designed to curb the violent demonstrations that had erupted this past spring and summer. They encouraged counter demonstrations and vigilante groups like the "Communist Hunting Command" who attacked liberal politicians.

Communist hunting was condoned; Nazi hunting was not. I wondered what the government would do if I handed a Nazi war criminal over to them. Would he still be extradited as Stangl had been? I decided not to worry about that now. I was too far into this case to quit. I'd just have to speed up my investigation while there was time.

A few days later, my chance came. Hector von Schee contacted me from Rio do Sul to tell me Dr. Mengele had been spotted leaving Dona Ema only two days before. This was the break I needed. Now I knew Mengele was in Brazil. I stepped up the pressure on my informants, traveling to as many small towns in the region as I could. Little by little the reports filtered in. Dr. Mengele had been spotted in the plaza of a small settlement near Guaraprava; he had reportedly stayed at a wealthy rancher's home in another town; he was said to be traveling on a letter of recommendation given him by a sympathetic military *delegado*. Always, the information came a day or two late. Mengele had already moved to a new location.

As I was sitting in my office with a map, plotting

Mengele's route north from Rio do Sul, I had a call from a restaurant owner whom I had working for me in Cascavel, a village on the road between Foz do Iguaçu and Curitiba. According to the restaurant owner, Dr. Mengele was staying at the ranch of a hide and wool wholesaler who lived outside of town. I thanked him for the tip and immediately made a call to Cascavel's *delegado*, giving him the information and location of the ranch and asking him to arrest Mengele immediately. As soon as I heard from him that he had Mengele under arrest, I would meet him in Cascavel.

I waited nervously all afternoon. When the *delegado* called again, he opened with an apology, and I knew that once again Mengele had slipped through the net. The *delegado* said Mengele had just left, only a few hours ahead of the arrest party. The same grapevine that was keeping me informed of Mengele's travels was evidently keeping the doctor up to date on police movements. Next time, I thought, I'll go myself.

For several days there was no word of Mengele. Evidently, he now knew he was being pursued and was hiding until it was safe to return to Paraguay. The problem was, where was he hiding? There were thousands of acres of uninhabited land between Cascavel and Paraguay and lots of isolated farms on which to hide.

On the twenty-fourth of June, I drove to Marechal Rondon to check personally with my contacts there, to see if they had heard of any unusual activity or seen any strangers in the area in the past few days. As I drove I tried to imagine what I would do if I were Mengele. Where would I hide? For how long? Where would I cross into Paraguay?

At Pôrto Mendes, I stopped at a small roadside restaurant owned by another of my informants, who was keeping an eye on Carl Kraft for me. As I pushed open the tattered screen door, I heard someone call my name.

197

Behind me was a friend from the federal police in Foz do Iguaçu. Roberto (not his real name, since he is still with the federal police as far as I know) had hoped he could catch me, he said. He had just received information that Mengele was hiding in a small village called Sao João de Alcaide, in northwest Paraná, about an eight hour drive from Foz do Iguaçu. A friend had given the doctor a job as foreman for a construction crew that was building a slaughterhouse there. According to his source, Mengele was traveling on a Paraguayan passport under the name of Cyrilo Chavez Flores.

Roberto wanted to be in on the capture, so we left the restaurant, soft drinks in hand, hopped back in our cars, and headed for Foz do Iguaçu. There we separated to round up some men and vehicles for the capture party.

A half hour later, I met Roberto outside police headquarters. I had convinced Captain Almeida, chief of the military police, to give me five of his men and a Jeep. I drove the Willys station wagon. Roberto had his Volkswagen and brought along two of his agents and an extra Jeep.

We drove until nightfall. Stopping only a few hours short of Sao João de Alcaide, we pulled off to the side of the road. I spent the night pacing up and down, fearing that once again the delay would give Mengele a chance to escape.

In the morning, we discussed our plan of attack over coffee. We knew the slaughterhouse was being built in the center of the small settlement next to the plaza, so we decided we would encircle the construction site. We timed our arrival for nine-thirty, giving Mengele plenty of time to show up for work. As I drove up the unpaved street into the town, I spotted the raw wood skeleton of the slaughterhouse, one of only six or seven buildings in the settlement. A small group of men stood near the site, and as I drove closer I could see that they were gathered around a short, thin man with a large, drooping mustache. He was dressed in a short sleeved white shirt and tan slacks, and had a deep suntan. Although the mustache was larger than I remembered and he no longer wore a beard, I recognized Joseph Mengele from the photographs I had found at Dona Ema.

The physician and his companions were gazing up at the roof, where two men were working. The sounds of a hammer echoed inside the structure. As a horsedrawn cart filled with corn rumbled by, temporarily screening me from view, I stepped out of the station wagon. I was only a few feet from Mengele. Behind me, Roberto signalled the other policemen already stationed on the four sides of the square. They got out of the Jeeps and drew their guns. Several men who had been standing in front of an adobe cafe broke into a run when they saw the military police Jeeps. Probably they were two of the hundreds of petty criminals who were constantly disappearing into this wild and isolated region.

One of the men standing with Mengele nudged him, and pointed toward the military policemen to my left. I took several steps and said, "Dr. Mengele, I am with the federal police. You're under arrest."

The other men backed off slowly, keeping their eyes on me. Mengele stood still, looking at me with a haughty expression. "You are mistaken," he announced in a clear calm voice, as if he had been prepared to meet me.

"I know who you are. I've seen your photograph before. You escaped me once, but not this time," I answered.

Still keeping his hands at his sides and his eyes fixed on my face. Mengele shook his head impatiently, as if trying to shake off a fly. When he spoke again, I noted the distinctive gap between his two front teeth that had been mentioned in the Interpol report. "I don't mean that. I mean you're making a mistake in arresting me. I'll be free tomorrow. There's nothing against me in Brazil."

Angered at his assurance, I told him we could argue that point later. Now, if he'd come with me. I asked for his identity papers, and he handed me his passport that, as we had been told, gave his name as Cyrilo Chavez Flores. I signalled to two of the federal agents and had them put Mengele into the back seat of the station wagon and handcuff him to the door handle. The town plaza had fallen silent; the hammering from the construction site stopped. The workers stared, some with curiosity, some with anger.

Ahead of us stretched a thirty-five hour drive to Curitiba, the nearest federal police headquarters, along an unpaved highway that twisted through the hills. The military policemen accompanied us part of the way, then turned off to Foz do Iguaçu. The federal agents and I took turns at the wheel, and most of the men caught catnaps when they weren't driving. I was too excited to think of sleep. I really had him. I turned, as if to convince myself that Mengele was sitting there. He was calmly gazing out the window. When I turned around, he returned my stare. His eyes reflected his hostility, but he showed no fear.

After peering intently at me for a few seconds he suddenly asked, "Are you really with the Brazilian police then? I thought you were an Israeli agent."

"No, I'm not with the Israelis." I told him I was opposed to the kind of extralegal action that had been used to capture Adolph Eichmann. As a law enforcement officer, I couldn't condone kidnapping, no matter how much I wanted people like Eichmann and him punished.

"Well, you better shoot *me* right now if you want vengeance. Because they'll just let me go." He laughed harshly. "But you wouldn't dare kill me yourself, would you?"

Once again his lack of concern rankled me. "Well,

you should know about killing," I snapped. "You've killed hundreds of thousands yourself."

Mengele raised his eyebrows in distaste at my outburst. "I never killed anybody," he said patiently, as if explaining to a child. "The people that died, it was their destiny. I had nothing to do with that. My work was strictly scientific.

"Everything has been overdramatized by the Americans. The Nazis were not so cruel as they'd like you to believe. Lampshades out of skulls and such nonsense!"

I ticked off on my fingers some of his more infamous medical experiments, glad now that I had done a little research.

"But these people were condemned already," Mengele protested. "You don't understand. What more beautiful death than in the service of humanity."

"Just a man of science," I muttered.

"Yes, only that." He missed the sarcasm and seemed hopeful that I was beginning to understand. "Only that. Politics doesn't interest me."

I closed my eyes, suddenly very tired. My anger dissolved into disgust. The excitement I felt at capturing Mengele had disappeared.

By early evening, Mengele had fallen asleep and was snoring loudly. This only angered me more. He couldn't be less concerned about his fate. I sat wide awake and stewed.

We stopped several times at small roadside cafés for coffee and sandwiches. Not wanting to take any chances, I left Mengele handcuffed in the car and brought him the food. At breakfast, he tried to start a conversation with me again.

"Who are you? Are you a Jew? Are you persecuting me because you're a Jew?"

I didn't answer, and he made no more attempts to talk with me. When we drove into Curitiba it was late evening of the next day. We went straight to federal police headquarters. I was anxious to hand my prisoner over to the authorities and leave.

A sleepy-looking cop was on duty. He listened stolidly as the federal agent explained who the prisoner was and how and where we had captured him. We handed him Mengele's passport and suggested the police check the fingerprints; it was impossible to alter them and I assumed if the passport was stolen, the fingerprints would be the original owner's. I watched the clerk sign in "Dr. Joseph Mengele," and phoned the airport to check on flights to Foz do Iguaçu. Luckily there was a flight later that evening. I made a reservation. I wanted to leave that night before the reporters had the story and began to hound me. I had been embarrassed by the earlier publicity and by the sensationalism of the newspaper accounts of the Dona Ema raid and the clean-up in Marechal Rondon.

I was tired, and my mind was fuzzy. Had I been more alert I might have stopped to consider that publicity was my one weapon against the reluctance of the federal government to deal with Mengele. By leaving Curitiba without alerting the newspapers, I was giving the government a chance to sidestep the problem.

On the plane to Foz do Iguaçu, I finally fell asleep, lulled by the steady drone of the airplane engines. It was an effort to walk from the plane to the cab stand and from there to my hotel room, where I collapsed fully dressed on the bed and fell into a deep sleep that lasted until late the next evening. It was the first sleep I had had in almost three days.

16

When I returned to my office the next day it was with a satisfied, almost smug feeling. The fugitives who had haunted me like ghosts for eighteen months were not mere figments of my imagination, nor were they criminal masterminds who always managed to stay one step ahead of justice. Joseph Mengele was safely locked in a cell and soon would be called to account for his crimes.

It was late afternoon when I had a call from a friend in federal police headquarters in Curitiba. I greeted him heartily. "This is confidential, Erico, but I thought you ought to know," he said in a hushed, conspiratorial voice. "Mengele was released about an hour ago."

"Who gave the order?" I gasped, the wind knocked out of me.

"General Lima Gomes, chief of the federal police." The telephone had been ringing constantly since we brought Mengele in forty-eight hours before, with calls from Army brass, SNI officials and government officials. The justification they contrived for the release was that, although the prisoner had been brought in as Dr. Mengele, his passport indicated he was Cyrilo Chavez Flores. I found out later the Flores was a convicted murderer from Paraguay who was wanted in three South

American countries, one of which was Brazil. Major Acosta told me later that the real Flores had been shot and killed by Paraguayan police, who had buried him in a pauper's grave in Asunción and for some reason had given his passport to Mengele. Even if the federal police had believed the prisoner was Flores, they should have held him on murder charges.

That night, after enough straight Scotch to make any man drunk, I sat stone sober in a small restaurant and bar run by a fellow Austrian. I was stunned, my mind still refusing to accept the fact that the federal police, with the acquiescence of the government, had just opened Mengele's cell and let him walk out, set free a man who was accused of killing thousands of innocent people. Mengele's mocking face as he predicted his release was fresh in my mind.

I had been contemptuous of him, sure that he would meet with justice soon enough. Had I been totally naive, I wondered, living in my own, old fashioned world of right and wrong? What had given me the idea that Mengele would be turned over to the Germans to stand trial?

I thought of the Stangl case and remembered how close he had come to escaping extradition. But the federal police *had* arrested him, *had* kept him in jail, and he *had* been extradited.

By the time I trudged through the streets to my hotel, it was almost dawn. Ahead of me scurried an Arab carrying a shapeless bundle. Glancing back at me, he ducked into an alleyway and disappeared. The shock was wearing off, and now anger boiled its way to the surface. I wanted to lash out, to fight back, but I felt hamstrung. What good would it do to arrest criminals if the government just unlocked their cells? I wanted to give up, but it isn't in my nature. I couldn't quit without bringing Joseph Mengele to justice. I couldn't round up every German war criminal in South America, or even in

Brazil, but I could deal with Mengele. Otherwise, that smug face would haunt me forever.

The problem wasn't recapturing him. I knew he would want to return to Paraguay as quickly as possible. I thought he'd be reluctant to cross legally because of the Flores passport, and I knew he'd be cocky because he'd shown me that he had more power than I did. He would think that he was free of me and therefore wouldn't be as cautious as he had been last time. All I had to do was to wait for him to cross the river. And I had a pretty good idea where he would do that.

The more important consideration was what to do with Mengele when I caught him. Even with a well-planned campaign of publicity, I couldn't trust the federal government not to release him again. In their campaign of repression against the Brazilian people, they had shown little regard for world opinion. Besides, too few people cared any more about Nazi war criminals. Most people, including many Jews, wanted to forget about the whole thing to avoid making waves. They remembered that after Eichmann's capture there had been violent outbreaks of anti-Semitism in cities throughout South America, including swastika painting, desecration of Jewish graveyards, and vandalism against Jewish merchants. The Israelis, anxious for world allies in their struggle against the Arabs, were no longer willing to offend other nations by invading their sovereignty and kidnapping their citizens.

What I needed was a government that would arrest and extradite Mengele. Stationed as I was on the border with Paraguay and Argentina, I could easily slip Mengele out of Brazil. Paraguay had to be ruled out as a possibility, but I knew Argentina had an extradition treaty with Germany. I had already discussed my investigation with Señor Rainer, the Argentine consul in Foz do Iguaçu and found him sympathetic. Now I approached him again and explained my predicament. I told him I planned to capture Mengele a second time, but hesitated to turn him over to the federal authorities. Rainer said he was sure that his government would take Mengele and promised to check with his superiors. A few days later, he told me that if I captured Mengele and could deliver him to Argentine soil, his government would extradite him. They still had an arrest warrant and extradition request from West Germany on file in Buenos Aires.

Soon I was working feverishly on a plan that would snare the doctor. At the same time, I knew that this was the last case I would work on in Brazil. I had to be prepared to leave the country with Mengele and never return.

Once again I alerted my contacts in Marechal Rondon, Pôrto Mendes, and Foz do Iguaçu to watch for anyone visiting local Nazis. In Marechal Rondon, I had several people keeping an eye on Isenberg's ranch. In Pôrto Mendes, I stationed one of my men to stake out Carl Kraft's farm. As far as I knew, it was the only river crossing used by the Nazis in this region.

I took two days out to fly to São Paulo to check with Ian Capps, the Reuter's correspondent who had been interested in the Nazi story from the beginning. He contacted his counterpart in Buenos Aires to expect my arrival and promised his assistance when I arrived there. I also checked with British intelligence, with whom I had kept in close contact since the war. They approved of my plan and promised whatever assistance they could give. They cautioned me that I should be prepared to leave South America for good when this was over. My life would be in danger from the many other war criminals who had found refuge in South America, and the government of Brazil would be embarrassed and angered because I had exceeded my authority. I was well aware that I was living on borrowed time.

For several weeks, I waited for the trap to spring. Betting that Mengele would try to cross into Paraguay on Carl Kraft's boat, I planned to intercept the German doctor at the river crossing, hold him for a day or two at a hunting cabin owned by an Arab friend, and then transfer him at night to a barge I would anchor in the river. When word came that the Argentine authorities were ready to move, I would take my prisoner by barge to Puerto Iguazú, a small tourist town on the Argentine side of the river.

My transportation to the barge would be provided by an Argentine secret agent to whom Ranier had referred me. His name was "El Gordo," which is roughly translated as Fatty, and he was as roly-poly as his name suggests, with dark thinning hair that he slicked back with oil. El Gordo owned a small restaurant on the bank of the river not far from Foz do Iguaçu and a rowboat he would be glad to lend me.

The third week of June, about three weeks after Mengele's release, I heard from a schoolteacher in Marechal Rondon who was one of my better informants. She told me that one of the farmers living on Isenberg's ranch had come into town to pick up some outboard motor parts that had been ordered from Argentina and, after inquiring casually among the farmers who lived nearby, she had discovered that there had been an unusual amount of activity at the ranch in the past few days.

Two days later, on July 28, the agent who was keeping an eye on Carl Kraft reported that the old man had had a visit from Walter Bernhardt, a Marechal Rondon man who was one of the *Graf Spee* crewmen interned in Argentina during the war. I knew that this must be the messenger setting up an appointment for the crossing. From my talk with Kraft, I knew that the old man usually received only a day's notice before his services were needed. Now I was sure that Mengele was on his way.

I went to my Arab friend and told him I wanted to do some hunting and wished to rent his cabin for a few days. The one-room cabin was just what I needed; it was in an isolated spot in the woods away from any settlements but near enough to Foz do Iguaçu and the river that I could easily transfer the prisoner to the barge in one night.

After negotiating an agreement with the Arab, I contacted four Paraguayans who owned a lumber barge. I told them only that I wanted to rent their barge for a few days to hide a man from the police. The boatmen, who made less than a handsome living from transporting lumber down the river from Paraguay to Argentina, were happy to do exactly what they were told—for a fee.

I ordered them to load the barge with lumber and anchor it off the island underneath the Friendship Bridge in the middle of the river. They were to wait there until I brought the prisoner. I deliberately picked this island because it was such a public spot that no one would think the boatmen had anything to hide. Barge owners usually lived on their boats, anchoring at a pleasant spot along the river until they were ready to deliver a load of lumber.

That same evening, I took Alberto and Juan, two police sergeants I had learned I could trust, to the river landing where Carl Kraft kept the *Lambari*. We pulled my car off the road, hid it well with branches, and walked down the path through the thick underbrush to the landing. The beach was about fifty yards wide at this point, the sand turning to red mud at the river's edge where the boat was beached. A few yards from the boat was a rickety lean-to where Kraft kept his supplies.

I stationed Juan behind a group of trees just to the right to the path that came from Kraft's house. Alberto and I waited behind the lean-to. The night was deadly still, with only the soft lapping of the water against the shore and an occasional screech from a water fowl. The sand flies helped keep us awake and restless. Towering cumulus clouds rolled across the sky, and I wondered if it was going to rain.

Just before dawn I heard the muffled sounds of men's voices coming down the path. As the voices became more distinct, I could pick out random German words. The men appeared out of the woods. I drew my gun, stood up, and stepped into view. I was about five feet from Mengele, who was wearing a jacket and a pair of old slacks. Next to him was a stocky, short man I had never seen before. He looked burly enough to be some kind of bodyguard. Bringing up the rear was Carl Kraft, who was lugging a small outboard motor. As I stepped from behind the lean-to, he dropped the motor in the mud and turned and scrambled up the slippery bank and into the woods. I shouted to Juan to let him go. I hadn't expected two men, and I wanted an extra hand. One of my men could pick up Kraft later, if it were even necessary.

Mengele was staring at me in disbelif. *"Schon wieder? What again?"* he snarled. His friend looked at him in surprise.

I kept my .38 trained on Mengele. "It's me again, and this time it's for keeps." I had already decided on a story that I hoped would keep Mengele quiet until I could deliver him to Argentina.

"I have information that a group of Israeli commandos are on the other side of the river waiting for you to cross. They've been tipped off about your arrest and release from prison. As I told you, I don't approve of their methods. They're likely to kill you on the spot."

"And what do you intend to do with me?" Mengele asked. For the first time he looked nervous. Beads of sweat had broken out on his upper lip when I mentioned the Israelis.

I told him I planned to take him to Argentina where

I would turn him over to the authorities for extradition to Germany. He pondered the alternatives for a few minutes, then nodded. He would take his chances with the Argentines rather than face the Israelis. His partner remained silent throughout the conversation.

I motioned Juan to handcuff the two men together and pointed with the gun toward the path. We walked in silence; Mengele seemed to be deep in thought. We went to where my car was hidden in the underbrush, put the two men in the back, and drove to the cabin, which was only about twenty minutes from the river.

When we reached the cabin, I motioned Mengele inside, leaving Alberto with the other prisoners. "Who's your friend?" I asked.

"Oh, he's Heinrich Mueller. He was head of the Gestapo, you know. He doesn't talk much."

I took this admission with a grain of salt. I couldn't believe that if the man were the former Gestapo chief, a man wanted for war crimes, Mengele would so casually reveal it to me. Perhaps it was just his idea of a joke, or perhaps he wanted me to claim that I had captured Heinrich Mueller only to have it turn out that the man was a complete unknown. I made a mental note to check my office files to see if I had any description or information about Mueller. I had met any number of men with the same name, including the Heinrich Mueller who ran the German/Brazilian Alliance in Curitiba. Most likely, the man was just a bodyguard.

I told Mengele that I would return soon to transfer him to a boat and take him to Argentina. Leaving Juan in charge of the two handcuffed prisoners, Alberto and I returned to Foz do Iguaçu. Once again I was excited by the capture and eager to move. I sent word through El Gordo to the Argentine consul informing him I had apprehended Mengele and another man, whose identity I did not yet know. I was awaiting instructions from his

210

government. Ranier sent back his promise to let me know as soon as he received word.

Next I checked on the barge, which I could see from the bridge was anchored on the island, half out of sight and loaded down with logs. It looked innocent and peaceful floating on the calm harbor. I stopped by El Gordo's restaurant and told him I would be by late the next night with the prisoners.

The next day I took some food to the cabin and talked further with Mengele. He was apprehensive about the Israelis, but seemed to have little concern about my plans for him. As long as he kept quiet, I didn't care. His companion lay on the cot where Alberto had handcuffed him and stared at the ceiling, refusing to speak or answer questions.

I waited until well past three o'clock that morning, when I knew that the casino had closed and the tourists would be back in their hotels. Then I returned to the cabin, picked up Juan and the prisoners, and drove to El Gordo's. The restaurant was dark and quiet. I knocked at the side door, according to the plan. El Gordo's eldest son, a thin boy of about sixteen, slipped out the door and led the way down the steep path to the river, where a long, slender rowboat was tied up at the dock. We transferred one man at a time to the barge, with El Gordo's son rowing and me in the back with my gun trained on the prisoner.

Once I had both men on board, I put them in the hold, in a small cabin with two cots and a hotplate. The Paraguayans looked over their guests with curiosity. I told them to keep an eye on the two men and assured them I would visit the next day. I paid them their day's wages before I left and told them I would bring more money tomorrow. I was afraid to give them more than a day's pay; they might decide to slip away that night and leave the prisoners to their own devices.

211

The days slipped by with no word. I checked on Mueller's description from my office files; the age, height, and complexion matched the second prisoner, but there was no way to confirm his identity without tipping my hand. Meanwhile the days became weeks, and still there was silence. Frantic, I spent my days pursuing my usual duties and my nights ferrying back and forth from the restaurant to the barge reassuring my nervous prisoners, who were beginning to get suspicious about my intentions, and greasing the palms of the Paraguayans who were also getting edgy. The bills mounting, I cabled Ian Capps for aid, and he sent some money to cover my expenses. Meanwhile I sent word to Ranier almost every day. He continued to counsel patience.

It was hard advice to follow. The first week of September I heard from a friend in Curitiba that the word had come down from federal authorities that I was to be recalled. Two days later, I had a call from Wilfred Pilloto, chief of the Paraná civil police and my direct superior. Before he could transmit the order, I asked for a leave of absence without pay, pleading personal business that had to be settled. He hesitated, and I knew that he understood what was happening. He agreed reluctantly, and before he hung up, asked me to take care.

On September 7, Foz do Iguaçu shook itself from its usual stupor to celebrate the nation's Independence Day with a parade. Although not as elaborate as the festivities in the large cities, it was still a major holiday for the townspeople. A wooden reviewing stand was erected on the main street and the military band was called out to lead contingents of school children and local fraternal organizations. The buildings along the route were smothered in clouds of dust kicked up by the marching groups and by hoards of small children who ran through the streets followed by a collection of stray dogs.

212

I walked over to the reviewing stand as the dignitaries began to take their places. Among them was my old friend Colonel Gralha, who gave me a disapproving look, and Captain Almeida of the military police, who smiled in conspiratorial fashion. He had taken me aside only a few days before to hint that he knew what I was up to, but he approved of my actions and was not about to say anything. I should understand, of course, that he knew nothing officially. He knew about Mengele, and that worried me. Who else knew my secret?

A few minutes later, Mr. Ranier hurried up to the stand. As he walked past me, he nodded slowly in my direction, looking right at me. I knew immediately that a go-ahead was imminent. Without either of us saying a word, he walked up the steps to the platform and greeted the other officials. In the distance, the band swung into a stirring march.

Three more days passed while I waited for exact instructions. In the meantime, I auctioned off my one valuable possession, a gold watch, to pay the debts I had accumulated in Foz do Iguaçu. I did not want to leave owing people money. I gathered the newspaper clippings and documents I had accumulated in my investigation of the Nazis and packed them in a battered suitcase. The rest of the time I followed my normal routine to avoid suspicion.

On September 14, I had a telephone call from my counterpart in Paraguay. I had talked with him before when he had asked me to turn over to him a man we had picked up in Foz do Iguaçu. The man was wanted for murder in Paraguay, so we agreed to send him back to stand trial. A few weeks later the police chief invited me to his office in Puerto Presidente Stroessner to tell him what I knew of the man's activities in Brazil.

While I was there, he had taken me to see his prisoner. The man I had sent to Paraguay was not the creature who crouched in the three-by-three foot cage, a ball and chain around his neck. The ragged animal twirled in the dust and screeched at me when he recognized the man who had sent him to this fate. The cell was the worst I had seen in my twenty years in South America. The police chief, who had seemed like a genial man, seemed almost proud of the jail's filthy condition.

Now the police chief, who seemed to consider us good friends because of the incident, had a warning for me. "Dr. Erico, you're going to get killed. There are three men and a woman driving a dark-colored Simca. They're Nazis and they're out to kill you and free Mengele. Be careful."

My secret obviously had been leaked in the weeks since I captured Mengele. I thanked the police chief for the tip and called Captain Almeida, knowing he could be trusted. I told him about the call and he picked me up a few minutes later in a Jeep. With him were a few of his men, armed with Tommy guns. Together we searched Foz do Iguaçu and the surrounding countryside for the Simca. About ten o'clock that evening we returned, exhausted and empty-handed. I went to the Austrian restaurant for some dinner. As I ate, I tried to figure out what to do now. It was obvious the word was out that I had Mengele. How long would it be before someone knew where I was holding him? Or did they already? I was exceeding my authority and disobeying orders to drop the investigation. This would give the government the excuse to pull me back to Curitiba, leave of absence notwithstanding.

Just as I was finishing dinner, Rainer walked into the restaurant. Without looking directly at me, he signalled me to follow him, and walked into the men's room. I waited a few minutes, then got up and went in after the consul. He was standing at the sink washing his hands. We were the only two people in the washroom.

"It's the Paraguayans who want to kill you, Erico. It's a trap. You must leave tonight. An Argentine boat will meet you off Puerto Iguazú." He wiped his hands on one of the paper towels stacked up on the window ledge and walked out. The adrenalin started to pump through my system. I had been tired; now I was awake and ready to move.

I didn't want to leave without taking the precaution of alerting Ian Capps, as I had promised. At night, the long-distance calls from Foz do Iguaçu had to be made by microwave. During the day, there was a line hooked up to police headquarters, but the microwave station closed at nine every night. I drove my car to the station and pounded on the door until I awakened the manager, who lived in the back.

Telling him I had emergency police business, I convinced him to open the station. Luckily, Ian Capps was home. I told him things were hot, and I had to leave that night. He assured me that he'd have everything arranged. I'd be met by a Reuter's man in Buenos Aires. British intelligence would make sure there were no slip-ups in my handing over the prisoner to the Argentine authorities.

I called El Gordo from a public telephone in town and told him to pick me up at four o'clock that morning. I drove back to my hotel, parked the car in a conspicuous spot in the street and sat in the bar, nervously fingering a drink, trying to think of what else I could do besides wait. A few minutes before four I went up to my room and picked up my suitcase. The little money I had left to my name, something under $200, I stuck in my wallet.

El Gordo drove up and parked his car just past the hotel entrance. At four o'clock sharp, I walked out, took a quick look around, and jumped into the front seat. The streets were dark and deserted. There was a thick cloud cover, and the air smelled like rain. We drove in a circuit-

215

ous route to his restaurant, both of us wondering if a car would appear suddenly out of the blackness. When we pulled up alongside his house, his son was waiting. I shook El Gordo's hand; he and his son were the only persons besides Ranier and Capps who knew I was leaving.

It was difficult to pick out the steps on the steep stairway, but once we reached the dock, I could see the rowboat and the dim outline of the island. We climbed into the boat. The sound of the oars being slipped into the pins and the slap of the water against the side of the boat as we pushed away seemed to reverberate across the water. I crouched in the back of the boat, afraid to smoke, and we rowed for the barge in darkness without even a flashlight to guide us.

My heart rose when I saw the barge still anchored in the same spot where I had left it the day before. The Paraguayans loomed out of the darkness, leaning over the edge as they watched the rowboat approach. They had never been awake before when I visited in the dead of night. I wondered why they were now, but the thought slipped away as they hauled me aboard, and El Gordo's son pushed off and began to row back to shore.

"We're leaving," I told them. "Get the two Germans and bring them up on deck." I told the head man to steer for the small harbor at Puerto Iguazú. He glared at me as he turned his back. The Paraguayans had obviously decided I was up to no good, not that it mattered now. I was less than a mile from Argentine territory. In a few minutes, the hard part of the job would be done.

Mengele and the other prisoner stumbled out of the cabin, trying to steady themselves on the deck. I removed their handcuffs so they could keep their balance and ordered them to stand against the cabin so I could keep my eye and my gun on them. Mengele appeared calm, as if he were taking a moonlight cruise on the river.

216

The barge maneuvered out of the sheltered harbor and into the main channel, heading downriver toward Argentina. It was brighter on the water, with glimpses of moonlight through the clouds.

Suddenly I saw Mengele stiffen as he looked back the way we had come. I turned and saw a black shadow looming in the darkness, not more than twenty yards from the barge. In the first instant, I thought it was the Argentine escort, then realized it was approaching from the wrong direction. Now it drew closer and I could make out the outlines of an outmoded motor launch with perhaps a dozen men on board. Two searchlights blazed out of the night, blinding me for a few seconds.

A burst of gunfire came from behind the searchlights. I ducked behind a pile of logs. From there, I could see six men wearing plain khaki uniforms, without insignia or caps, standing on the deck of the launch firing submachine guns. I recognized them immediately as Paraguayan soldiers. My lumbermen ran for the other boat and reached out to try to pull the two boats together. I cursed them and suddenly understood they had sold me out.

As the launch closed in, Mengele and his friend broke for safety. I shouted *"Para!* Stop!" Two Paraguayan soldiers leapt onto our barge to grab the Germans. I raised my gun and fired four bullets at Mengele. They struck him in the chest and side. He turned toward me, stared at me with a surprised expression, and I shot again. This time it was a direct hit in the throat. His body jerked violently, and he fell over the side of the barge headfirst into the water. His feet caught in some ropes that were laying on the deck; they held him face down in the water. The Paraguayans, who had dropped back when I fired, now grabbed the other German and jumped for the launch. I shot again, and saw my second prisoner stumble and grab for his leg.

I heard a shout from the other side of the barge, turned, and saw a huge patrol boat bearing the blue and white Argentine flag. The Argentines shouted at the Paraguayans, who screeched back in their native Guarani. Bullets whizzed past my head, and for a few minutes there was bedlam, with the shouting and the gunfire mingling in a terrifying racket.

The Paraguayans, seeing they were outgunned by the larger boat, gave covering fire to two of their men, who fished Mengele out of the water just as the launch began to pull away. His body was limp, and I knew that he was dead. He had been in the water at least five minutes.

The Argentines helped me aboard. The shots subsided as the opposing boats pulled away from the empty barge. I turned, ears still ringing as an eerie silence descended over the river. At some point it had started to rain, and now the water danced madly, as if to a frantic tune. The rain gained momentum until the water seemed to fall in solid sheets. Thunder rumbled across the sky. I checked myself for injuries, but had none . . . only a dull ache and an occasional pang from the old face wound.

I sat on the deck, barely listening to the boat's captain who was telling me the post commander would be awaiting me at Puerto Iguazú and would arrange for my transportation to Posadas, and then on to Buenos Aires where the British would take over to fly me to London.

I walked back to the rear deck and stood in the downpour, staring back toward the island, the bridge, and the hulking shadow of Brazil. As the rain beat on my head and shoulders, I wondered how it had led to this. Once again I was leaving my home, in secret, with no money, no possessions. Once again I was an exile.

I saw before me Mengele's body slumped into the water. One Nazi dead. But what did it matter? A Nazi never dies. He will appear again tomorrow with a different face a different name, a different language perhaps, but the same old ideas. I was suddenly very tired.

EPILOGUE

Erich Erdstein arrived at London's Heathrow Airport on September 22, 1968, where he was met by reporters who had been alerted to the Mengele shooting and by British intelligence, who questioned him over a period of several weeks.

After recuperating in England, he traveled extensively in Europe before settling in Canada in 1970, where he now has landed immigrant status.

Erdstein still carries his Austrian passport although he has refused, because of his memories, to return to the country of his birth or to accept reparation payments offered him by the Austrian government after the war. Erdstein never became a citizen of any of the countries he served, considering it untruthful to state, "I am a Uruguayan, or Brazilian, or Canadian." He considers himself an international citizen.

He is a member of Amnesty International and is committed to that organization's attempt to secure civil liberties and human rights for people throughout the world. Erdstein is involved in hunting down terrorist groups acting on the American continent and is convinced after 30 years' experience that these movements, whether on the left or right of the political spectrum, have a common purpose: to undermine democracy. Often they work together toward that aim.

Since his departure from South America, eight of twelve South American governments have succumbed to military rule. In Brazil, President Ernesto Geisel is under increasing attack for political repression and use of torture. In a conspiracy in 1975, a number of Brazilians were arrested and harassed as suspected "Communists." Violations of human rights, arbitrary arrest, and detention are still not uncommon.

There has been no confirmation of Mengele's death, nor confirmation of Bormann's whereabouts in the years since Erdstein left South America. Various persons have claimed to have seen Mengele in Paraguay; others have been sure that they located Bormann. But the rumors remain unconfirmed. No Nazi war criminals have been extradited from South America since Franz Stangl ws returned to Germany to stand trial in 1967.

2.—

Also by Steve Martin

NOVELS

The Pleasure of My Company

Shopgirl

PLAYS

Picasso at the Lapin Agile

WASP

NONFICTION

Pure Drivel

Cruel Shoes

SCREENPLAYS

Shopgirl

Bowfinger

L.A. Story

Roxanne

The Jerk (coauthor)

Born

Standing

Up

A Comic's Life

Steve Martin

SCRIBNER

New York London Toronto Sydney

Scribner
A Division of Simon & Schuster, Inc.
1230 Avenue of the Americas
New York, NY 10020

First Scribner hardcover edition November 2007

Scribner and design are trademarks of
Macmillan Library Reference USA, Inc., used under license
by Simon & Schuster, the publisher of this work.

For information about special discounts for bulk purchases,
please contact Simon & Schuster Special Sales:
1-800-456-6798 or business@simonandschuster.com.

Designed by C. Linda Dingler

Text set in Scala

Manufactured in the United States of America

1 3 5 7 9 10 8 6 4 2

Library of Congress Cataloging-in-Publication Data

Martin, Steve, 1945–
Born standing up: a comic's life/by Steve Martin.
p. cm.
1. Martin, Steve, 1945– 2. Entertainers—United States—Biography.
I. Title.
PN2287.M522A3 2007
792.7'028092—dc22
[B]
2007027143

ISBN-13: 978–1–4165–5364–9
ISBN-10:   1–4165–5364–9

Photograph credits appear on page 209.

To my father, mother,
and sister, Melinda

Contents

Born
Standing
Up

My decade is the seventies, with several years extending on either side. Though my general recall of the period is precise, my memory of specific shows is faint. I stood onstage, blinded by lights, looking into blackness, which made every place the same. Darkness is essential: If light is thrown on the audience, they don't laugh; I might as well have told them to sit still and be quiet. The audience necessarily remained a thing unseen except for a few front rows, where one sourpuss could send me into panic and desperation. The comedian's slang for a successful show is "I murdered them," which I'm sure came about because you finally realize that the audience is capable of murdering you.

Stand-up is seldom performed in ideal circumstances. Comedy's enemy is distraction, and rarely do comedians get a pristine performing environment. I worried about the sound system, ambient noise, hecklers, drunks, lighting, sudden clangs, latecomers, and loud talkers, not to mention the nagging concern "Is this funny?" Yet the seedier the circumstances, the funnier one can be. I suppose these worries keep the mind sharp and the senses active. I can remember instantly retiming a punch line to fit around the crash of a dropped glass of wine, or raising my voice to cover a patron's ill-timed sneeze, seemingly microseconds before the interruption happened.

I was seeking comic originality, and fame fell on me as a by-product. The course was more plodding than heroic: I did not strive valiantly against doubters but took incremental steps studded with a few intuitive leaps. I was not naturally talented—I didn't sing, dance, or act—though working around that minor detail made me inventive. I was not self-destructive, though I almost destroyed myself. In the end, I turned away from stand-up with a tired swivel of my head and never looked back, until now. A few years ago, I began researching and recalling the details of this crucial part of my professional life—which inevitably touches upon my personal life—and was reminded why I did stand-up and why I walked away.

In a sense, this book is not an autobiography but a biography, because I am writing about someone I used to know. Yes, these events are true, yet sometimes they seemed to have happened to someone else, and I often felt like a curious onlooker or someone trying to remember a dream. I ignored my stand-up career for twenty-five years, but now, having finished this memoir, I view this time with surprising warmth. One can have, it turns out, an affection for the war years.

Coffee and Confusion

ON A HUMID MONDAY NIGHT in the summer of 1965, after finding an eight-dollar hotel room in the then economically friendly city of San Francisco, I lugged my banjo and black, hard-shell prop case ten sweaty blocks uphill to the Coffee and Confusion, where I had signed up to play for free. The club was tiny and makeshift, decorated with chairs, tables, a couple of bare lightbulbs, and nothing else. I had romanticized San Francisco as an exotic destination, away from friends and family and toward mystery and adventure, so I often drove my twenty-year-old self up from Los Angeles to audition my fledgling comedy act at a club or to play banjo on the street for tips. I would either sleep in my VW van, camp out in Golden Gate Park, pay for a cheap hotel, or snag a free room in a Haight-Ashbury Victorian crash pad by making an instant friend. At this point, my act was a catchall, cobbled together from the disparate universes of juggling, comedy, banjo playing, weird bits I'd written in college, and magic tricks. I was strictly Monday-night quality, the night when, traditionally, anyone could get up to perform. All we entertainers knew Mondays were really audition nights for the club.

The Coffee and Confusion, ca. 1965.

I walked past Broadway and Columbus, where Lawrence Ferlinghetti's ramshackle City Lights Books was jam-packed with thin small-press publications offering way-out poetry and reissues of long-ago-banned erotic novels. Around the corner on Broadway was Mike's Pool

Hall, where bikers and hippies first laid eyes on each other, unsure whether they should beat each other up or just smoke pot and forget about it. Steps away was the hungry i, a nightclub that had launched a thousand careers, including those of the Smothers Brothers, the Kingston Trio, and Lenny Bruce, but I had to trudge on by. Just up Columbus, I passed the Condor, the first of a sudden explosion of topless clubs, where Carol Doda, in a newfangled bathing suit that exposed her recently inflated basketball breasts, descended from the ceiling on a grand piano that was painted virginal white. This cultural mélange—and the growing presence of drugs—made the crowded streets of North Beach simmer with toxic vitality.

The Coffee and Confusion was nearby on Grant Avenue, a street dotted with used-clothing stores and incense shops. I nervously entered the club, and Ivan Ultz, the show runner, slotted me into the lineup. I lingered at the back, waiting for my turn, and surveyed the audience of about fifteen people. They were arrayed in patchwork jeans with tie-dyed tops, and the room was thick with an illegal aroma. In the audience was a street poet, dressed in rags and bearded like a yeti, who had a plastic machine gun that shot Ping-Pong balls, which he unloaded on performers he didn't like. I was still untouched by the rapidly changing fashion scene; my short hair and conservative clothes weren't going to help me with this crowd.

Ivan introduced me. My opening line, "Hello. I'm Steve Martin, and I'll be out here in a minute," was met

7

with one lone chuckle. I struggled through the first few minutes, keeping a wary eye on Mr. Ping-Pong Ball, and filled in the dead air with some banjo tunes that went just okay. I could see Ivan standing nearby, concerned. I began to strum the banjo, singing a song that I told the audience my grandmother had taught me:

Be courteous, kind, and forgiving.
Be gentle and peaceful each day.
Be warm and human and grateful,
And have a good thing to say.

Be thoughtful and trustful and childlike,
Be witty and happy and wise.
Be honest and love all your neighbors,
Be obsequious, purple, and clairvoyant.

Be pompous, obese, and eat cactus.
Be dull and boring and omnipresent.
Criticize things you don't know about.
Be oblong and have your knees removed.

Be sure to stop at stop signs,
And drive fifty-five miles an hour.
Pick up hitchhikers foaming at the mouth,
And when you get home get a master's degree in
    geology.

8
—

Be tasteless, rude, and offensive.
Live in a swamp and be three-dimensional.
Put a live chicken in your underwear.
Go into a closet and suck eggs.

Then I said, "Now, everyone," and I repeated the entire thing, adding in:

Ladies only!: Never make love to Bigfoot.
Men only!: Hello, my name is Bigfoot.

Not many people sang along. I thought I was dead, but I wasn't. "And now," I announced, "the napkin trick." Unfolding a paper napkin, I grandly displayed it on both sides, held it up to my face, and stuck my wet tongue through it. I bowed deeply, as though what I had just done was unique in the history of show business. No Ping-Pong balls came my way, only a nice curious laugh that perked up the rest of my show and seemed to make the audience think that what they were seeing might be okay.

I got word from the club's owner, Sylvia Fennell, that the Coffee and Confusion would like to try me for a week as an opening act. Sylvia was a tough but likable New Yorker who had moved west to enter the nightclub business and whose width, height, and depth were the same measurement. She didn't know much about show business, having once told a ventriloquist to move the

9

dummy closer to the microphone. She was, however, savvy about the bottom line, as evidenced by a sign in the kitchen that said: ANYONE GIVING MONEY TO JANIS JOPLIN BEFORE HER LAST SET IS FIRED! AND IF THEY ARE A CUSTOMER, THEY'RE 86'ED! Later, I found out that the main reason I was hired was because I was a member of the musicians' union, which I joined only because I thought I had to be in at least one performers' union, and the musicians' was the cheapest. Sylvia had been told that if she didn't hire a union worker, pronto, the place would be shut down.

The night of my first appearance, Gaylord the bartender—the separate syllables of his name correctly described his sexual orientation and his demeanor—came to me and said it was time to start. "But," I said as I waved my hand to indicate the stone-empty club, "there's nobody here." He pointed to the large window that looked onto the sidewalk, and explained that my job was to be onstage so passersby could see a show going on and be lured in. I said that I wasn't a singer, I was a comedian, and doing comedy for absolutely no one posed a problem. So? he implied. Dave Archer, the amiable doorman, seconded him, telling me that this was the way the evening always began, so I went onstage and started talking. Talking to no one. The first couple who walked through the door did a whiplash scan of the vacant room and immediately left. But more than a few came in, looked around, saw nobody, shrugged an "Oh well," and sat down, especially after Dave offered them a free coffee.

The cheapness of the place gave me some opportunity for laughs. The lights were controlled with wall switches just behind the performer. Saying I wanted a "mood change," I gave an imperious order to the light man, who, the audience soon realized, was me. I reached back and twiddled the rheostat while feigning indignation.

One night I started a serious banjo tune and, sensing the audience's boredom, stopped and said, "I like to keep the laughs rolling even while I'm playing. . . ." I reached down to my prop table and put on my arrow-through-the-head, purchased on a whim at a Hollywood Boulevard magic store, and finished the song. Then I forgot to take it off. Every earnest thing I said was contradicted and deflated by this silly novelty. Sylvia Fennell's advice about the arrow—which was to become my most famous prop—was "Lose it."

I had a strong closer, an absurdist version of a balloon-animal act in which all the balloon animals were unrecognizable. I would end up with the balloons on my head, nose glasses on my face, and bunny ears. The point was to look as stupid as possible, then pause thoughtfully and say, "And now I'd like to get serious for a moment. I know what you're thinking. You're thinking, 'Oh, this is just another banjo-magic act.' "

I was contracted to be onstage for twenty-five minutes. I had a solid ten minutes, and the rest of my material

11

was unreliable. If I got some laughs, I could almost make it, but if the audience was dead, my twenty-five-minute show would shrink to about twelve. Afraid of falling short, I ad-libbed, wandered around the audience, talked to patrons, joked with waitresses, and took note of anything unusual that was happening in the crowd and addressed it for laughs, in the hope of keeping my written material in reserve so I could fill my time quota. The format stuck. Years later, it was this pastiche element that made my performances seem unstructured and modern.

That week at the Coffee and Confusion, something started to make sense. My act, having begun three years earlier as a conventional attempt to enter regular show business, was becoming a parody of comedy. I was an entertainer who was playing an entertainer, a not so good one, and this embryonic notion drove me to work on other material in that vein.

After my last show on Sunday, I walked a few doors up to the Coffee Gallery, another Grant Avenue folk club, and sat alone in an empty showroom. On the jukebox was the haunting voice of Frank Sinatra singing ". . . When I was seventeen, it was a very good year." Each successive stanza advanced the narrator by a decade, causing me to reflect on something I could not possibly reflect on: my future. The next song was the Beatles' "Norwegian Wood," and its modal tones underscored the moody darkness. I felt an internal stillness, much like the moment of

12

silence a performer seeks before he goes onstage. I know now why this memory has stuck with me so vividly. My ties to home were broken, I had a new group of friends, I was loose and independent, I had my first job where I slept in a hotel at night instead of my own bed. I was about to start my life.

Comedy Through the Airwaves

MY FATHER WANTED TO BE AN ACTOR and my
mother hated the Texas heat, so in 1950, when I was five
years old, our family moved from Waco to Hollywood. To
maintain family ties, we motored between Texas and California several times over the next few years. On these
road trips, I was introduced to comedy. As evening closed
around us, my father would turn on the car radio, and
with my sister, Melinda, and me nestled in the backseat,
we would listen to Bob Hope, Abbott and Costello, the hilarious but now exiled Amos 'n' Andy, and the delight
that was *The Jack Benny Program*. These were only voices,
heard but unseen, yet they were vivid and vital characters
in our imaginations. We laughed out loud as our tubby

15

Our family in a Texas diner, ca. 1949. Me, my mother, my father, and Melinda. I don't know who the woman in the middle is, unless we happened to be having lunch with Virginia Woolf.

Nash Airflyte glided down the isolated southwestern highways. Listening to comedy was one of the few things our family did together.

My father got a job at the Hollywood Ranch Market on Vine Street, sorting fruit. I was taken to see him act in a play, though I was so young I didn't quite understand what a play was. The performance was at the Callboard Theater on Melrose Place in Los Angeles, and my mother and I sat until the third act, when my father finally came onstage to deliver a drink on a tray and then exit. My father's acting career stopped soon after that, and I had no understanding that he had been interested in show business until I was an adult.

A few months later, we moved from Hollywood to Inglewood, California, and lived in a small bungalow on Venice Way, directly across from Highland Elementary School. This was the site of my first stage performance, where, in kindergarten, I appeared as Rudolph the Red-nosed Reindeer. My matronly teacher, who was probably twenty-two, explained that I would be dressed up like Rudolph and—this was the best part—I would wear a bright red nose made from a Ping-Pong ball. As show time neared, my excitement built. I had the furry suit, the furry feet, and the cardboard antlers. Finally, I asked, "Where's the Ping-Pong ball?" She told me that the Ping-Pong ball would be replaced with lipstick that would be smeared on my nose. What had been delivered as a casual aside, I had taken as a solemn promise; there had never been, I now realized, a serious intent to get a Ping-Pong ball, even though this was my main reason for taking the gig. I went on, did my best Rudolph, and because lipstick doesn't wash off that easily, walked back home hiding my still-crimson nose under my mother's knee-length top-coat. One coat, four legs extending beneath.

I was five years old when television entered the Martin household. A plastic black box wired to a rooftop an-tenna sat in our living room, and on it appeared what had to be the world's longest continuous showing of B Westerns. I had never seen anything with a plot, so even the corniest, most predictable stories were new to me, and I rode the Wild West by sitting astride a blanket I had placed on the back of an overstuffed chair and gal-

17
—

TV!

loped along with the posse. I provided hoof noises by slapping my hands alternately on my thighs and the chair, which made enough variation in the sound effect to give it a bit of authenticity.

The TV also brought into my life two appealing characters named Laurel and Hardy, whom I found clever and gentle, in contrast to the Three Stooges, who were blatant and violent. Laurel and Hardy's work, already thirty years old, had survived the decades with no hint of cobwebs. They were also touching and affectionate, and I believe this is where I got the idea that jokes are funniest when played upon oneself. Jack Benny, always his own victim, had a variety show that turned into a brilliant half-hour situation comedy; his likable troupe was now cavorting in my living room, and I was captivated. His slow burn—slower than slow—made me laugh every time. *The Red Skelton Show* aired on Tuesday evening, and I would memorize Red's routines about two pooping seagulls, Gertrude and Heathcliffe, or his bit about how different people walk through a rain puddle, and perform them the next day during Wednesday morning's "sharing time" at my grade school.

My life on Venice Way was spent in close proximity to my mother—the tininess of our house assured it—and I can remember no strife or unpleasantness about our time there. Unpleasantness began to creep into our lives after we moved a few miles away to 720 South Freeman in Inglewood.

MY FATHER, GLENN VERNON MARTIN, died in 1997 at age eighty-three, and afterward his friends told me how much they had loved him. They told me how enjoyable he was, how outgoing he was, how funny and caring he was. I was surprised by these descriptions, because the number of funny or caring words that had passed between my father and me was few. He had evidently saved his vibrant personality for use outside the family. When I was seven or eight years old, he suggested we play catch in the front yard. This offer to spend time together was so rare that I was confused about what I was supposed to do. We tossed the ball back and forth with cheerless formality.

real estate instead of pursuing acting was that my mother had pressured him to get a real job. But when she was older and I presented this idea to her, she said, "Oh, no, I wanted your father to be a star," and she went on to say that it was he who hadn't followed his dream. My mother was the daughter of a strict Baptist matriarch who barred dancing, dating, and cardplaying, and she must have viewed her marriage to my theatrically inclined father as an exciting alternative to small-town life. But my father overpowered her easily intimidated personality, and she only escaped from one repressive situation into another.

My sister and me in haute couture,
hand-sewn by my mother.

STEVE MARTIN

Though I was just eight years old, I was, like most children in that benign era, allowed to walk alone the few blocks to my new school, Oak Street Elementary, which opened in the 1920s and is still operating today. It has a wee bit of architecture about it, featuring an inner Spanish courtyard with six shady ficus trees. It is directly under the flight path of LAX, and our routine civil defense drills had us convinced that every commercial jet roaring overhead was really a Russian plane about to discharge A-bombs. One rainy day, fooled by a loud clap of thunder, we dived under our desks and covered our heads, believing we were seconds away from annihilation.

At Oak Street School I gave my second performance onstage, which introduced me to an unexpected phenomenon: knocking knees. I had seen knocking knees in animated cartoons but hadn't believed they afflicted small boys. As I got onstage for the Christmas pageant—was I Joseph?—my knees vibrated like a tuning fork. I never experienced the sensation again, but I wonder if I would have preferred it to the chilly pre-show anxiety that I sometimes felt later in my performing career. This mild but persistent adrenal rush beginning days before important performances kept the pounds off and, I swear, kept colds away. I would love to see a scientific study of how many performers come down with the flu twenty-four hours after a show is over, once the body's jazzed-up defenses have collapsed in exhaustion.

• • •

MY FATHER HAD A RESONANT VOICE, and he liked to sing around the house. He emulated Bing Crosby and Dean Martin, and my mother loved it when he crooned the popular songs of the day. She was a good piano player and kept encouraging me to sing for her, I suppose to find out if I had inherited my father's voice. I was shy at home and kept refusing, but one day after her final push, I agreed. I went to the garage, where I could practice "America the Beautiful" in private. A few hours later, I was ready. She got out the sheet music, placed it on the piano, and I stood before her. After the downbeat, what came out of my mouth was an eight-year-old boy's attempt to imitate his dad's deep baritone. I plunged my voice down as low as it could go, and began to croon the song like Dean Martin might have done at a baseball game. My mother, as much as she wanted to continue, collapsed in laughter and could not stop. Her eyes reddened with tears of affection, and the control she tried to exert over herself made her laugh even more, with her forearm falling on the piano keys as she tried to hide her face from me, filling our small living room with laughter and dissonance. She explained, as kindly as she could, that I was charming, not ridiculous, but I was forever after reluctant to sing in public.

Having been given a few store-bought magic tricks by an uncle, I developed a boy's interest in conjuring and felt a glow of specialness as the sole possessor—at least locally—of its secrets. My meager repertoire of tricks quintupled when my parents gave me a Mysto Magic set, a cherished Christmas gift. The apparatus was flimsy, the instructions indecipherable, and a few of the effects were deeply uninteresting. Out of a box of ten tricks, only four were useful. But even four tricks required practice, so I stood in front of a mirror for hours to master the Linking Rings or the Ball and Vase. My first shows were performed

My mother and father, and my Linking Rings, Christmas 1953.

in my third-grade class, using an upturned apple crate for my magic table. I can still remember the moment when my wooden "billiard balls," intended to multiply and vanish right before your eyes, slipped from between my fingers and bounced around the schoolroom with a humiliating clatter as I scrambled to pick them up. The balls were bright red, and so was I.

My father was the generous one in the family (my mother promoted penny-pinching habits lingering from her Great Depression childhood; her practice of scrimping on household heat nearly froze us into statues on frosty winter mornings). He annoyed my mother by occasionally lending what little leftover money we had to pals in need, but when my mother objected, my father would sternly remind her that they had been able to buy their first house because of the generosity of a family friend. I loved comic books, especially the funny ones, like *Little Lulu,* and man oh man, if Uncle Scrooge was in the latest episode of *Donald Duck,* I was in heaven. My father financed my subscriptions, and I ended up, after one year, owing him five dollars. Though he never dogged me for it, I'm sure he kept this debt on the books to teach me the value of money. As the balance grew, I was nauseated whenever I thought of it. One birthday, he forgave my debt, and I soared with relief. In my adult life, I have never bought anything on credit.

In spite of these sincere efforts at parenting, my father seemed to have a mysterious and growing anger toward me. He was increasingly volatile, and eventually, in my teen years, he fell into enraged silences. I knew that money issues plagued him and that we were always dependent on the next hypothetical real estate sale, and perhaps this was the source of his anger. But I suspect that as his show business dream slipped further into the sunset, he chose to blame his family who needed food, shelter, and attention. Though my sister seemed to escape his wrath, my mother grew more and more submissive to my father in order to avoid his temper. Timid and secretive, she whispered her thoughts to me with the caveat "Now, don't tell anyone I said that," filling me with a belief, which took years to correct, that it was dangerous to express one's true opinion. Melinda, four years older than I, always went to a different school, and a sibling bond never coalesced until decades later, when she phoned me and said, "I want to know my brother," initiating a lasting communication between us.

I was punished for my worst transgressions by spankings with switches or a paddle, a holdover from any Texas childhood of that time, and when my mother warned, "Just wait till Glenn gets home," I would be sick with fear, dreading nightfall, dreading the moment when he would walk through the door. His growing moodiness made each episode of punishment more unpredictable—and hence, more frightening—and once, when I was about nine years old, he went too far. That evening, his mood was ominous as we indulged in a rare family treat, eating

27

Disneyland

A WIDE SWATH OF our Inglewood neighborhood was scheduled to be flattened by the impending construction of the San Diego freeway. The steamrollers were soon to be barreling down on our little house, so the search was on for a new place to live. My father's decision profoundly affected my life. Orange County, California, forty-five minutes south of Inglewood, was a real estate boomtown created from the sprawl of Los Angeles. It consisted of interlocking rectangles of orange groves and tract homes and was perfectly suited to my father's profession. Housing developments rose out of the ground like spring wells, changing the color of the landscape from desert brown to lawn green, and my parents purchased a brand-new tract home for sixteen thousand dollars. I was ten years old when my family moved from complicated and historic Los Angeles to uncomplicated and nonhistoric Garden Grove, where the sky was blue and vast but without the drama of Wyoming, just a flat dead sky of ease. Everything from our toes to the horizon was the same, except for the occasional massive and regal oak tree that had defied the developer's scythe. This area of Orange County gleamed with newness, and the move enabled me to place my small hand on Opportunity's doorknob.

In the summer of 1955, Disneyland opened in Anaheim, California, on a day so sweltering the asphalt on Main Street was as soft as a yoga mat. Two-inch headlines announced the event as though it were a victory at sea. A few months later, when a school friend told me that kids our age were being hired to sell Disneyland guidebooks on weekends and in the summer, I couldn't wait. I pedaled my bicycle the two miles to Disneyland, parked it in the bike rack—locks were unnecessary—and looked up to see a locomotive from yesteryear, its whistle blowing loudly and its smokestack filling the air with white steam, chugging into the turn-of-the-century depot just above a giant image of Mickey Mouse rendered in vibrantly colored flowers. I went to the exit, told a hand-stamper that I was applying for a job, and was directed toward a souvenir stand a few steps inside the main gate. I spoke with a cigar-chomping vendor named Joe and told him my résumé: no experience at anything. This must have impressed Joe, because I was issued a candy-striped shirt, a garter for my sleeve, a vest with a watch pocket, a straw boater hat, and a stack of guidebooks to be sold for twenty-five cents each, from which I was to receive the enormous sum of two cents per book. The two dollars in cash I earned that day made me feel like a millionaire.

Guidebooks were sold only in the morning, when thousands of people poured through the gates. By noon I was done, but I didn't have to leave. I had free admission to the park. I roamed through the Penny Arcade, watched the Disneyland Band as they marched around the plaza, and even found an "A" ticket in the street, allowing me to choose between the green-and-gold-painted streetcar or the surrey ride up Main Street. Because I wisely kept on my little outfit, signifying that I was an official employee, and maybe because of the look of longing on my face, I was given a free ride on the Tomorrowland rocket to the moon, which blasted me into the cosmos. I passed by Mr. Toad and Peter Pan rides, toured pirate ships and Western forts. Disneyland, and the idea of it, seemed so glorious that I believed it should be in some faraway, impossible-to-visit Shangri-la, not two miles from the house where I was about to grow up. With its pale blue castle flying pennants emblazoned with a made-up Disney family crest, its precise gardens and horse-drawn carriages maintained to jewel-box perfection, Disneyland was my Versailles.

I became a regular employee, age ten. I blazed short-cuts through Disneyland's maze of pathways, finding the

33

most direct route from the Chicken of the Sea pirate ship to the Autopia, or the back way to Adventureland from Main Street. I learned speed-walking, and I could slip like a water moccasin through dense throngs of people, a technique I still use at airports and on the sidewalks of Manhattan. Though my mother provided fifty cents for lunch (the Carnation lunch counter offered a grilled cheese sandwich for thirty-five cents and a large cherry phosphate with a genuine red-dye-number-two cherry for fifteen cents), the big difference in my life was that I was self-reliant and funded. I was so proud to be employed that some years later—still at Disneyland—I harbored a secret sense of superiority over my teenage peers who had suntans, because I knew it meant they weren't working.

In Frontierland, I was fascinated by a true cowboy named Eddie Adamek, who twirled lariats and pitched his homemade product, a prefab lasso that enabled youngsters to make perfect circles just like their cowboy heroes. Eddie, I discerned, was living with a woman not his wife, the 1955 equivalent of devil worship. But I didn't mind, because his patronage enabled me to learn rope tricks, including the Butterfly, Threading the Needle, and the Skip-Step. A few years later, after my tenure as guide-book salesman ended—perhaps at thirteen I was too old—I became Eddie's trick-rope demonstrator, fitting in as much work as I could around my C-average high school studies.

34

In my mapping of the Disney territory, two places captivated me. One was Merlin's Magic Shop, just inside the Fantasyland castle gate, where a young and funny magician named Jim Barlow sold and demonstrated magic tricks. The other was Pepsi-Cola's Golden Horseshoe Revue in Frontierland, where Wally Boag, the first comedian I ever saw in person, plied a hilarious trade of gags and offbeat skills such as gun twirling and balloon animals, and brought the house down when he turned his wig around backward. He wowed every audience every time.

The theater, built with Disneyland's dedication to craftsmanship, had a horseshoe-shaped interior adorned with lush gay-nineties decor. Oak tables and chairs crowded the saloon's main floor, and a spectacular mirrored bar with a gleaming foot rail ran along one side. Polished brass lamps with real flames gave off an orangey glow, and on the stage hung a plush golden curtain tied back with a thickly woven cord. A balcony lined with steers' horns looped around the interior, and customers dangled their arms and heads over the railing during the show. Four theater boxes stood on either side of the stage, where VIPs would be seated ceremoniously behind a velvet rope. Young girls in low-cut dance-hall dresses served paper cups brimming with Pepsi that seemed to have an exceptionally stinging carbonated fizz, and the three-piece band made the theater jump with liveliness. In the summer the powerful air-conditioning made it a welcome icebox.

35

The admission price, always free to everyone, made me a regular. Here I had my first lessons in performing, though I never was on the stage. I absorbed Wally Boag's timing, saying his next line in my head ("When they operated on Father, they opened Mother's male"), and took the audience's response as though it were mine. I studied where the big laughs were, learned how Wally got the small ones, and saw tiny nuances that kept the thing alive between lines. Wally shone in these performances, and in my first shows, I tried to imitate his amiable casualness. My fantasy was that one day Wally would be sick with the flu, and a desperate stage manager would come out and ask the audience if there was an adolescent boy who could possibly fill in.

Merlin's Magic Shop was the next best thing to the cheering audiences at the Golden Horseshoe. Tricks were demonstrated in front of crowds of two or three people, and twenty-year-old Jim Barlow took the concept of a joke shop far beyond what the Disney brass would have officially allowed, except it was clear that the customers enjoyed his kidding. Coiled springs of snakes shot out of fake peanut-brittle cans, attacking the unsuspecting customer who walked through the door. Jim's greeting to browsers was, "Can I take your money—I mean help you?" After a sale, he would say loudly, "This trick is guaranteed! . . . to break before you get home." Like Wally, Jim was genuinely funny, and his broad smile and innocent blond flattop smoothed the way for his prankster style. I loitered in the shop so often that Jim and I became buddies as I memorized his routines, and I wanted more than ever to be a magician.

The paraphernalia sold in the magic store was exotic, and I was dazzled by the tricks' secret mechanics. The Sucker Die Box, with its tricky false fronts and gimmicked door pulls, thrilled me. At home, I would peruse magic catalogs for hours. I was spellbound by the graphics of another era, unchanged since the thirties, of tubes that produced silks, water bowls that poured endlessly, and magic wands that did nothing. I dreamed of owning color-changing scarves and amazing swords that could spear the selected card when the deck was thrown into the air. I read advertising pamphlets from distant companies in Ohio that offered collapsible opera hats, pre-owned tuxedos, and white-tipped canes. I had fantasies of levitation and awesome power and, with no Harry Potter to be compared to, my store-bought tricks could go a long way toward making me feel special. With any spare money I had, I bought tricks, memorized their accompanying standard patter, and assembled a magic show that I would perform for anyone who would watch, mostly my parents and their tolerant bridge partners.

One afternoon I was in the audience at the Golden Horseshoe, sipping my Pepsi and mouthing along with Wally Boag, when I blacked out and collapsed. I remember my head striking the table. A few seconds later, I was sitting back up but unnerved. Nobody noticed, but I re-

37

I loved my derby hat and cane,
both purchased by mail.

ported this incident to my mother, and she called Dr. Kus-
nitz, perhaps Orange County's only Jewish doctor, who
lived next door. "What was it?" he asked. "It was a thump
in my chest," I said. Tests confirmed I had a heart murmur,
more spookily expressed as a prolapsed mitral valve, a
mostly benign malady that was predicted to go away as I
aged. It did, but it planted in me a seed of hypochondria
that poisonously bloomed years later.

After poor sales ended my trick-roping days, I spent a year working away from the action, in the sheet-metal-gray storage room of Tiki's Tropical Imports in Adventureland, where I pinned finger-piercing price tags onto straw hats (I'm sure my bloody screams alarmed the nearby dock loaders). On my infrequent trips to the actual store, I was entertained by a vibrant Biloxi-born store manager named Irene, who, I now realize, was probably the first neurotic I ever met. Her favorite saying—"Well, excuse me for livin'!"—stuck in my head. I had heard rumors of a job opening up at the magic shop, and longing to be free of the sunless warehouse, I went over and successfully applied, making that day the happiest of my life so far. I began my show business career a few days later, at age fifteen, in August 1960. I stood behind a counter eight hours a day, shuffling Svengali decks, manipulating Wizard decks and Mental Photography cards, and performing the Cups and Balls trick on a rectangle of padded green felt. A few customers would gather, usually a young couple on a date, or a mom and dad with kids. I tried my first jokes—all lifted from Jim's funny patter—and had my first audience that wasn't friends or family. My weekends and holidays were now spent in long hours at Disneyland, made possible by lax child labor laws and my high school, which assigned no homework. At closing time, I would stock the shelves, sweep the floor, count out the register, and then bicycle home in the dark.

At the magic shop.

The magic shop purveyed such goodies as the arrow-through-the-head and nose glasses, props I turned into professional assets later on. Posted behind the scenes, too risqué for Disneyland's tourists, was a little gag postcard that had been printed in Japan. It said, "Happy Feet," and featured the outline of the bottoms of four feet, two pointed up, two pointed down. After I studied it for about an hour, Jim Barlow explained that it was the long-end view of a couple making love.

There were two magic shops—the other was on Main Street—and I ran between them as necessary. In the Main Street store, there was a booth, really an alcove, where you could get your name printed in a headline, WANTED, HORSE THIEF, YOUR NAME HERE, and I mastered the soon-to-be-useless art of hand typesetting. The proprietor, Jim—a different Jim—laughed at me because I insisted on wearing gardening gloves while I worked with the printing press. I couldn't let the ink stain my hands; it would look unsightly when I was demonstrating cards. At the print shop I learned my first life lesson. One day I was particularly gloomy, and Jim asked me what the matter was. I told him my high school girlfriend (for all of two weeks) had broken up with me. He said, "Oh, that'll happen a lot." The knowledge that this horrid grief was simply a part of life's routine cheered me up almost instantly.

Merlin's was run by Leo Behnke, a fine card and coin manipulator who was the first person to let me in on the inner secrets of magic, and who endorsed a strict code of practice and discipline that I took to heart. But Leo had another quality that transfixed me. He handled cards with delicacy; there was a rhythm to his movements that was mildly hypnotic. He could shuffle the deck without ever lifting it from the tabletop: After an almost invisible riffle, every card was interlaced exactly with the next, a perfect shuffle. Then, with the elegance of Fred Astaire, he squared the cards by running his fingers smoothly around the edges of the deck. Leo taught me his perfect shuffle (called the faro shuffle), which I perfected a mere

41

four months later, and I squared the deck just like he did. I enjoyed making the sleights imperceptible and moving my fingers around the cards with Leo's grace and ease. A magician's hands are often hiding things, and I learned that stillness can be as deceptive as motion. It was my first experience with the pleasure and subtlety of physical expression, and I became aware of the potency of movement.

Because I was demonstrating tricks eight to twelve hours a day, I got better and better. I could even duplicate the effects of trick decks with a regular deck. I was able to afford more professional equipment, including, at a price of four dollars and fifty cents, the Zombie, a floating silver ball that danced behind a silk scarf to bewildering effect. I put together a magic act, complete with music, that required a friend to put the needle down on a record at exactly the right moment, in exactly the right groove. Jim Barlow connected me to a network of desperate Cub Scout troops seeking entertainment, and the minuscule prestige from my magic shop gig enabled me to work for free or sometimes for five dollars at the local Kiwanis Club. I was now performing at the hectic pace of one show every two or three months. Later in life, I wondered why the Kiwanis Club or the Rotary Club, comprised of grown men, would hire a fifteen-year-old boy magician to entertain at their dinners. Only one answer makes sense: out of the goodness of their hearts.

Claude Plum, a suspender-wearing oddnik who, among

Performing for Cub Scouts.

other things, collected thousands of B-movie stills from the 1940s, wrote a mimeographed in-house newsletter for Disneyland and supplied gags for Wally Boag: "I'm in the dark side of the cattle business." "Do you rustle?" "Only when I wear taffeta shorts." He would lend me his copies of Robert Orben's joke books, filled with musty one-liners from other comedians' acts, but to me they were as new as sunrise. These books were like the Bible and I scoured them for usable passages. For five dollars, a major investment, I hired Claude to write some material for my floating silver ball routine: "With the advent of the space age," I squeaked, "scientists have been searching for a metal that can defy gravity. . . . "

The magic shop put me in daily contact with people, and when I was fifteen, there was only one kind of people: girls. I have a clear memory of standing behind the counter watching a girl in shorts turn away from me, and being confronted by the alarmingly pleasant sight of her rear end and all its curvy virtues. My body flooded with chemistry, and the female behind was instantly added to my growing list of turn-ons, which up till then included only faces, hair, and that which I will call brassieres, because actual breasts were still unseen and never experienced. The Main Street store was run by Aldini the Magician— real name Alex Weiner—a mustachioed, tart-tongued spiel-meister who taught me all the Yiddish words I know, including the invaluable *tuchis* (meaning "ass"), which he used as a code word to indicate that a sexy girl had come into the shop.

I did have a life outside Disneyland. I had been attending Rancho Alamitos High School, but in the fall of 1962, redistricting moved me across town to Garden Grove High School, where I was happy to discard my old personality and adopt a new one defined by the word of the day, "nonconformist." Of course, the difference between my old personality and my new personality was probably imperceptible, so I was lucky to have all-new classmates who would not remember my old conformist ways.

On my first day of school, the student body was called together for an assembly, and this was when I saw the face of God. The Don Wash Auditorium seated fifteen hundred people, and its interior narrowed like a funnel to focus all eyes on its polished hardwood stage. The proscenium was framed by heavy velvet curtains, and the acoustics were—and still are—brilliant and sharp, making microphones unnecessary. I sat in the audience, looking up at the stage, surrounded by high-energy, adolescent chatter. The house lights dimmed dramatically, and when the crisp ice-blue spotlight illuminated center stage in anticipation of parting curtains and grand entrances, I knew I wanted to be up there rather than down here.

When Claude Plum asked me to appear in a vaudeville show featuring Wally Boag, coincidentally staged at this auditorium, my heart leaped. I was to perform a five-minute act, billed as "Steve Martin: Youth and Magic," in an evening show for Wally's fans. The programs appeared from the printer with the perfect prescient typo: "Steve Martin: Mouth and Magic." I couldn't judge how it went, since it was my first show in front of a sizable audience, but I don't remember a standing ovation. Claude Plum appeared in the program, too, but he listed his name as Clyde Primm in order to escape creditors. Years later, I ran into him working at Larry Edmunds's rare-book store on Hollywood Boulevard. Claude was still weird and mysterious, a bit of a pigpen, still with a one-inch stub of smoldering cigarette pursed in his lips, still collecting artifacts of forties film noir.

45

The daily excitement of my life at Disneyland and high school was in stark contrast to my life at home. Silent family dinners, the general taboo on free talk and opinion, my father's unpredictable temper, and the stubborn grudges I collected and held toward him meant that the family never gelled. But when I was away from home, my high school pals and I enjoyed endless conversation and laughter, and my enthusiasm for what I was doing—working at Disneyland, clowning with friends, and being swept up in the early rock and roll of AM radio—made life seem joyful and limitless. When I moved out of the house at eighteen, I rarely called home to check up on my parents or tell them how I was doing. Why? The answer shocks me as I write it: I didn't know I was supposed to.

• • •

THINGS WERE CHANGING at the magic shop. Leo Behnke left to consult on a television show, and our store needed a new manager. Leo's replacement was a fortunate choice for me. Dave Steward, emaciated, lanky, and deadpan, was an actual former vaudevillian who had worked the circuits with a magic act. He went by the name Lord Chesterfield, later changed to David and Company because, he said, the "company" implied two people, and he could ask for more money. His act had been that of a stone-faced, bungling magician, which appealed to me because Jim Barlow's and my hero at the time was the king of bungling magicians, Carl Ballantine, whose legendary appearances on *The Ed Sullivan Show* nudged every young magician toward comedy.

Dave Steward's vaudeville act had involved an ordinary-looking violin that he was always about to play but never did. His big finish, enabled by old-world craftsmanship, was its instantaneous transformation into a bouquet of flowers. One day he brought his trick violin to the store to share with this sixteen-year-old boy. He flicked a hidden switch, and I watched as the violin changed into a colorful bouquet of feather-flowers. Nice, but then he showed me his opening joke: He walked from behind the counter and stood on the floor of the magic shop, announcing, "And now, the glove into dove trick!" He threw a white magician's glove into the air. It hit the floor and lay there. He stared at it and then went on to the next trick. It was the

47

Dave Steward's vaudeville publicity photo.

48

first time I had ever seen laughter created out of absence. I found this gag so funny that I asked permission to use it in my youthful magic act, and he said yes.

He told me another bit. He would take out a white handkerchief, pretend to mop his brow, and then, thanks to a rubber ball sewn into the cloth, absentmindedly bounce it on the floor. I didn't really get the joke, but the concept stuck. I took a high-bounce juggling ball and sewed it inside a realistic-looking cloth rabbit. Producing the bunny from a tube painted with Chinese symbols, I would say, "And now, a live bouncing baby rabbit!" Then, to everyone's shock and eventual laughter, I would bounce the rabbit on the floor. I had my first original gag.

Dave Steward's stories intrigued me, and I developed an interest in the history of vaudeville. I read up on the subject, studying Joe Laurie's book *Vaudeville,* and was captivated by its descriptions of each old-time act. It mentioned the Cherry Sisters, and it was here that I first heard an act described as "so bad it was good." The five screeching sisters elicited boos and vegetables from the audience and yet still made it to Broadway, a concept that the off-pitch singer Mrs. Miller succeeded with in the sixties and that Andy Kaufman took to the limit in the eighties. My interests widened to carnival scams, thanks to the nearby Long Beach Pike and its boardwalk games and sideshow featuring Zuzu the Monkey Girl; Electra (a woman who could light lightbulbs in her bare hand); and a two-headed baby

49

resting in formaldehyde that was actually a convincing rubber facsimile. There was also a roller coaster called the Cyclone Racer, whose behemoth wooden skeleton extended out over the sea. I was hoping the carnies would let me in on their secrets, but they never did. Maybe it was my Ivy League button-down shirts that kept them from thinking I was one of them.

The Main Street shop sold magic books. Rarely purchased, they gathered dust on a high shelf. A yellow cover caught my eye, and this book turned out to be more important to me than *The Catcher in the Rye*. It was Dariel Fitzkee's *Showmanship for Magicians*, first published in 1943. A terse Internet bio of Mr. Fitzkee (who turned out, coincidentally, to be a distant relative by marriage) describes him this way:

> Born in Annawan, Illinois. Pen name of Dariel Fitzroy. Acoustical engineer in San Rafael, California. Semi-pro magician. Toured an unsuccessful full-evening show 1939–40. Reportedly dropped magic in disgust.

Showmanship for Magicians is a handbook meant to turn amateurs into professionals. Its subtitle is *Complete Discussions of Audience Appeals and Fundamentals of Showmanship and Presentation*. I held my first copy and solemnly turned the pages, reading each sentence so slowly that it's a miracle I could remember what the verb was. The cover was plain-faced—like a secret manifesto that should be hidden under your mattress—and the pages were as thick as rags. Fitzkee starts by denigrating the current state of magic, saying it is old-fashioned. Though published in 1943, this statement contains an enduring truth. All entertainment is or is about to become old-fashioned. There is room, he implies, for something new. To a young performer, this is a relief. My references were all in the past, and in just one chapter, these roots were severed, or at least choked. Fitzkee then goes on to break down a show into elements such as Music, Rhythm, Comedy, Sex Appeal, Personality, and Selling Yourself, and he concludes that attention to each is vital and necessary. Why not throw everything in the book at the audience, like an opera does? Costumes, lights, music, everything? He also talks about something that was to land on me with a thud six years later: the importance of originality. "So what," I thought at the time. "Who cares?"

Following the advice in *Showmanship for Magicians,* I kept scrupulous records of how each gag played after my local shows for the Cub Scouts or Kiwanis Club. "Excellent!" or "Big laugh!" or "Quiet," I would write in the margins of my Big Indian tablet; then I would summarize how I could make the show better next time. I was still motivated to do a magic show with standard patter, but the nice response to a few gags had planted a nagging thought that contradicted my magical goal: They love it when the tricks don't work. I started to think that the

51
—

Notes

Leave out unessasary ~~and~~ jokes, change
patter for sq. cicle, Relax, dont shake,

Hindu Rope
Hippity Hops
Routine w/ 20th century silks w/ Kid
  Went Real goodr work on and put
in reg. act.

          En Rapport
      Get a connection with The audience like
at work. lengen act.

      Show went over good in spite of all
correcTions. , Chorge money

      Good gag

The show was for Fed-marT. when
Brakaway wand broke I said " Gee, I
goT iT aT C.M.A. Too."

My performing notes, from age fifteen, complete with misspellings.

future of a serious magician was limited. Plus, I was
priced out of the market by the impossible cost of
advanced stage illusions: Sawing a Lady in Half, two hundred dollars. By doing comedy, however, I could be more
like Stan Laurel and Jack Benny, more like Wally Boag.
I was still using Claude's somber introduction to my
floating silver ball routine, but I added a twist at the end

of the long-winded speech: "And now, ladies and gentlemen, the toilet float trick."

My time at the magic shop gave me a taste of performing and convinced me that I never wanted to wait on customers again. I didn't have the patience; my smile was becoming plastered on. I then crossed all kinds of jobs off my list of potentials, such as waiting tables or working in stores or driving trucks: How could my delicate fingertips, now dedicated to the swift execution of the Two-handed Pass, clutch the heavy, callus-inducing steering wheel of a ten-ton semi?

But there was a problem. At age eighteen, I had absolutely no gifts. I could not sing or dance, and the only acting I did was really just shouting. Thankfully, perseverance is a great substitute for talent. Having been motivated by Earl Scruggs's rendition of "Foggy Mountain Breakdown," I had learned, barely, to play the banjo. I had taught myself by slowing down banjo records on my turntable and picking out the songs note by note, with a helpful assist from my high school friend John McEuen, already an accomplished player. The only place to practice without agonizing everyone in the house was in my car, parked on the street with the windows rolled up, even in the middle of August. Also, I could juggle passably, a feat I had learned from the talented Fantasyland court jester Christopher Fair (who could juggle five balls while riding a high unicycle) and which I practiced in my backyard using heavy wooden croquet balls that would clack

53

against each other, pinching my swollen fingers in between. Despite a lack of natural ability, I did have the one element necessary to all early creativity: naïveté, that fabulous quality that keeps you from knowing just how unsuited you are for what you are about to do.

After high school graduation, I halfheartedly applied to and was accepted at Santa Ana Junior College, where I took drama classes and pursued an unexpected interest in English poetry from Donne to Eliot. I had heard about a theater at Disneyland's friendly, striving rival, Knott's Berry Farm, that needed entertainers with short acts. One afternoon I successfully auditioned with my thin magic act at a small theater on the grounds, making this the second happiest day of my life so far.

My final day at the magic shop, I stood behind the counter where I had pitched Svengali decks and the Incredible Shrinking Die, and I felt an emotional contradiction: nostalgia for the present. Somehow, even though I had stopped working only minutes earlier, my future fondness for the store was clear, and I experienced a sadness like that of looking at a photo of an old, favorite pooch. It was dusk by the time I left the shop, and I was redirected by a security guard who explained that a photographer was taking a picture and would I please use the side exit. I did, and saw a small, thin woman with hacked brown hair aim her large-format camera directly at the dramatically lit castle, where white swans floated in the moat underneath the functioning drawbridge. Almost forty years later, when I was in my early fifties, I purchased that photo as a collectible, and it still hangs in my house. The photographer, it turned out, was Diane Arbus. I try to square the photo's breathtakingly romantic image with the rest of her extreme subject matter, and I assume she saw this facsimile of a castle as though it were a kitsch roadside statue of Paul Bunyan. Or perhaps she saw it as I did: beautiful.

The Bird Cage Theatre

DURING THE 1960s, the five-foot-high hand-painted placard in front of the Bird Cage Theatre at Knott's Berry Farm read WORLD'S GREATEST ENTERTAIMENT. The missing "n" in "entertainment" was overlooked by staff, audience, and visitors for an entire decade. I worked there between the ages of eighteen and twenty-two as an actor in melodramas. Knott's Berry Farm didn't have the flash of its younger sibling, Disneyland, but it was authentic and charming. Knott's Berry Farm began in the 1930s, when Walter and Cordelia Knott put up a roadside berry stand. A few years later, Cordelia opened her chicken-dinner restaurant, and Walter bought pieces of a ghost town and moved the Old West buildings to his burgeoning tourist

57

destination. Squawking peacocks roamed the grounds, and there was a little wooden chapel that played organ music while you stared at a picture of Jesus and watched his eyes magically open.

My first performances for a paying audience were at the Bird Cage, a wooden theater with a canvas roof. Inside, two hundred folding chairs sat on risers, and a thrust Masonite stage sat behind a patch of fake grass. A painted cutout of a birdcage, worthy of a Sotheby's folk art auction, hung over center stage, and painted representations of drapes framed the proscenium. The actors swept the stage, raised and lowered the curtains, cleaned the house of trash, and went out on the grounds pitching the show to visitors strolling around the park. I was being paid two dollars a show, twenty-five shows a week. Even in 1963, the rate was considered low.

The show consisted of a twenty-five-minute melodrama in which the audience was encouraged to cheer the hero and boo the villain. I appeared in *The Bungling Burglar,* performing the role of Hamilton Brainwood, a detective who was attracted to the provocatively named soubrette, Dimples Reardon. Fortunately, I ended up with the virtuous heroine, Angela Trueheart. My opening night was attended by my high school girlfriend, Linda Rasmussen, and her parents, who, it turned out, were more nervous for me than I was. The play was followed by a ten-minute "olio" segment involving two five-minute routines where the actors did their specialties, usually songs or

Performing the olio at the Bird Cage.

short comedy acts. Though I didn't do an olio that night, the Bird Cage was the first place where I was able to work steadily on my magic act, six minutes at a time, four times a day, five on Sunday, for three years.

The Bird Cage was a normal theatrical nuthouse. Missed cues caused noisy pileups in the wings, or a missing prop left us hanging while we ad-libbed excuses to leave the stage and retrieve it. A forgotten line would hang in the dead air, searching for someone, anyone, to say it. The theater was run by Woody Wilson, a dead ringer for W. C. Fields, and a boozer, too, and the likable George Stuart, who, on Saturday night, would entertain the crowd with a monologue that had them roaring: "You're from Tucson? I spent a week there one night!" Four paying customers, in a house that seated two hundred, was officially an audience, so we often did shows to resonating silence. Woody Wilson, on one of these dead afternoons, peed so loudly in the echoing bathroom that it broke up us actors and got laughs from our conservative family audience.

The theater was stocked with genuine characters. Ronnie Morgon, rail thin, would dress up as Lincoln and read the Gettysburg Address for local elementary schools. On a good day, he would show us young lads cheesecake photos of his wife in a leopard-skin bikini, and even at age eighteen, we thought it was weird. There was Joe Carney, a blustery and funny actor who opened the lavatory door from the top to avoid germs. Paul Shackleton

Me, Terri Jo Flynn, Ronnie Morgon, and George Stuart in a publicity photo, though we never got any publicity.

was the son of a preacher and could not tolerate a swear word, but he once laughed till he cried when we sat down under a eucalyptus tree to drink our Cokes and a bird shit on my head. His laughter made me think it was funny, too, and for days we could not look each other in the eye without breaking into uncontrollable hysterics. John Stuart, a talented tenor with a mischievous sense of humor, once secretly put talcum powder in my top hat. Onstage, whenever I popped the hat on or off, a mushroom cloud of smoke bloomed from my head, causing an unscheduled laugh from the audience.

Kathy Westmoreland, another actress at the theater, had attended Garden Grove High School at the same time I did and was the first indisputably talented person

61

I ever met. She sang like the Swedish Nightingale and, later in life, achieved a strange kind of celebrity. As a backup singer for Elvis, she became his confidante and then, quietly, his lover. Years later, after his death, she wrote a book revealing her secret, making her the focus of overwrought Elvis fans.

Kathy and I developed a hillbilly routine, she on washtub bass and I on banjo. It was my first foray into comedy without magic to back me up. She blacked out a tooth, and the act included crossed eyes and corny jokes, and it absolutely killed. We soon ascended to the premier slot for the Bird Cage's olio acts, the Saturday-night nine o'clock performance. The audience would howl and weep and thrash about, and the laughs would double the length of our five-minute show.

We decided to take our act to the Golden Bear for a Monday tryout. The "Bear" was a folk music club in Huntington Beach, California, where all the big names played, including Kenny Rankin, John Mayall, Jackson Browne, and Hoyt Axton (an accomplished performer and songwriter himself—author of the oddly unforgettable lyric "Jeremiah was a bullfrog!"—but it's hard to forget that his mother cowrote "Heartbreak Hotel"). I was smug about presenting our fully broken-in and seemingly invulnerable act. My belief in the inevitability of our success charged me up before, during, and after the show, and it was not until days later when I acknowledged to myself that our debut in the tougher world of real show business had been met with only a polite response. Kathy and I were probably too corny for an exploding folk scene that was producing many serious and spectacular artists. The willing and forgiving audiences at the Bird Cage did not necessarily reflect those at hip folk clubs.

And then there was Stormie.

Stormie Sherk, later to become an enormously successful Christian author and proselytizer under her married name, Stormie Omartian, was beautiful, witty, bright, and filled with an engaging spirit that was not yet holy. We performed in plays together; my role was either the comic or the leading man, depending on the day of the week. She wore antique calico dresses that complemented her strawberry-blond hair and vanilla skin. Soon we were in love and would roam around Knott's in our period clothes and find a period place to sit, mostly by the period church next to the man-made lake, where we would stare endlessly into each other's eyes. We developed a love duet for the Bird Cage in which she would sing "Gypsy Rover" while I accompanied her on the five-string. When she sang the song, the lyric that affected me the most was—believe it or not—"La dee do la dee do dum day." We would talk of a wedding in a lilac-covered dale, and I could fill any conversational gaps with ardent recitations of Keats and Shelley. Finally, the inevitable happened. I was a late-blooming eighteen-year-old when I had my first sexual experience, involving a

63

condom (swiped from my parents' drawer) and the front seat of my car, whose windows became befogged with desire. Later, Stormie wrote in her autobiography that when she was a girl, her severely mentally ill mother would lock her in a dark closet for days, cruelly abusing her. I had no idea.

If Stormie had said I would look good in a burgundy

Stormie, me.

ball gown, I would have gone out and bought a burgundy ball gown. Instead, she suggested that I read W. Somerset Maugham's *The Razor's Edge*. *The Razor's Edge* is a book about a quest for knowledge. Universal, final, unquestionable knowledge. I was swept up in the book's glorification of learning and the idea that, like a stage magician, I could have secrets possessed by only a few. Santa Ana Junior College offered no philosophy classes, so I immediately applied to Long Beach State College (later renamed the loftier-sounding California State University at Long Beach) and enrolled with a major in philosophy. I paid for schooling out of my Bird Cage wages, aided in my second year by a dean's list scholarship (one hundred eighty dollars a year) achieved through my impassioned studying, fueled by *Razor's Edge* romanticism. I rented a small apartment near school, so small that its street number was 1059 $^1/_4$. Stormie eventually moved an hour north to attend UCLA, and we struggled for a while to see each other, but without the metaphor of the nineteenth century to enchant us, we realized that our real lives lay before us, and, painfully for me, we drifted apart.

At the Bird Cage, I formed the soft, primordial core of what became my comedy act. Over the three years I worked there, I strung together everything I knew, including Dave Steward's glove into dove trick, some comedy juggling, a few standard magic routines, a banjo song, and some very old jokes. My act was eclectic, and

65

it took ten more years for me to make sense of it. However, the opportunity to perform four and five times a day gave me confidence and poise. Even though my material had few distinguishing features, the repetition made me lose my amateur rattle.

Catalyzed by the popularity of the folk group the Kingston Trio, small music clubs began to sprout in every unlikely venue. Shopping malls and restaurant cellars now had corner-stage showrooms that sometimes did and sometimes didn't serve alcohol. There were no clubs dedicated to comedy—they did not exist for at least fifteen years—so every comedian was an outsider. The Paradox, in Tustin, was where I first saw the Dillards, a bluegrass group that played hard and made us laugh, too, and featured the whizbang five-string banjo picker Doug Dillard, who looked like a grin on a stick but played with staggering speed and clarity. There was the Rouge et Noir in Seal Beach, where I saw David-Troy (aka David Somerville, aka Diamond Dave), a singer-guitarist who had the ladies swooning and who had been, years earlier, the lead singer on the Diamonds' monster hit "Little Darlin'." I didn't realize I was hearing one of the most famous voices in early rock and roll. At the Mecca, in Buena Park, I saw the up-and-coming comedian Pat Paulsen, who opened with this funny line: "I've had a great life, with the exception of 1959, when, unfortunately, I passed away." (The best opening line I ever heard was from Sam Kinison. In the late eighties, playing the Comedy Store in Los Angeles, he said, "You're going to see a lot of comedians to-night; some will be good, some will be okay. But there's a difference between me and them. Them, you might want to see again sometime." But wait—maybe the best opening line I heard was Richard Pryor's, after he started two hours late in front of a potentially miffed crowd at the Troubadour in Los Angeles. He said simply, "Hope I'm funny.")

Using the Bird Cage as a home base, I flirted with out-side work, auditioning for gigs while keeping my class load at school as light as possible. The Prison of Socrates was a music club in the T-shirts-and-shorts beach town of Balboa. The Prison's main star was a charismatic sandal-clad folksinger named Tim Morgon, who was so popular that for several months in Southern California, his record outsold the Beatles' *A Hard Day's Night*. My Monday-night audition at the Prison was marginal, but because the open-ing acts were usually marginal anyway, I was hired for a weekend tryout. I now had my first job outside Knott's Berry Farm, which presented a particular difficulty. It was one thing to do five minutes at the Bird Cage, or ten min-utes at a "hoot," but it was another thing to do twenty min-utes for paying customers. Furiously trying to expand the act before my three-day gig, I threw in earnest readings of the poets e. e. cummings, T. S. Eliot, Carl Sandburg, and Stephen Vincent Benét, all aimed at stretching my act to show length. Nobody cared about hearing Eliot and cum-mings in a nightclub, but the Benét piece, a socko narra-

67

tive poem about a fiddle contest in Georgia, stayed in the act for at least a year until I canned it.

Opening night, I stood in the parking lot behind the club, going over my material and warming up on the banjo. Adjacent to garbage cans and blowing with beach sand, the parking lot was where the opening acts tuned up and rehearsed, as there was no place else to practice out of the audience's earshot. I performed to a sparse crowd, among them my college friend Phil Carey, his brothers, and their dates. How did it go? I have no idea. My only memories of it are the unsettling echo of chairs screeching on the concrete floor as patrons adjusted their seats. After the show, I was informed by my college friends that I had mispronounced the word "incomparable."

I now had two credits, the Bird Cage and the Prison of Socrates—my Disneyland credit was not quite professional—and I was able to land intermittent jobs, among them the Ice House in Pasadena, which had been converted from—guess what—an icehouse. Many earnest folk musicians appeared there, strumming guitars and wearing shirts with puffy sleeves. At the Ice House, I faced a real nightclub audience and performed almost as frequently as I did at the Bird Cage. Three shows a night was standard at these small clubs. Eventually, I ingratiated myself with enough venues that I wondered if I could possibly finance my life without the security of my steady job at Knott's Berry Farm.

68

Having no agent or any hopes of finding one, I could

Onstage at the Ice House, doing my parody
of male models.

not audition for movies or television or even learn where
auditions were held. I didn't know about trade papers—
Variety or *The Hollywood Reporter*—from which I might
have gathered some information. I lived in suburbia at a
time when a one-hour drive to Los Angeles in my first
great car—a white 1957 Chevy Bel Air, which, despite its
beauty, guzzled quarts of oil, then spewed it back into the
air in the form of white smoke—seemed like a trip across

the continent in a Conestoga wagon. But the local folk clubs thrived on single acts, and, as usual, their Monday nights were reserved for budding talent. Stand-up comedy felt like an open door. It was possible to assemble a few minutes of material and be onstage *that week,* as opposed to standing in line in some mysterious world in Hollywood, getting no response, no phone calls returned, and no opportunity to perform. On Mondays, I could tour around Orange County, visit three clubs in one night, and be onstage, live, in front of an audience. If I flopped at the Paradox in Tustin, I might succeed an hour later at the Rouge et Noir. I found myself confining the magic to its own segment so I wouldn't be called a magician. Even though the idea of doing comedy had sounded risky when I compared it to the safety of doing trick after trick, I wanted, needed, to be called a comedian. I discovered it was not magic I was interested in but performing in general. Why? Was I in a competition with my father? No, because I wasn't aware of his interest in showbiz until years later. Was my ego out of control and looking for glory? I don't think so; I am fundamentally shy and still feel slightly embarrassed at disproportionate attention. My answer to the question is simple: Who wouldn't want to be in show business?

I looked around the Bird Cage and saw actors who had worked there fifteen years and counting, and I knew it could be a trap for me. With some trepidation, I gave notice. Stormie was gone, Kathy was gone, John Stuart and Paul Shackleton were gone, too, so there were no actual tearful goodbyes. Handshakes with George and Woody. At age twenty-one, three years after I had started at the Bird Cage, I slipped away almost unnoticed.

I CONTINUED TO ATTEND Long Beach State College, taking Stormie-inspired courses in metaphysics, ethics, and logic. New and exhilarating words such as "epistemology," "ontology," "pragmatism," and "existentialism"—words whose definitions alone were stimulating—swirled through my head and reconfigured my thinking. One semester I was taking Philosophy of Language, Continental Rationalism (whatever that is; what, Descartes?), History of Ethics, and to complete the group, Self-Defense, which I found especially humiliating when, one afternoon in class, I was nearly beaten up by a girl wearing boxing gloves. A course in music appreciation focused me on classical music, causing me to miss the pop music of my own era, so I got into the Beatles several years late. I was fixated on studying, and even though I kept my outside jobs, my drive for learning led to a significant improvement from my dismal high school grade average. I was now an A student. I switched to cotton pants called peggers, because I had vowed to grow up and abandon jeans. My look was strictly wholesome Baptist.

A friend lent me some comedy records. There were three by Nichols and May, several by Lenny Bruce, and

71

one by Tom Lehrer, the great song parodist. Mike Nichols and Elaine May recorded without an audience, and I fixated on every nuance. Their comedy was sometimes created by only a subtle vocal shift: "Tell me Dr. Schweitzer, what is this *reverence for life*?" Lenny Bruce, on the records I heard, was doing mostly nonpolitical bits that were hilarious. Warden at a prison riot: "We're giving in to your demands, men! Except the vibrators!" Tom Lehrer influenced me with one bizarre joke: "My brother Henry was a nonconformist. To show you what a nonconformist he was, he spelled his name H-E-N-3-R-Y." Some people fall asleep at night listening to music; I fell asleep to Lenny, Tom, and Mike and Elaine. These albums broke ground and led me to a Darwinian discovery: Comedy could evolve.

On campus I experienced two moments of illumination, both appropriately occurring in the bright sun. Now comfortable with indulging in overthinking, I was walking across the quad when a thought came to me, one that was nearly devastating. To implement the new concept called originality that I had been first introduced to in *Showmanship for Magicians,* and was now presenting itself again in my classes in literature, poetry, and philosophy, I would have to write everything in the act myself. Any line or idea with even a vague feeling of familiarity or provenance had to be expunged. There could be nothing that made the audience feel they weren't seeing something utterly new.

This realization mortified me. I did not know how to write comedy—at all. But I did know I would have to drop some of my best one-liners, all pilfered from gag books and other people's routines, and consequently lose ten minutes from my already strained act. Worse, I would lose another prime gag I had lifted, Carl Ballantine's never-fail Appearing Dove, which had been appropriated by almost every comic magician under the age of twenty. Ballantine would blow up a paper bag and announce that he was going to produce a dove. "Come out flyin'!" he would say. Then he would pop the bag with his hands, and an anemic flutter of feathers would poof out from the sack. The thought of losing all this material was depressing. After several years of working up my weak twenty minutes, I was now starting from almost zero.

I came up with several schemes for developing material. "I laugh in life," I thought, "so why not observe what it is that makes me laugh?" And if I did spot something that was funny, I decided not to just describe it as happening to someone else, but to translate it into the first person, so it was happening *to me*. A guy didn't walk into a bar, I did. I didn't want it to appear that others were nuts; I wanted it to appear that *I* was nuts.

Another method was to idly and abstractedly dream up bits. Sitting in a science class, I stared at the periodic table of the elements that hung behind the professor. That weekend I went onstage at the Ice House and announced, "And now I would like to do a dramatic reading of the periodic table of the elements. Fe . . . Au . . . He . . ." I said. That bit didn't last long.

In logic class, I opened my textbook—the last place I was expecting to find comic inspiration—and was startled to find that Lewis Carroll, the supremely witty author of *Alice's Adventures in Wonderland,* was also a logician. He wrote logic textbooks and included argument forms based on the syllogism, normally presented in logic books this way:

All men are mortal.
Socrates is a man.

Therefore, Socrates is mortal.

But Carroll's were more convoluted, and they struck me as funny in a new way:

1) Babies are illogical.
2) Nobody is despised who can manage a crocodile.
3) Illogical persons are despised.

Therefore, babies cannot manage crocodiles.

And:

1) No interesting poems are unpopular among people of real taste.
2) No modern poetry is free from affectation.
3) All your poems are on the subject of soap bubbles.

4) No affected poetry is popular among people of taste.

5) Only a modern poem would be on the subject of soap bubbles.

Therefore, all your poems are uninteresting.

These word games bothered and intrigued me. Appearing to be silly nonsense, on examination they were *absolutely logical*—yet they were still funny. The comedy doors opened wide, and Lewis Carroll's clever fancies from the nineteenth century expanded my notion of what comedy could be. I began closing my show by announcing, "I'm not going home tonight; I'm going to Bananaland, a place where only two things are true, only two things: One, all chairs are green; and two, no chairs are green." Not at Lewis Carroll's level, but the line worked for my contemporaries, and I loved implying that the one thing I believed in was a contradiction.

I also was enamored of the rhythmic poetry of e. e. cummings, and a tantalizing quote from one of his recorded lectures stayed in my head. When asked why he became a poet, he said, "Like the burlesque comedian, I am abnormally fond of that precision which creates movement." The line, with its intriguing reference to comedy, was enigmatic, and it took me ten years to work out its meaning.

The second illuminating moment occurred when I was walking to class from a parking lot so far from campus that I could see the curvature of the earth. Again under the bright California sun, I saw a girl with short black hair, pertly walking in faded blue jeans. I was nervous about saying hello, but she offered me a welcoming smile that said it was okay. She had an unmelodic name—Nina Goldblatt—and she was a professional dancer. We started running into each other accidentally at every opportunity. I only had to get over the hurdle of her dating the handsome actor Vince Edwards, who played the TV doctor Ben Casey, and who was sending limos down to Long Beach to chauffeur her to Hollywood. Somehow I did, and a new romance was on.

Nina was a dancer in *The Mickey Finn Show,* a banjo and pizza whoop-de-do, with an upcoming appearance in Las Vegas on the fabled Strip. I drove five hours to spend the weekend with her and was captivated by the city, but my excitement was dampened by having only four dollars in my pocket. I was so broke that when I hit a nickel slot for fifty cents, it momentarily changed the quality of my life. It was Nina who had the dough, and we learned that Vegas could support even the poorly heeled by offering dollar-twenty-five all-you-can-eat buffets. Nina treated me to some Vegas nightclubs and I fantasized about starring as a lounge act at a spiffy hotel. We went to see the Jets, a two-man comedy-music team whose gags included passing through the audience, using the microphone as a "falsie detector." I enjoyed my time with Nina—she was funny and saucy as well as

Nina and me, ca. 1965.

cute—and one year later, she was to have a significant effect on my professional life.

My college roommate, Phil Carey, was an artist and musician. He sang bass, not in a barbershop quartet but for a sophisticated chorale that featured music with complicated rhythms and mismatched twelve-tone arrangements. Phil's contagious enthusiasm got me excited about art, particularly the avant-garde, and we quickly noted that the campus art scene was also a great arena to meet girls. We loved reading magazine reports of New York galleries stuffed with Warhol's Brillo boxes and giant flowers, Lichtenstein's cartoon panels, and throngs of

77

people dressed in black. One afternoon I donned Phil's beret—which meant I was disguised as an artist—and sneaked into his life drawing class, where an attractive nude blonde was casually displaying herself. I was all business on the outside, but on the inside I was shouting, "Yeehaw!" Phil had a developed sense of humor: His cat was named Miles, and when asked if the cat was named after Miles Davis, Phil would say no, it was "and miles to go before I sleep."

Working on a college project, Phil landed an interview with the great American composer Aaron Copland. However, he would have to drive from Los Angeles to Peekskill, New York, to conduct it. I jumped at the chance to go along. In the summer of 1966—I was still twenty and proud that I would make it to New York City before I turned twenty-one—we installed a makeshift cot in the back of my coughing blue windowless VW bus, and we drove across America without stopping. I was trying to write like e. e. cummings, so my correspondence to Nina, all highly romantic, goopy, and filled with references to flowers and stars, read like amateur versions of his poems. Nina saved the letters, but they are too embarrassing to reproduce here.

Three days after we left Los Angeles, Phil and I arrived at Aaron Copland's house, a low-slung A-frame with floor-to-ceiling windows, set in a dappled forest by the road. We knocked on the door, Copland answered it, and over his shoulder we saw a group of men sitting in the living room wearing only skimpy black thongs. He escorted us to his flagstone patio, where I had the demanding job of turning the tape recorder on and off while Phil asked questions about Copland's musical process. We emerged a half hour later with the coveted interview and got in the car, never mentioning the men in skimpy black thongs, because, like trigonometry, we couldn't quite comprehend it. We drove to West Redding, Connecticut, for a tour of the house of another great American composer, the late Charles Ives. Speaking with Ives's son-in-law, George Tyler, we learned the peculiar fact that Ives was an avant-garde composer by night and an insurance agent by day. After a detour to Cambridge, Massachusetts, to cruise the home of my idol cummings, we drove in to glorious Manhattan. Saucer-eyed, we hustled over to the Museum of Modern Art, where we saw, among the Cézannes and Matisses, Dalí's famous painting of melting clocks, the shockingly tiny *The Persistence of Memory*. We were dismayed to find that Warhol and Lichtenstein had not yet been ordained. We drove to Eighth Avenue, and Phil circled the block while I retrieved from the imposing central New York post office a lively and welcome letter from Nina, sent to me care of General Delivery, New York City. I bounded down the massive steps, waving the onionskin envelope aloft for Phil to see, as though it were the lost map of the Incas.

Before we left Cambridge, I sent this postcard to Nina:

Dear Nina,

Today (about an hour ago) I stood in front of e. e. cummings's home at Harvard; his wife is still living there—we saw her. But the most fantastic thing was when we asked directions to Irving Street, the person we asked said to tell Mrs. Cummings hello from the Jameses! She turned out to be William James's great-granddaughter!

Then I added:

I have decided my act is going to go avant-garde. It is the only way to do what I want.

I'm not sure what I meant, but I wanted to use the lingo, and it was seductive to make these pronouncements. Through the years, I have learned there is no harm in charging oneself up with delusions between moments of valid inspiration.

AT THE ICE HOUSE, I had met the comedian George McKelvey. George had an actual career and was quite funny. In reference to radio's invisible crime fighter, the Shadow, he would ask, "If you could be invisible, what would you do? [long pause] Fight crime?" He was in Aspen, Colorado, during spring break, about to work a small folk club, when he broke his leg skiing. Could I fill in for him? he asked. He generously offered me all his salary—I think it was three hundred dollars for the two weeks—which would be more than I had ever earned, anywhere, anytime. I was twenty-one years old in March of 1967 when I headed for the notorious ski resort.

I arrived at a Pan-Abode house—a cedar cabin made from a kit—just outside Aspen. Visiting entertainers were bunked there, and after I made my way through the crunchy snow and stowed my suitcase under my bed, several of us introduced ourselves. One was my co-bill, John McClure, a lanky guitarist with an acute sense of humor. Wandering in later was a pretty waitress named Linda Byers who, I assumed, would fall for me because of my carefully designed, poetry-quoting artist's persona, but who, to my shock, chose John, and they formed a long-term relationship. Also in the house was one of the few English comedians working in America, Jonathan Moore, who played a bagpipe to open his show, scaring the audience with its ancient howl as he entered the club from behind them. Jonathan was older than we were, had been around, wore sunglasses indoors, and had the charm of a well-spoken cynic. His sheepdog, an ecstatic, ball-chasing mop named Winston, dove repeatedly into the deep snowy banks to retrieve our enthusiastically thrown snowballs. Winston didn't seem to mind that they would vanish white on white, and he earnestly pursued the impossible, digging, digging, digging. Jonathan Moore also said something in passing that put my hypochondriacal senses on

81

alert. A local Aspenite had died, and Jonathan offered, "You can't live at this altitude with a bad heart." From then on, whenever I was in Aspen, I had a barely manageable fear that I would suddenly be struck down.

Jonathan's girlfriend Linda Quaderer, Jonathan Moore, Linda Byers, John McClure, Winston, and me.

The nightclub, the Abbey Cellar on Galena Street, was at basement level in the middle of town and hard to find even for us. John and I, in order to drum up business, left little cards on the tables in the upstairs restaurant that read STEVE MARTIN / JOHN MCCLURE, ENTERTAINMENT ORDINAIRE, which to me was hilariously funny, but never seemed to be noticed as a joke.

Entertainment 'Ordinaire' STEVE MARTIN JOHN McCLURE Abbey Cellar 9:30–2 am

Aspen was no place for poetry readings, and they were stripped permanently from my act. I was now doing my triptych of banjo playing, comedy, and magic. One evening at the Abbey Cellar, I had my first experience with a serious heckler, who, sitting at the front table with his wife and another straight-looking couple, stood up and said, "See if you think this is funny," and threw a glass of red wine on me. The problem for him was, at this point in the evening, the employees outnumbered the audience. A few seconds later, John McClure and the rough, tough bartender, an Irishman named Mike, appeared like centurions and escorted him out. Eventually, his friends slunk out, too. The expulsion had a downside: The audience was now one third as large and in shock, and remained in stunned silence for the rest of my show. Later, I developed a few defensive lines to use against the

83

unruly: "Oh, I remember when I had my first beer," and if that didn't cool them off, I would use a psychological trick. I would lower my voice and continue with my act, talking almost inaudibly. The audience couldn't hear the show, and they would shut the heckler up on their own.

I was in awe of the red-bearded Mike, who seemed so confident in the divided world of Aspen, where locals with a sense of entitlement were pitted against developers with a sense of condominiums. One evening after closing, I watched him crack open an amyl nitrate, a potent drug for the heart and a dangerous one to fool around with, but rumored to enhance sex. With a long, deep breath, he inhaled its fumes in one nostril, then did the same extended inhale through the other nostril. "Do you want some? It only lasts a few seconds," he said. Not really, but I leaned over and, with the ampoule held far away from my nose, gave it the most tentative sniff possible. My brain exploded. I walked around the club feeling like a colossus with a four-foot-wide lightbulb where my head was supposed to be. Alarmed and anxious, I went sliding into the icy streets, trying to calm down. As for it lasting seconds, I was still vibrating twenty-four hours later. What, I wondered, must Mike feel as he inhaled the freshly broken capsule into both lungs with an effort worthy of the Big Bad Wolf?

The next night I was picked up by a local woman. She was older and looking for sex and, since my boyfriend status with Nina had recently unraveled, I was eager to oblige. Even though I was still reeling from the previous night, we went to her second-floor apartment in a hundred-year-old building and wasted no time. In the middle of this experience, I heard the pop of an amyl nitrate, and then she shoved it toward my nose. I had barely come down from the previous night's blast and I wasn't about to have my head ripped off again. I breathed out and tried to make it appear as though I were breathing in, determined that none of the molecules should get anywhere near me. I was successful but had to act as though I was wowed beyond belief. "Yes, yes!" I lied. After this mess was over, she asked if she could take my picture. I said sure, and she went to get her camera. I moved into her living room, where I casually picked up from her coffee table a wood-bound scrapbook bearing the image of a sleeping Mexican on its cover. Pasted inside were dozens of photos of guys sitting in the chair I was now occupying.

My experience at the Abbey Cellar was important to me, but not as important as what was going on after hours. John and I shared a room, and his future partner, Linda, would join us for lengthy chats. What we discussed was the new zeitgeist. I don't know how it got to this bedroom in Aspen, but it was creeping everywhere simultaneously. I didn't yet know its name but found out later it was called Flower Power, and I was excited to learn that we were now living in the Age of Aquarius, an age when, at least astrologically, the world would be taken over by macramé. Anticorporate, individual, and freak-based, it

85

proposed that all we had to do was love each other and there would be no more wars or strife. Nothing could have been newer or more appealing. The vast numbers of us who changed our thoughts and lives for this belief proved that, yes, it is possible to fool all of the people some of the time. The word "love" was being tossed around as though only we insiders knew its definition. But any new social philosophy is good for creativity. New music was springing up, new graphics twisted and swirled as if on LSD, and an older generation was being glacially inched aside to make room for the freshly weaned new one. The art world, always contrarian, responded to psychedelia with monochrome and minimalism. It was fun trying to "turn" a young conservative, which was easy because our music was better. I remember trying to convince a member of the Dallas Ski Club that "Yummy, Yummy, Yummy (I've Got Love in My Tummy)" was not really a good song no matter how much he liked it. After two weeks in Aspen, I went back to Los Angeles feeling like an anointed prophet, taking my friends aside and burping out the new philosophy.

I CONTINUED TO PURSUE my studies and half believed I might try for a doctorate in philosophy and become a teacher, as teaching is, after all, a form of show business. I'm not sure what the purpose of fooling myself was, but I toyed with the idea for several semesters. I concluded that not to continue with comedy would place a question in my mind that would nag me for the rest of my life: Could I have had a career in performing? Everything was dragging me toward the arts; even the study of modern philosophy suggested that philosophy was nonsense. A classmate, Ron Barnett, and I spent hours engaged in late-night mind-altering dialogues in Laundromats and parking lots, discussing Ludwig Wittgenstein, the great Austrian semanticist. Wittgenstein's investigations disallowed so many types of philosophical discussions that we were convinced the very discussion we were having was impossible. Soon I felt that a career in the irrational world of creativity not only made sense but had moral purpose.

I was living several lives at once: I was a student at Long Beach State; I sometimes filled in at the Bird Cage Theatre; and at night I performed in various folk clubs with an eclectic, homemade comedy act that wasn't to reach its flash point for another decade. One of the clubs I played was Ledbetter's, a comparatively classy beer-and-wine nightspot a few blocks from UCLA that catered to the college crowd. I was taken under the wing of its owner, Randy Sparks, a theatrical entrepreneur who had founded the New Christy Minstrels, a highly successful folk act. I opened the show for his new acts, the Back Porch Majority and the New Society, two massive, stage-filling folk groups who offered wholesome high spirits and some pretty funny comedy to the Westwood Village audiences. Fats Johnson, a jovial folksinger who dressed to kill in black

87
—

suits with white ruffled shirts and wore elaborate rings on his guitar-strumming hand, often headlined the club. When I asked him about his philosophy of dressing for the stage, he said firmly, "Always look better than they do."

Now that most of my work was in Westwood, Long Beach State College, forty miles away, seemed like Siberia. I transferred to my third college, UCLA, so I could be closer to the action, and I took several courses there. One was an acting class, the kind that feels like prison camp and treats students like detainees who need to be broken; another was a course in television writing, which seemed practical. I also continued my studies in philosophy. I had done pretty well in symbolic logic at Long Beach, so I signed up for Advanced Symbolic Logic at my new school. Saying that I was studying Advanced Symbolic Logic at UCLA had a nice ring; what had been nerdy in high school now had mystique. However, I went to class the first day and discovered that UCLA used a different set of symbols from those I had learned at Long Beach. To catch up, I added a class in Logic 101, which meant I was studying beginning logic and advanced logic at the same time. I was overwhelmed, and shocked to find that I couldn't keep up. I had reached my math limit as well as my philosophy limit. I abruptly changed my major to theater and, free from the workload of my logic classes, took a relaxing inhale of crisp California air. But on the exhale, I realized that I was now investing in no other future but show business.

The physical distance from each other had permanently

broken up Nina and me, and she had left school to pursue her dancing career. But overnight, there were dozens of new people in my life. Pot smoking was de rigueur—this being the sixties—and since I was now a regular at Ledbetter's, I was living rent-free over the garage of a mansion in the exclusive area of Bel Air, thanks to the generosity of Randy Sparks and his wife, Diane. Even though I was armed with only a comedy act that was at best hit-and-miss, I was fearless and ready to go. Among the crowd of singers and musicians whose local fame I assumed was worldwide was a sylph-like figure, a nonsinger and nonmusician who nonetheless seemed to be regarded quite highly in this small showbiz matrix. Her name was Melissa, but her friends called her Mitzi. She was twenty years old, with a Katharine Hepburn beauty and a similarly willowy frame. She was intelligent, energetic, and lit from inside. Her hair was ash brown, and always at the end of one of her long and slender arms was a Nikon camera with a lens the size of a can of Campbell's soup.

When her current romance withered, Mitzi and I became entwined. After several weeks of courtship, I was ready for family inspection and she invited me to her parents' house for dinner. Mitzi's last name was Trumbo. Her father was screenwriter Dalton Trumbo, one of the notorious Hollywood Ten, a group of writers and directors who were blacklisted during the Red Scare of the early fifties. During his congressional hearing,

Trumbo vociferously challenged the right of his inquisitors to interrogate him, prompting a frustrated committee member to scream, "You are out of order, sir! You are out of order!" in a futile attempt to get him to shut up. It

Mitzi Trumbo, 1965.

was Trumbo who wrote the screenplays for *Spartacus, Lonely Are the Brave, Hawaii, Exodus,* and *Papillon;* whose personal letters read like Swiftian essays; who had to flee to Mexico for several years and write under pseudonyms such as Sam Jackson and James Bonham in order to escape McCarthyism; and whom, at this stage in my tunnel-visioned life, I had never heard of. Mitzi later told me that there were no wrong numbers in their household because any unknown name the caller asked for was assumed to be one of Trumbo's aliases.

90

From my perspective, Mitzi was a sophisticate. She had traveled. She was politically aware and had attended Reed College in Oregon, a bastion of liberal thought. Her intelligence was informed by her family history. When I went to dinner at her home in the Hollywood Hills, I did not know that the few months I would spend in this family's graces would broaden my life.

My first glimpse of Dalton Trumbo revealed an engrossed intellect—not finessing his latest screenplay but sorting the seeds and stems from a brick of pot. "Pop smokes marijuana," Mitzi explained, "with the wishful thought of cutting down on his drinking." Sometimes, from their balcony, I would see Trumbo walking laps around the perimeter of the pool. He held a small counter in one hand and clicked it every time he passed the diving board. These health walks were compromised by the cigarette he constantly held in his other hand.

Dalton Trumbo was the first raconteur I ever met. The family dinners—frequented by art dealers, actors, and artists of all kinds, including the screenwriters Hugo Butler and Ring Lardner, Jr., and the director George Roy Hill—were lively, political, and funny. I had never been in a house where conversations were held during dinner or where food was placed before me after being prepared behind closed doors. It was also the first time I ever heard swear words spoken by adults in front of their offspring. Lyndon Johnson's Vietnam bombing policy dominated the conversation, and the government's ironfisted response to war protesters rankled the dinner guests, since the Hollywood Ten were long familiar with oppression. Trumbo had a patriarchal delivery whether he was on a rant or discussing art or slinging wit, but nothing he said was elitist—though I do remember him saying, as he spread his arms to indicate the china and silver serving ladles, "Admittedly, we do live well."

Trumbo's wife, Cleo, beautiful like Mitzi, was at the head of the table when Trumbo was downstairs writing. Cleo was the person actually in charge and could not have been more welcoming. She extended an open dinner invitation to Mitzi and me, and as I was deeply broke, we always accepted. The food was delicious and the company spectacular, so we did not regret missing out on the "health salads" served at our local incense-burning restaurants—gunky concoctions of cheese-laden, ham-draped iceberg lettuce doused with creamy dressing.

One evening after dinner, we adjourned to the living room—something else I had never done before—and I was surprised to see a marijuana cigarette passed among the guests. The joint finally got to Trumbo, and he clasped it between his knuckles like a German officer in a movie. He didn't pass it along, just held it and puffed on it but did not inhale. With a broad grin, Mitzi leaned over to me and said, "Pop doesn't know how to smoke pot. He thinks you smoke it like a cigar, and he never gets high."

The family's liberal bent was never fully tested. When I asked Mitzi if her parents knew about my slipping in the garden door of her bedroom late at night and leaving at daybreak, she said that Cleo knew but Pop would not be pleased. Hence, in the early mornings, I started my car gingerly, thinking that if I turned the key slowly, the engine would not make so much noise.

The Trumbo house was modern, built on a hillside, and extended down three floors into a ravine. The walls in the living room were large, and they give me my most vivid memory of the house, for they were covered with art. Political art. I had never seen real paintings in a

Dancing with Mitzi
in front of the Hiram Williams painting.

93

house, and this might have been where my own inclination toward owning pictures began. In the entry was an eight-foot-high Baconesque painting by Hiram Williams, a picture of several businessmen, their hands bloody, emerging from a white background. In the dining room was a William Gropper, depicting members of the House Un-American Activities Committee grotesquely outlined in fluorescent green against a murky background. There was a Raphael Soyer, a Moses Soyer, and a Jack Levine painting of Hindenburg making Hitler chancellor. These

An ad for the Ice House; photo by Mitzi Trumbo.

artists are obscure today but not forgotten. Gropper's art depicted politicos as porcine bullies, and Jack Levine's well-brushed social realism had a biting edge and fit the politics of the family perfectly.

Mitzi became my official photographer, and she snapped dozens of rolls of film, all to find the perfect publicity photo. It being the sixties, there were many shots of me with a flower on my head or a daisy between my teeth. We spent one morning taking photos in Fern Dell, where a stream flowed down the concrete center of a man-made mini–tropical rain forest set in the heart of Los Angeles, which up to that point was the most lush place I had ever seen. Later that day, we attended an anti–Vietnam War protest where I was lucky to get—then unlucky enough to lose—my draft card autographed by Cassius Clay, soon to be the most famous person in the world, Muhammad Ali.

The war was rapidly consuming young men, and the draft was closing in. The thought of being shipped off to Vietnam for possible dismemberment scared me, especially after I read Dalton Trumbo's antiwar book, *Johnny Got His Gun,* the story of a young soldier who wakes to discover he has lost his legs, arms, mouth, nose, eyes, and ears and is left with only the ability to think. In the face of this war, which snared so many, I had a case of rolling luck. First I was exempt because I was in college. When the college deferment lifted, I became 1-Y, unacceptable because of migraine headaches, which I had exaggerated. When the definition of 1-Y was tightened and I was moved up to 1-A, the draft went to a lottery, and I drew a middling number. As my number approached, the army went to all-volunteer, and I was saved from an alternate life. But I cannot end this story without a solemn bow to those who weren't so fortunate.

I got a one-show job performing near the Russian River in Northern California. I drove there in my second great car, a yellow 1966 Ford Mustang (my third and last great car was a yellow 1967 Jaguar XK-E. Then I lost all interest in cars). Up north, I reconnoitered with Mitzi, and she took photos of me canoeing. Unfortunately, she didn't photograph the job I had, performing at a drive-in theater at three P.M. under the afternoon sun while a dozen cars hooked up to the sound system listened through window speakers. If the drive-in patrons thought a joke was funny, they honked. You might think I'm exaggerating, but I'm not.

Once, on the way to the Trumbo house, Mitzi warned me, "Pop's in a bad mood today. He's got a screenplay due in four days and he hasn't started it yet." The screenplay was for the movie *The Fixer,* starring Alan Bates. Eventually, the work got done and the movie was ready to shoot. Trumbo encouraged Mitzi to join him and she was whisked off to Budapest for the duration of the film. After I'd received several charming letters from her and then noticed a lag in the regularity of their arrival, Mitzi sent me a gentle and direct Dear John letter. She had been swept away by the director John Frankenheimer, who, twenty years later, tried and failed to seduce my then wife, the actress Victoria Tennant, whom he was directing in a movie. Mitzi was simply too alluring to be left alone in a foreign country, and I was too hormonal to be left alone in Hollywood. Incidentally, Frankenheimer died a few years ago, but it was not I who killed him.

Television

I WAS STILL TWENTY-ONE when I was politely booted from Randy and Diane Sparks's garage apartment. I moved to an unincorporated area called Palms, adjacent to the historic MGM Studios, and shared a small guesthouse with the sharp, deadpan comedian Gary Mule Deer ("I think we should put pictures of missing transvestites on cartons of half-and-half") and the lonely-voiced singer-guitarist Michael Johnson. I continued to work at Ledbetter's and attend classes at UCLA. But while I studied halfheartedly in Westwood, Nina had entered the world of real show business. She had changed her name to the more mellifluous Nina Lawrence and landed a job dancing on *The Smothers Brothers Comedy Hour,* the hippest thing on television and Flower-Powered all over the place. She had begun dating Mason Williams, the head writer on the show. I still had an affectionate crush on her and was glad for her and sick all at the same time. Mason Williams, exuberant, infused with creativity, and the future composer of the smash hit "Classical Gas," drove an elegant 1938 Pierce-Arrow and could talk the new aesthetic—essentially, the appreciation for all things quirky and creative—much better than I could. Where I could only recite poetry, Mason actually was a poet. He lived in a rented house in the Hollywood Hills with sparkling views of Los Angeles out the bedroom's vast picture window. I imagined Mason and Nina doing it every which-a-way for anyone with a pair of binoculars to see. But these days, who could mind? We weren't a couple anymore, and Free Love, man, Free Love! Which, by the way, was the single greatest concept a young man has ever heard. This was a time when intercourse, or some version of it, was a way of saying hello. About three years later, women got wise and my frustration returned to normal levels.

I was almost but not quite in a financial bind when Nina phoned me to say that the Smothers Brothers—exercising the slogan of the day, "Never Trust Anyone over Thirty"—wanted to experiment and hire a few young writers for their hit TV show. In college, influenced by Jack Douglas's book *My Brother Was an Only Child* and Mason Williams's *The Mason Williams Reading*

Matter, I had composed, as a defiant alternative to coherent essay writing, some goofy one-paragraph stories with such titles as "The Day the Dopes Came Over," "What to Say When the Ducks Show Up," and "Cruel Shoes." Nina told me to send over my stories. I did, and she gave them to Mason.

The collection of scraps I sent was sketchy, half-baked material that I never would have submitted to a college English class for fear of expulsion. But Mason liked it, or maybe he just liked Nina, and having never written anything professionally in my life, I was hired as a tryout for the few remaining weeks of the *Smothers* season. I gingerly went to my television writing instructor at UCLA and told him I had to resign from the class—and school—because I had gotten a job writing for television. Years later, I learned that because my material had not made it past the final judges at the top, Mason, in an act of artistic generosity, had paid this newcomer out of his own pocket.

My professional writing career started off painfully. The older writers were rightfully suspicious of this kid, especially since my only qualification was being under thirty, and I felt the pressure to deliver. I was timid and unsure of myself in this suddenly wider world. If I was asked to write an intro for the folksinger Judy Collins, I would write, "And now, ladies and gentlemen, here's folksinger Judy Collins!" One afternoon I was in the studio, watching a rehearsal of a sketch dealing with television.

Tommy Smothers came up to me and said directly, "We need an intro for this bit. Can you write it?" This question was put to me with a clear implication that my job was on the line. I said yes but meant no. I went upstairs to my office as if I were on a march to the gallows; my mind was blank. Blanker than blank. I was a tabula rasa. I put paper in the typewriter and impotently stared at it. Finally, a great line occurred to me, except it belonged to my roommate, the comedian Gary Mule Deer. But it was perfect for this intro, so why not call him and ask if I could use it? By a miracle, he was home. I explained that I was stuck. He said sure, use it. I went downstairs, handed in the line, and Dick Smothers read the joke: "It has been proven that more Americans watch television than any other appliance." Two highly experienced writers, Hal Goodman and Al Goldman, with credits extending back to Jack Benny, came up to me and said, "Did you write that joke?" "Yes," I said. "Good work," they said. If, at that moment, I had been hooked up to a lie detector, it would have spewed smoke. The event must have been cathartic, because afterward, I relaxed and was able to contribute fully to the show.

The season ended, and I was asked to work on a summer replacement show, the malappropriately titled *The Summer Brothers Smothers Show*, starring Glen Campbell. Glen was a former studio musician who had just risen to stardom with his first big hit, John Hartford's "Gentle on My Mind." I was twenty-two years old when I found myself standing in a small room at CBS on Fairfax with a few other writers, including John Hartford, while Pete Seeger strummed his banjo not five feet from me. Around the calfskin head of Pete's banjo was written in ink, THIS MACHINE SURROUNDS HATE AND FORCES IT TO SURRENDER (an allusion to Woody Guthrie's earlier guitar slogan, THIS MACHINE KILLS FASCISTS). We pitched concepts for Pete's appearance, but his idea was the best. He would sing "Waist Deep in the Big Muddy (and the Big Fool Says to Push On)" over images of the increasingly tragic war in Vietnam. Glen Campbell probably hadn't known what he was getting into, but he endorsed us all the way.

I was teamed with the hilarious Bob Einstein—an advertising writer who had found his way to CBS—and fortunately, as we shared a windowless office and worked together fourteen hours a day, we became inseparable friends. Bob and I were perfect writing foils. We had a mutual regard for Laurel and Hardy, Jerry Lewis, Daffy Duck, and Mel Blanc's peculiar genius, and we could make each other laugh until we were breathless. If I accidentally banged my head on a stage pipe, Bob would collapse in hysterics and, following his lead, so would I. At least eight of our fourteen working hours were spent laughing until we were in pain, then trying to decide if what we were laughing at was usable or just comic delirium. Bob later achieved fame as Super Dave, a bumbling TV daredevil.

Though Bob and I were a team, I sometimes worked

103

BORN STANDING UP

with another young writer/performer, Rob Reiner, later to make his mark as the director of, among other films, *When Harry Met Sally* and the classic *This Is Spinal Tap*. Rob, in a coincidence that was yet to happen, was the son of my future film director, Carl Reiner. Rob and I closed our first season with a strong finish. We wrote a ten-minute finale combining short sketches with classic rock songs from the fifties. At that time "oldies but goodies" was a new concept. The segment was a hit and Rob and I gave ourselves credit, whether it was accurate or not, for starting a fifties music revival. We wrote it for Glen Campbell and Bobbie Gentry (who was still riding on the success of "Ode to Billy Joe"), and when Bobbie appeared onstage in an "itsy-bitsy teeny-weeny yellow polka-dot bikini," all the writers' jaws dropped. We hadn't known she'd started as a chorus girl in Las Vegas.

I had a short-lived but troublesome worry. What if writing comedy was a dead end because one day everything would have been done and we writers would just run out of stuff? I assuaged myself with my own homegrown homily: Comedy is a distortion of what is happening, and there will always be something happening. This problem solved, I grew more confident as a writer and slid into steady work the following season, thanks to an endorsement from Bob Einstein, on *The Smothers Brothers Comedy Hour*. I even had a few walk-on appearances where I inevitably played "the hippie." The satirical show had taken a big left turn, which suited my politics perfectly. Constantly making news because of CBS's censorship policy, *The Smothers Brothers Comedy Hour* was the only source on prime-time television for both satire and contemporary music acts such as the Doors and the Beatles.

Bob Einstein, Nina Lawrence, Don Wyatt, and me, in costume for a *Smothers* sketch.

Though the new writing job frequently required all-nighters, I continued to service my stand-up career. I would bomb regularly at the Ice House, but the audiences were so sparse that the proprietor, Bob Stane, couldn't tell if I was flopping or the house was too empty. One night I realized I had been on for twenty minutes and had not gotten a single laugh from the dead Tuesday-night crowd. I thought, "Why not go for the record?" I set my mind to it and finished the show without having roused one

105

snicker. However, there was a sign of encouragement from these early jobs, and years later I heard it phrased perfectly by Bill Cosby. He said that early in his career, when the audience wasn't laughing, he could hear the waitresses laughing, and they saw the show night after night. I noticed that the waitresses were laughing.

MY LIFE HAD BEEN ALTERNATELY inching or leaping upward: I was proud of my job on the Smothers Brothers' show. I had some cash. My sex life was abundant and selfish. Things were rolling along nicely when I experienced a crushing psychological surprise. One night I was off to the movies with my friends John McClure, George McKelvey, and his wife, Carole. We were going to see Mel Brooks's *The Producers,* and we decided to smoke a little pot, which had become a dietary staple for me. So now I was high. In the car on the way to the theater, I felt my mind being torn from its present location and lifted into the ether. My discomfort intensified, and I experienced an eerie distancing from my own self that crystallized into morbid doom. I mutely waited for the feeling to pass. It didn't, and I finally said, "I feel strange." We got out of the car, and John, George, and Carole walked me along Sunset Boulevard in the night. I decided to go into the theater, thinking it might be distracting. During the film, I sat in stoic silence as my heart began to race above two hundred beats per minute and the saliva drained from my mouth so completely that I could not move my tongue. I assumed this was the heart attack I had been waiting for, though I wasn't feeling pain. I was, however, experiencing extreme fear; I thought I was dying, and I can't explain to you why I just sat there. After the movie, I considered checking myself in to a hospital. But if I went to the hospital, I would miss work the next day, which might make me expendable at CBS, where my career was just launching. My friends walked me along Sunset again, and I remember humming, "Whenever I feel afraid, I hold my head erect and whistle a happy tune" from *The King and I*. I spent the night on George and Carole's couch in absolute terror. I kept wondering, "Am I dying?" but was more concerned with the question "Do I have to quit my job?"

I survived the night and struggled in to work the next morning. I was not relieved, but I was calmer; I confessed to Bob Einstein what had happened and found that as soon as I discussed the symptoms, they arose again with full intensity. However, I somehow maintained my implacable façade.

The cycle was unbreakable. Any relief was followed by the worry of recurrence, which itself provoked the symptoms. After a few weeks, a list of triggers developed. I couldn't go back into a movie theater, and I didn't for at least ten years. I never smoked pot again, or got involved in the era's preoccupation with illicit substances (I'm sure this event helped me avoid the scourge of cocaine).

107

However, the worst trigger was a certain event that, cruelly, happened every day. It was *night*. Eventually, I could find my way through the daytime, but as I left work, winding my way up the canyon streets as the sun set, I imagined feeling the slight rise in elevation and the air getting thinner. Nuts, I know. As a teenager, I had mixed a somber home life with a jubilant life away from the house. Now I could be funny, alert, and involved while nursing internal chaos, believing that death was inching nearer with each eroding episode of terror. I learned over the next months that I could do several things at once: be a comedy writer, be a stand-up comedian, and endure private mortal fear. Thankfully, after a difficult year, my specific dread of nightfall faded. I suppose I was too practical to have such an inconvenient phobia.

I discovered there was a name for what was happening to me. Reading medical and psychology books, I found my symptoms exactly described and named as an anxiety attack. I felt a sense of relief from the simple understanding that I was not alone. I read that these panic attacks were not dangerous, just gravely unpleasant. The symptoms were comparable to the biological changes the body experiences when put in danger, as if you were standing in front of an object of fear, such as an unleashed lion. In an anxiety attack you have all the symptoms of fear, yet there is no lion. I could not let self-doubt or lack of talent cause me to fail at this new writing job—this lion—which was the gateway to my next life as an entertainer. I carefully buried this fear; I was in over my head, but my conscious mind wouldn't allow that thought to exist, and my body rebelled that night at the movie theater. At least this is my ten-cent diagnosis. I continued to suffer the attacks while I went on with my work, refusing to let this inner nightmare affect my performing or writing career. Though panic attacks are gone from my life now—they receded as slowly as the ice around Greenland—they were woven throughout two decades of my life. When I think of the moments of elation I have experienced over some of my successes, I am astounded at the number of times they have been accompanied by elation's hellish opposite.

IN THE LATE SIXTIES, comedy was in transition. The older school told jokes and stories, punctuated with the drummer's rim shot. Of the new school, Bill Cosby—one of the first to tell stories you actually believed were true—and Bob Newhart—who startled everyone with innovative, low-key delivery and original material—had achieved icon status. Mort Sahl tweaked both sides of the political fence with his college-prof delivery, but soon the audiences were too stoned to follow his coherent sentences. George Carlin and Richard Pryor, though very funny, were still a few years away from their final artistic breakthroughs. Lenny Bruce had died several years earlier, fighting both the system and drugs, and his work was already in revival because of his caustic brilliance that made authority nervous. Vietnam, the first televised war, split the country, and one's left or right bent could be recognized by haircuts and clothes. The country was angry, and so was comedy, which was addressed to insiders. Cheech and Chong spoke to the expanding underground by rolling the world's largest doobie on film. There were exceptions: Don Rickles seemed to glide over the generation gap with killer appearances on *The Tonight Show,* and Johnny Carson remained a gentle satirist while maintaining a nice glossary of naughty-boy breast jokes. Tim Conway and Harvey Korman, two great comic sketch actors working for the affable genius Carol Burnett, were deeply funny. The television free-for-all called *Laugh-In* kept its sense of joy, thanks in part to Goldie Hawn's unabashed goofiness and producer George Schlatter's perceptive use of her screwups, but even that show had high political content. In general, however, a comedian in shackles for indecent language, or a singer's arrest for obscene gestures, thrilled the growing underground audience. Silliness was just not appropriate for hip culture. It was this circumstance that set the stage for my success eight years later.

IN A COLLEGE PSYCHOLOGY CLASS, I had read a treatise on comedy explaining that a laugh was formed when the storyteller created tension, then, with the punch line, released it. I didn't quite get this concept, nor do I still, but it stayed with me and eventually sparked my second wave of insights. With conventional joke telling, there's a moment when the comedian delivers the punch line, and the audience knows it's the punch line, and their response ranges from polite to uproarious. What bothered me about this formula was the nature of the laugh it inspired, a vocal acknowledgment that a joke had been told, like automatic applause at the end of a song.

A skillful comedian could coax a laugh with tiny indicators such as a vocal tic (Bob Hope's "But I wanna tell ya") or even a slight body shift. Jack E. Leonard used to punctuate jokes by slapping his stomach with his hand. One night, watching him on *The Tonight Show,* I noticed that several of his punch lines had been unintelligible, and the audience had actually laughed at nothing but the cue of his hand slap.

These notions stayed with me for months, until they formed an idea that revolutionized my comic direction: What if there were no punch lines? What if there were no indicators? What if I created tension and never released it? What if I headed for a climax, but all I delivered was an anticlimax? What would the audience do with all that tension? Theoretically, it would have to come out sometime. But if I kept denying them the formality of a punch line, the audience would eventually pick their own place to laugh, essentially out of desperation. This type of laugh seemed stronger to me, as they would be laughing at something *they chose,* rather than being told exactly when to laugh.

To test my idea, at my next appearance at the Ice House, I went onstage and began: "I'd like to open up with sort of a 'funny comedy bit.' This has really been a big one for me . . . it's the one that put me where I am today. I'm sure most of you will recognize the title when I mention it; it's the Nose on Microphone routine [pause for imagined applause]. And it's always funny, no matter how many times you see it."

I leaned in and placed my nose on the mike for a few long seconds. Then I stopped and took several bows, saying, "Thank you very much." "That's it?" they thought. Yes, that was it. The laugh came not then, but only after they realized I had already moved on to the next bit.

Now that I had assigned myself to an act without jokes, I gave myself a rule. Never let them know I was bombing: *This is funny, you just haven't gotten it yet.* If I wasn't offering punch lines, I'd never be standing there with egg on my face. It was essential that I never show doubt about what I was doing. I would move through my act without pausing for the laugh, as though everything were an aside. Eventually, I thought, the laughs would be playing catch-up to what I was doing. Everything would be either delivered in passing, or the opposite, an elaborate presentation that climaxed in pointlessness. Another rule was to make the audience believe that I thought I was fantastic, that my confidence could not be shattered. They had to believe that I didn't care if they laughed at all, and that this act was going on with or without them.

I was having trouble ending my show. I thought, "Why not make a virtue of it?" I started closing with extended bowing, as though I heard heavy applause. I kept insisting that I needed to "beg off." *No, nothing, not even this ovation I am imagining, can make me stay.* My goal was to make the audience laugh but leave them unable to describe what it was that had made them laugh. In other words, like the helpless state of giddiness experienced by close friends tuned in to each other's sense of humor, *you had to be there.*

At least that was the theory. And for the next eight years, I rolled it up a hill like Sisyphus.

My first reviews came in. One said, "This so-called 'comedian' should be told that jokes are supposed to have punch lines." Another said I represented "the most serious booking error in the history of Los Angeles music."

"Wait," I thought, "let me explain my theory!"

MY JOB WITH THE SMOTHERS BROTHERS allowed me to move to the hippie center of Southern California, Laurel Canyon. In 1968 Laurel Canyon was considered by the in crowd to be a nature reserve because of the presence of trees, even though the democratic Los Angeles smog covered all areas. Joni Mitchell lived there, so did Carole King, so did Kenny Loggins and Frank Zappa. I never met any of them, but I did reconnect with the person who, for the next fifteen years, would be the most significant figure in my performing life. His name was Bill McEuen, and he was the older brother of my high school friend John McEuen. John, a musician since the ninth grade, had joined a group, the Nitty Gritty Dirt Band, and Bill, who aspired to be a showbiz entrepreneur in the mold of Elvis's Colonel Parker, was managing them. It was simply coincidence that Bill and I had both moved, with intermittent stops, from Garden Grove to Laurel Canyon.

Bill had a deep love of early blues, country, and bluegrass music. He would pick up his guitar and sing Jimmie Rodgers's line, "He's in the jailhouse now!" and

In my Laurel Canyon apartment. Notice the Ed Kienholz on the wall, one of the first artworks I ever bought, acquired from a local gallery.

STEVE MARTIN

snap a string, giving the note a slight percussion. He also spotted genius. At Pepe's, a dinky club in St. Louis, he saw an act called the Allman Joys and brought them to Hollywood. They changed their name to Hour Glass, and he represented them for a while before they became the Allman Brothers Band. A few years later, he would create and produce a revered country music album, *Will the Circle Be Unbroken,* for which, it seems to me, everyone gets credit but him, even though Bill dreamed it all up and made it happen. He corralled some recording time for me at those Nashville sessions—after Mother Maybelle Carter, Doc Watson, Earl Scruggs, and Jimmy Martin had gone home for the evening—to lay down some banjo tunes I had written. In 1981 the songs appeared on my final last-gasp comedy album, *The Steve Martin Brothers.*

Bill McEuen was rebellious, defiant, and loved to watch the big guy squirm. After I had achieved success, he said to me, "Right now there are a lot of old-time comedians saying, 'What the fuck?'" He had banged his way out of nowhere, too, living just a few miles from me in Garden Grove and growing up under the thumb of a critical father. He had long hair before it was fashionable and kept it not only after it was unfashionable but forever. He also loved comedy. We were united in our worship of Johnny Carson, Don Rickles, Steve Allen, and Jerry Lewis. You can hear Bill's laugh buried somewhere on each of my albums. He even came up with one of my staple jokes of the period: "Do you mind if I smoke? Uh, no, do you mind if I fart?"

We started hanging around together—breakfast, lunch, and dinner—along with his beautiful wife, Alice, who was an excellent photographer. My MGB GT seated two, which meant one of us had to ride in the hatchback trunk, and it was always Bill, who, at six-four, had to curl up like a cat to fit into the car. Bill, after seeing my act a hundred times, asked if he could manage me. "What's a manager?" I said. After he explained, I didn't quite understand, and I don't think he did, either, but we struck a handshake deal for no other reason than that we had nothing to lose.

Bill and Alice McEuen, me, and their cat "White Cat," in Laurel Canyon.

STEVE MARTIN

John McEuen, whom I hadn't seen in about a year, came to the house. He had been on the road and grown his hair long, which surprised me, because I was still resisting. He noted my response, stroked his locks, and said, "Part of the business." Soon after, I grew my hair long and with my earnings from *The Smothers Brothers Comedy Hour,* financed a garish collection of turquoise jewelry that I would wear onstage. I was now a full-blown hippie, though not walking around stoned because of my earlier disastrous experience. I riffed on the drug era with this bit, which was delivered in a secretive, low whisper:

"I'm on drugs. . . . You know what I'm talking about. . . . I like to get small. . . . It's very dangerous for kids, because they get realllly small. . . . I know I shouldn't get small when I'm driving, but I was drivin' around the other day and a cop pulls me over . . . says, 'Hey, are you small?' I say, 'No, I'm tall, I'm tall!' He says, 'I'm gonna have to measure you.' They give you a little test with a balloon. If you can get inside it, they know you're small . . . and they can't put you in a regular cell, either, 'cause you walk right out."

The Smothers Brothers show continued to rankle the brass at both CBS and the federal halls of power. Sketches dealing with race, war, and politics, mixed in with anomalies such as Kate Smith singing "God Bless America," made it a hit in the ratings and at the watercooler. It thrived on controversy, but we writers didn't know the

No comment.

level of rancor the Brothers were facing. One morning in 1969, I was driving to work when I heard on the radio that the Smothers Brothers show had been ignominiously axed. Ostensibly, CBS canceled the show because of late delivery of an episode, but I knew what really had canceled it: a trickle-down from President Nixon. The Brothers had surely made Nixon's enemies list, and probably all of us writers had, too, and the political pressure must have been too much for lumbering CBS, which didn't need static from the FCC. After the show's demise, our team of eight writers won Emmys, the academy's defiant response to the CBS brass. Even after this gold-plated recognition, my father still urged me to go back to college so I would "have something to fall back on."

Comedy was now fully charged with political energy. George Carlin transformed himself from the Hippy Dippy Weatherman into a true social commentator. So did the volatile Richard Pryor, who dropped the gags, appealed to the underground audience, and used "motherfucker" as poetic punctuation. Robert Klein was the educated one; you sat in the audience nodding in agreement with his tart observations. After *The Smothers Brothers Comedy Hour* fell, I joined in with my never-miss Nixon jokes ("Nixon's best friend is Bebe Rebozo, a name that means 'to have bozo-ed again'"). All I had to do was mention Nixon's name, and there were laughs from my collegiate audiences.

Bob Einstein and I had become a solid workhorse writing team. When *The Smothers Brothers* ended, we continued to get jobs, including *The Sonny & Cher Comedy Hour,* which kept me busy for seven months out of the year. During the hiatuses, I would slog away at my act. Bill had put me on the road, opening the show for the Nitty Gritty Dirt Band, and I am grateful to them because they really didn't need me. We went everywhere. Atlanta, Spokane, Madison, Little Rock, Tallahassee, you name it, I was there. Colleges, clubs, and concert halls in what

119

seemed like every state in the union. One magical night, on a lonely road in upstate New York, the bus pulled over and we all got out for a stretch of the legs. We looked north into the moonless black sky. Above us, in this low latitude, shimmered the aurora borealis.

Mostly, I was alone on these road trips, and I would while away the solitary daytime hours by indulging my growing interest in American art of the nineteenth and twentieth centuries. I haunted museums and galleries, making quick visual checks in the local antique stores in hopes of finding a Winslow Homer that had gone astray. I never did, but I managed to buy a nineteenth-century picture by the English artist John Everett Millais, thinking I had made the find of the century, only to discover that it was a tired old fake that had been around the art market for years. This was a cheap lesson in my art-collecting hobby, which would develop fully a decade later. I also killed time in college libraries, browsing for books on American art. After spotting a rare and valuable book in the stacks at the University of Tulsa—it was Mabel Dodge Luhan's early treatise on southwestern painting, *Taos and Its Artists*—I wondered if I could smuggle it past the low-tech librarian. But my better judgment prevailed, and I left it in place.

IN LOS ANGELES, there was an exploding number of new afternoon television talk shows. *The Della Reese Show,*

The Merv Griffin Show, The Virginia Graham Show, The Dinah Shore Show, The Mike Douglas Show, and my favorite, *The Steve Allen Show.* Steve Allen had a vibrant comedy spirit, and if you tuned in, you might catch him playing Ping-Pong while suspended from a crane a hundred feet in the air, or becoming a human tea bag by dropping himself in a tank of water filled with lemons. In his standard warm-up for the studio audience, when he was asked, "Do they get this show in Omaha?" Steve would answer, "They see it, but they don't get it."

I had developed a small reputation from my appearances at the Ice House, and on May 6, 1969, I wrangled a meeting and auditioned in an office for Steve Allen's two producers, Elias Davis and David Pollock. They accepted me with more ease than I expected, and when I spoke with them afterward, they commented, "There seems to be a dearth of young comedians right now." I looked puzzled. I said, "That's odd, I don't think there are many at all." Their stares made me realize my blunder. I knew the word, but I had the definition backward.

For my first appearance on *The Steve Allen Show*—which was also my first appearance on television as a stand-up—I wore black pants and a bright blue marching-band coat I had picked up in a San Francisco thrift shop. Steve's introduction of me was ad-libbed perfectly. "This next young man is a comedian, and . . ." he stammered, ". . . at first you might not get it"—he stammered again—"but then you think about it for a while, and you still don't get it"—stammer, stammer—"then, you might want to come up onstage and talk to him about it."

The *Steve Allen* appearance went well—he loved the offbeat, and his cackle was enough to make any comedian feel confident. Seated on the sofa, though, I was hammered by another guest, *The Dick Van Dyke Show*'s Morey Amsterdam, for being unconventional. But I bore no grudge; I was so naive I didn't even know I had been insulted. The *Steve Allen* credit opened a few doors, and I bounced around all of the afternoon shows, juggling material, trying not to repeat myself. I developed a formula of convenience: "If I do a bit on *Merv Griffin,* which comes on at two P.M., it's okay to repeat the material on *Virginia Graham,* which comes on at four P.M. If I do a piece on *Steve Allen,* which comes on at five P.M. on Wednesdays, I can do the same bit on *Mike Douglas,* which comes on at three P.M. on Fridays." Or something like that. Through the three or four years I did these shows, I appeared probably fifty times.

I recently viewed a musty video of an appearance on *The Virginia Graham Show,* circa 1970, unseen since its airing. I looked grotesque. I had a hairdo like a helmet, which I blow-dried to a puffy bouffant, for reasons I no longer understand. I wore a frock coat and a silk shirt, and my delivery was mannered, slow, and self-aware. I had absolutely no authority. After reviewing the show, I was—especially since I was writing an autobiography documenting my success—depressed for a week. But later, searching my mind for at least one redeeming quality in the performance, I became aware that not one joke was normal, that even though I was the one who said the lines, I did not know what was coming next. The audience might have thought what I am thinking now: "Was that terrible? Or was it good?"

Weird hair on *The Virginia Graham Show.*

FROM THESE TELEVISION APPEARANCES, I got a welcome job in 1971 with Ann-Margret, five weeks opening the show for her at the International Hilton in Vegas, a huge, unfunny barn with sculptured pink cherubs hanging from the corners of the proscenium. Laughter in these poorly designed places rose a few feet into the air and dissipated like steam, always giving me the feeling I was bombing. One night, from my dressing room, I saw

123

a vision in white gliding down the hall—a tall, striking woman, moving like an apparition along the backstage corridor. It turned out to be Priscilla Presley, coming to visit Ann-Margret backstage after having seen the show. When she turned the corner, she revealed an even more indelible presence walking behind her. Elvis. Dressed in white. Jet-black hair. A diamond-studded buckle.

When Priscilla revealed Elvis to me, I was also revealed to Elvis. I'm sure he noticed that this twenty-five-year-old stick figure was frozen firmly to the ground. About to pass me by, Elvis stopped, looked at me, and said in his beautiful Mississippi drawl: "Son, you have an ob-leek sense of humor."

Later, after his visit with Ann-Margret, he stopped by my dressing room and told Bill and me that he, too, had an oblique sense of humor—which he did—but that his audience didn't get it. Then he said, "Do you want to see my guns?" After emptying the bullets into his palm, he showed us two pistols and a derringer.

Ann-Margret and her husband, Roger Smith, were, and still are, a fun and generous couple, and they provided me with work when others wouldn't. The next year they asked if I would open for Ann-Margret at the Fontainebleau Hotel in Miami Beach. I arrived at the hotel, which at the time was very old-world, with an even older clientele. I still had my helmet hair, long black frock coat, and turquoise jewelry, and I'd added a really unattractive beard. Opening night, I peeked at the audience. Older Jewish couples. I smelled disaster. Jerry Lewis once described standing backstage before a show and, listening to the tone of the audience, concluding: "I knew I was dead." I could hear the echoing rattle of forks on plates and the low, enervated dinner chitchat. I went on . . . and killed. Night after night. I was going over like it was a raucous college campus. Why? I wondered. I was baffled until Roger Smith explained it to me. "They look at you in your hippie clothes and beard and think, 'Aw, it's my son.'"

THE PLUM TELEVISION APPEARANCE during the sixties and seventies was *The Tonight Show Starring Johnny Carson.* Bob Shayne, who in the late sixties booked *The Steve Allen Show,* had moved over to *The Tonight Show* and mentioned me to its producer, Freddy De Cordova. Bob showed Freddy a kinescope (an expensive sixteen-millimeter film financed by my bank account) of my appearance on *The Steve Allen Show,* and Fred replied, "I don't think he's for us." But Bob persisted, and Johnny saw the film and said, "Let's give him a try." To close the deal, I went to NBC one afternoon and auditioned on the soundstage, in front of staff and crew, while cables were being pulled and cameras were being moved. I was booked on the show in October 1972.

There was a belief that one appearance on *The Tonight Show* made you a star. But here are the facts. The first time you do the show, nothing. The second time you do the show, nothing. The sixth time you do the show, someone

125

might come up to you and say, "Hi, I think we met at Harry's Christmas party." The tenth time you do the show, you could conceivably be remembered as being seen somewhere on television. The twelfth time you do the show, you might hear, "Oh, I know you. You're that guy."

But I didn't know that. Before the show, as I stood in the backstage darkness behind the curtain of *The Tonight Show,* hearing the muffled laughter while Johnny spoke and waiting for the tap on the shoulder that would tell me I was on, an italicized sentence ticker-taped through my head: "*I am about to do* The Tonight Show." Then I walked out onstage, started my act, and thought, "*I am doing* The Tonight Show." I finished my act and thought, "*I have just done* The Tonight Show." What happened while I was out there was very similar to an alien abduction: I remember very little of it, though I'm convinced it occurred.

I was booked back and did the show successfully several times. I was doing material from my act, best stuff first, and after two or three appearances, I realized how little best stuff I had. After I'd gone through my stage material, I started doing some nice but oddball bits such as Comedy Act for Dogs (first done on *Steve Allen*), in which I said, "A lot of dogs watch TV but there's really nothing on for them, so call your dog over and let him watch because I think you're going to see him crack up for the first time." Then I brought out four dogs "that I can perform to so I can get the timing down." While I did terrible canine-related jokes, the dogs would walk off one at a time, with the last dog lifting his leg on me. The studio audience saw several trainers out of camera range, making drastic hand signals, but the home TV audience saw only the dogs doing their canine best.

Another time I claimed that I could read from the phone book and make it funny. I opened the book and droned the names to the predictable silence, then I pretended to grow more and more desperate and began to do retro shtick such as cracking eggs on my head. I got word that Johnny was not thrilled, and I was demoted to appearing with guest hosts, which I tried not to admit to myself was a devastating blow.

I WAS GROWING FRUSTRATED with writing for television. Although the income was financing my performing career, I was marking time, and the prize of performing regularly on one of the shows was not materializing. I realized that the performers were just using my material as a starting point and, of course, I thought the better joke was to do it as written. On *The Sonny & Cher Comedy Hour*, I was thrown the occasional performing bone, appearing as a walk-on with a line or two in a sketch, but I felt no resonance from the producers or audience. There was a baffling moment when Sonny Bono and his partner, Denis Pregnolato, who were becoming showbiz entrepreneurs, approached me at work and took me aside. Sonny and Denis had seen me perform—I don't know where—and

Sonny said, "Steve, we've been watching you. We think you are the next big thing, bigger than David Brenner, bigger than Albert Brooks. We would like to work with you and develop a show for you." I nodded my excitement and never heard from them again, not one word.

In the early seventies, I had two memorable auditions. One was for Greg Garrison, the producer of *The Dean Martin Show*. The audition went like this: I did my act for his secretary, then she did it for Greg. She even borrowed a prop from me to take into his office. My other audition began with a call from a producer who told me about a sitcom pilot called *The Fireman's Ball*. "They specifically asked for you," he said. I heard this sentence as "They specifically asked *only* for you." I practiced the scene, went to the audition, and was surprised to see at least a dozen other young guys marching around a foyer holding scripts and inaudibly mouthing their lines. I didn't get hired, but the experience was significant for me. I understood I would never be hired in that situation, that the odds of confluence on a certain day of the producers' desires, my talent, and a good reading were low, and that the audition process was a dead end. I decided to leave Hollywood and go on the road.

I resigned from television writing against the advice of my agent, a man who had wisely vacuumed up all the young talent discovered by the Smothers Brothers. He said plainly, "Stick to writing." Which was a polite way of saying that my performing was headed nowhere. I took this warning with a strange delight. It was, in a way, the necessary ingredient in any young career, like when Al Jolson was told in *The Jazz Singer*, "Jolie, you'll never become a sing-gah!"

Bill McEuen had moved to Aspen, Colorado, for the skiing, and I moved to Santa Fe, New Mexico, to escape the Los Angeles smog and traffic. I was twenty-eight years old when a bleak thought occurred to me: "What if nothing happens?" I had never really imagined success; I was just trying to be a performer, but I could not see myself playing dreary nightclubs into my thirties, forties, and fifties. I would have struggled composing a real-world résumé, as my abilities were at best vague and at worst unusable. I decided to give it until I was thirty, and then I would have to figure out something else to do.

The Road

MY DEPARTURE FROM TELEVISION WRITING meant that I was now adrift. I had lost my financial support and my hyphen and now was only a comedian. A club owner in Denver, Chet Hansen, started up a small agency, and even though comedy clubs did not exist yet, he somehow produced wide-ranging bookings that involved planes, trains, and automobiles. For the next few years, I was on the road with an itinerary designed by the Marquis de Sade. But there was a sexy anonymity about the travel; I was living the folkie myth of having no ties to anyone, working small clubs and colleges in improvised folk rooms that were usually subterranean. However, the travel isolated me. Friends were available only through

131

BORN STANDING UP

costly phone calls, and contact with my parents and sister spiraled down to a pinpoint.

In this netherworld, I was free to experiment. These out-of-the-way and varied places provided a tough comedy education. There were no mentors to tell me what to do; there were no guidebooks for doing stand-up. Everything was learned in practice, and the lonely road, with no critical eyes watching, was the place to dig up my boldest, or dumbest, ideas and put them onstage. At night, preoccupied by the success or failure of that evening's show, I would return to my motel room and glumly watch the three TV channels sign off the air at eleven-thirty, knowing I had at least two more hours of ceiling staring to do before the adrenaline eased off and I could fall asleep.

While I toured around the country, Bill had found a Los Angeles agent whom we both adored: Marty Klein. Marty, who loved gold cigarette lighters, fancy eyeglasses, and quality suits, made sure I saw the old-time world of show business before it was gone, taking me to the Brown Derby restaurant in Hollywood, where the walls were lined with celebrity caricatures from the thirties and forties, and the Sands Hotel in Vegas, where the Rat Pack had cavorted. Bill was also promoting my name to record companies. A recording contract was our quest, though I secretly worried about a record's potential, as my act was becoming more and more visual. "And now," I would announce, "my impression of the Incredible Shrinking Man!" I would ask the audience to close their eyes for a

132

moment, and when they reopened them, I had raised the microphone several feet. Another bit: I would wonder what it would be like if the human body had only one arm right in the center of our chest. How would we applaud? Putting my elbow in the center of my torso, I would then slap myself in the face a dozen times.

I took on an excellent roadie, Maple Byrne, whom I met at a defunct recording studio where he lived in the echo chamber. He was a real Deadhead who had to vanish now and then to see a Grateful Dead concert. He booked my travel, set up the props, checked the sound, and ran the lights. Despite his presence, on the road I was fundamentally a loner, withdrawn and solitary, and his introduction of mournful Irish folk music into my life didn't help my mood. We would drive at night from job to job, listening to cassette tapes of the Bothy Band. Sad, lonely songs for the sad, lonely road. One of the tunes, "The Maid of Coolmore," inspired a film I wrote twelve years later, *L.A. Story*.

When necessary, I could still manage to have a personality, and sometimes I was rescued by a local girl who actually liked me. Occasionally the result was an erotic tryst enhanced by loneliness. Perhaps the women saw it as I did, an encounter free from obligation: the next day I would be gone. I had also refined my pickup technique. If I knew I would be returning to a club, I tweaked my hard-learned rule, "Never hit on a waitress the first night," to "Never hit on a waitress for six months." I came off as coolly reserved, as I would harmlessly flirt on my first visit; by my next visit, everything was in place. Soon the six months caught up with me, and I always had someone I could latch on to as I rolled from town to town.

I did have interludes of monogamy with a few women. Iris C. was an aspiring actress who, coincidentally, lived next door, which cut down on travel time for sudden sleepover urges. Chris Gooch, a fragile, ethereal blonde, seemed to float into the club I was playing, the Vanguard, in Kansas City, Missouri. We lived together in Los Angeles for a while. Sandee Oliver—her last name described the color of her skin—lived in Atlanta, and we rendezvoused in towns across America. Were they beautiful? We were all beautiful. We were in our twenties.

I alternated obscure appearances across America with higher-profile opening-act jobs at the Boarding House in San Francisco, the Troubadour in Los Angeles, and the Great Southeast Music Hall in Atlanta, where I first performed with the singer/comedian Martin Mull. Martin's wit was Sahara-dry; he performed onstage sitting on living room furniture and sang his own comic songs, with titles like "Noses Run in My Family," "I'm Everyone I Ever Loved," "(How Could I Not Miss) A Girl Your Size," and "Jesus Christ, Football Star." On opening night at the Great Southeast Music Hall, we were both nervous about meeting each other. I was sitting in my open dressing room when Martin walked by, carrying his stage clothes on a hanger. Unsure whether to say something to me, he kept going. After a few steps, I called out, "Nice meeting you, too." We've been friends ever since.

Martin suggested me to his recording label, Capricorn Records. The response from the producer, Phil Walden, was "Too visual; he's too visual." Later, after my first record shipped platinum (meaning it had already sold a million before it was released), Phil called up Martin: "Hey, Mull, you know any more of those visual guys?"

Yes, I suppose I was visual.

In Los Angeles, the Troubadour was my hangout, and the girls did indeed get prettier as closing time neared, or maybe it was I who got prettier to them. The Troubadour's regulars included Michael Nesmith, Jackson Browne, Joni Mitchell, Glenn Frey, Don Henley, and all the others whose music was a siren call to a perceptive record executive named David Geffen. One week I opened the show for Linda Ronstadt; she sang barefoot on a raised stage and wore a silver lamé dress that stopped a millimeter below her panties, causing the floor of the Troubadour to be slick with drool. Linda and I saw each other for a while, but I was so intimidated by her talent and street smarts that, after the ninth date, she finally said, "Steve, do you often date girls and not try to sleep with them?" We parted chaste.

One late night I was lingering in the bar and talking to Glenn Frey, who was just leaving his duo, Longbranch Pennywhistle. He said he was considering a name for his new five-man group. "What is it?" I said. He said, "Eagles." I said, "You mean, *the* Eagles." He said, "No, Eagles." I said, "You mean, *the* Eagles?" He said, "No, I mean Eagles." The name of the group remains, of course, Eagles.

Mixed reviews continued. At the end of my closing-night show at the Troubadour, I stood onstage and took out five bananas. I peeled them, put one on my head, one in each pocket, and squeezed one in each hand. Then I read the last line of my latest bad review: "Sharing the bill with Poco this week is comedian Steve

Linda onstage at the Troubadour.

Martin . . . his twenty-five-minute routine failed to establish any comic identity that would make the audience remember him or the material." Then I walked off the stage.

IN CASE I AD-LIBBED something wonderful, I began taping my shows with a chintzy cassette recorder. I had a

137

The Troubadour, 1968.

routine in which I played a smug party guy with a drink in his hand. When the bit started, the waitresses brought me a glass of wine that I would use as a prop. When that glass was empty, they would bring me another. One night I listened to the tape and could hear myself slurring. I never had a drink before or during a show again.

I made another correction based on the tapes. Texas-born and California-raised, I realized I was dropping my "ings"—runnin', walkin', and talkin'—and I worked like Eliza Doolittle to elevate my speech. It was a struggle; at first I thought I sounded pretentious and unnatural. But I did it, though now and then I slip back into my natural way of speakin'.

THE CONSISTENT WORK enhanced my act. I learned a lesson: It was easy to be great. Every entertainer has a night when everything is clicking. These nights are accidental and statistical: Like lucky cards in poker, you can count on them occurring over time. What was hard was to be *good*, consistently good, night after night, no matter what the abominable circumstances. Performing in so many varied situations made every predicament manageable, from Toronto, where I performed next to an active salad bar, to the well-paying but soul-killing Playboy Clubs, where I was almost but not quite able to go over. But as I continued to work, my material grew; I came up with odd little gags such as "How many people have never raised their hands before?" I was now capable of doing two different twenty-five-minute sets per evening, in case some of the audience stayed over for the second show.

Because I was generally unknown, in the smaller venues I was free to gamble with material, and there were a few evenings when crucial mutations affected my developing act. At Vanderbilt University in Nashville, I played for approximately a hundred students in a classroom with a stage at one end. I did the show, and it went fine. However, when it was over, something odd happened. The audience didn't leave. The stage had no

139
—

wings, no place for me to go, but I still had to pack up my props. I indicated that the show had ended, but they just sat there, even after I said flatly, "It's over." They thought this was all part of the act, and I couldn't convince them otherwise. Then I realized there were no exits from the stage and that the only way out was to go through the audience. So I kept talking. I passed among them, ad-libbing comments along the way. I walked out into the hallway, trying to finish the show, but they followed me there, too. A reluctant pied piper, I went outside onto the campus, and they stayed right behind me. I came across a drained swimming pool. I asked the audience to get into it—"Everybody into the pool!"—and they did. Then I said I was going to swim across the top of them, and the crowd knew exactly what to do: I was passed hand over hand as I did the crawl. That night I went to bed feeling I had entered new comic territory. My show was becoming something else, something free and unpredictable, and the doing of it thrilled me, because each new performance brought my view of comedy into sharper focus.

The act tightened. It became more physical. It was true I couldn't sing or dance, but singing *funny* and dancing *funny* were another matter. All I had to do was free my mind and start. I would abruptly stop the show and sing loudly, in my best lounge-singer voice, "Grampa bought a rubber." Walking up to the mike, I would say, "Here's something you don't often see," and I'd spread my mouth

wide with my fingers and leap into the air while screaming. Or, invoking a remembered phrase from the magic
shop, I would shout, "Uh-oh, I'm getting happy feet!" and
then dance uncontrollably across the stage, my feet
moving like Balla's painting of a futurist dog, while my
face told the audience that I wanted to stop but couldn't.
Closing the show, I'd say, "I'd like to thank each and every
one of you for coming here tonight." Then I would walk
into the audience and, in fast motion, thank everyone in-
dividually. My set lists, written on notepad paper and kept
in my coat pocket, were becoming drenched with sweat.

The new physicality brought an unexpected element
into the act: precision. My routines wove the verbal with
the physical and I found pleasure trying to bring them in
line. Each spoken idea had to be physically expressed as
well. My teenage attempt at a magician's grace was being
transformed into an awkward comic grace. I felt as though
every part of me was working. Some nights it seemed that
it wasn't the line that got the laugh, but the tip of my finger.
I tried to make voice and posture as crucial as jokes and
gags. Silence, too, brought forth laughs. Sometimes I
would stop and, saying nothing, stare at the audience with
a look of mock disdain, and on a good night, it struck us all
as funny, as if we were in on the joke even though there
was no actual joke we could point to. Finally, I understood
the cummings quote I had puzzled over in college: "Like
the burlesque comedian, I am abnormally fond of that precision which creates movement." Precision was moving

141

the plot forward, was filling every moment with content, was keeping the audience engaged.

The act was becoming simultaneously smart and stupid. My version of smart was to imbue a hint of conceptualism into the whole affair: My sing-along had some funny lyrics, but it was also impossible to sing along with. My version of stupid: "Oh, gosh! My shoelace is untied!" I would bend down, see that my shoelace was not untied, stand up, and say, "Oh, I love playing jokes on myself!"

I had the plumber joke, which was impossible to understand even for plumbers:

"Okay, I don't like to gear my material to the audience, but I'd like to make an exception, because I was told that there is a convention of plumbers in town this week— I understand about thirty of them came down to the show tonight—so before I came out, I worked up a joke especially for the plumbers. Those of you who aren't plumbers probably won't get this and won't think it's funny, but I think those of you who are plumbers will really enjoy this.

"This lawn supervisor was out on a sprinkler maintenance job, and he started working on a Findlay sprinkler head with a Langstrom seven-inch gangly wrench. Just then this little apprentice leaned over and said, 'You can't work on a Findlay sprinkler head with a Langstrom seven-inch wrench.' Well, this infuriated the supervisor, so he went and got volume fourteen of the Kinsley manual, and he reads to him and says, 'The Langstrom seven-inch wrench can be used with the Findlay sprocket.' Just then the little apprentice leaned over and says, 'It says sprocket, not socket!'

[*Worried pause.*]

"Were these plumbers supposed to be here this show?"

One of my favorite bits to perform evolved at the Troubadour in Los Angeles. After I finished my act, I would go up to the sound booth, where there was an open mike out of sight of the audience, and say, "They can't hear me out there, can they?" "No," the coached soundman would reply. Then I would say, "What a bunch of assholes. Where can I get some pot?" I would continue my arrogant comments until the bit ran dry.

On the road, the daylight hours moved slowly, filled with aimless wandering through malls and museums. But at night, onstage, *every second mattered. Every gesture mattered.* The few hours I spent in the clubs and coffeehouses seemed like a full existence.

When I had new material to try, I would break it down into its smallest elements, literally a gesture or a few words, then sneak it into the act in its shortest form, being careful not to disrupt the flow of the show. If it worked, the next night I would add the next discreet packet until the bit either filled out or died. I can remember bailing out of a bit because I didn't want to be trapped in it for the next five minutes. The easiest way was to pretend I'd gotten distracted by something and then completely change tack.

Around this time I smelled a rat. The rat was the Age of Aquarius. Though the era's hairstyles, clothes, and lingo still dominated youth culture, by 1972 the movement was tired and breaking down. Drugs had killed people, and so had Charles Manson. The war in Vietnam was near its official end, but its devastating losses had embittered and divided America. The political scene was exhausting, and many people, including me, were alienated from government. Murders and beatings at campus protests weren't going to be resolved by sticking a daisy into the pointy end of a rifle. Flower Power was waning, but no one wanted to believe it yet, because we had all invested so much of ourselves in its message. Change was imminent.

I cut my hair, shaved my beard, and put on a suit. I stripped the act of all political references, which I felt was an act of defiance. To politics I was saying, "I'll get along without you very well. It's time to be funny." Overnight, I was no longer at the tail end of an old movement but at the front end of a new one. Instead of looking like another freak with a crazy act, I now looked like a visitor from the straight world who had gone seriously awry. The act's unbridled nonsense was taking the audience—and me—on a wild ride, and my growing professionalism, founded on thousands of shows, created a subliminal sense of authority that made the audience feel they weren't being had.

Between 1973 and 1975, my one-man vaudeville show turned fully toward the surreal. I was linking the unlinkable, blending economy and extravagance, non sequiturs with the conventional. I was all over the place, sluicing the gold from the dirt, honing the edge that confidence

Cut my hair, put on a suit.

brings. I cannot say I was fearless, because I was acutely aware of any audience drift, and if I sensed trouble, I would swerve around it. I believed it was important to be funny now, while the audience was watching, but it was also important to be funny later, when the audience was home and thinking about it. I didn't worry if a bit got no response, as long as I believed it had enough strangeness to linger. My friend Rick Moranis (whose imitation of Woody Allen was so precise that it made

145

Woody seem like a faker) called my act's final manifestation "anti-comedy."

ONE WEEKEND I WAS PLAYING at the Boarding House in San Francisco, opening for a talented mountain-man folksinger named U. Utah Philips. My shows went well, very well. I waited for the reviews, but there was scant mention. Five paragraphs devoted to Utah, and a line or two about me. I noticed it in Los Angeles, too, at the Troubadour. Large thoughtful reviews of the headliner, little or nothing about the opening act. I was learning something about the audience and critics: They aren't there to see the opener. The implied power of the headliner cannot be challenged by a pleasant opening act. But I was not a headliner; I had no following, and I was nearing my arbitrary thirty-year cutoff point. I was consistently appearing on TV shows, even *The Tonight Show,* but what filled folk clubs was underground word of mouth, usually generated by record sales, not late-night TV watchers. I decided to headline only, win or lose. This meant no more Boarding House, no more Troubadour. It meant that the size of the house I could play would drop significantly. I held firmly to this idea, and within the year, I was completely broke.

I called the comedian David Brenner for advice. David was successfully guest-hosting *The Tonight Show* and filling theaters and clubs. Our paths had crossed, and we had exchanged phone numbers. I explained that I was getting jobs, but the travel costs were killing me. If I got five hundred dollars for an appearance, it would cost me three hundred just to get to it. He told me the deal he always proposed to club owners. He would take the door, and they would take the bar. He said he would hire someone to stand at the entrance with a mechanical counter to make sure he wasn't being cheated. I didn't have the chutzpah to "audit" this way, but otherwise it seemed like a fair gambit. I wanted to either get in or get out of the business. I would be paid according to how many people I drew, and that satisfied my Protestant inclination to earn my keep.

I proposed this deal immediately to an amenable club owner—after all, he didn't have to put any money up front—and in October 1973 I got a job at Bubbas in Coconut Grove, Florida, now vanished into the folkie sinkhole. It held about ninety people, seated in the worst configuration a club could have. Directly in front of the stage were seats for about ten; extending to the performer's right were the other eighty seats. There was no depth at all, and most of the audience saw only a side view of the performer. These lopsided arrangements were never conducive to laughter because the audience couldn't quite unite. I arrived a day early, in time to see the closing night of another performer, a comedian who, at least in the show I saw, lifted a line or two from Lenny Bruce. Doing other people's material was on my taboo list, but he was a nice

147

guy and still funny, and when we met after the show, he knew that I knew that he knew that I knew, but we ignored it.

The next night I opened, and business was slow. However, I was ready to put my experience at Vanderbilt into effect. The Florida night was balmy and I was able to take the audience outside into the street and roam around in front of the club, making wisecracks. I didn't quite know how to end the show. First I started hitchhiking; a few cars passed me by. Then a taxi came by. I hailed it and got in. I went around the block, returned and waved at the audience—still standing there—then drove off and never came back. The next morning I received one of the most crucial reviews of my life. John Huddy, the respected entertainment critic for *The Miami Herald,* devoted his entire column to my act. Without qualification, he raved in paragraph after paragraph, starting with HE PARADES HIS HILARITY RIGHT OUT INTO THE STREET, and concluded with: "Steve Martin is the brightest, cleverest, wackiest new comedian around." Oh, and the next night the club owner made sure all tabs had been paid before I took the audience outside.

Roger Smith had told me that when he came to Hollywood from El Paso to be an actor, he had given himself six months to get work. The time elapsed, and he packed up his car, which was parked on Sunset Boulevard, where his final audition would be. Informed that he was not right for the job, he went out and started up his car. He was about to

BUBBAS

FINE·FOOD BEER WINE

2990 Grand Avenue
Coconut Grove

for reservations
call 444-9582

Playbill~ oct. 1-13

live music
mon. thru sat.!

Steve Goodman
oct. 1~6 (mon.~sat.)

City of New Orleans has been called "the best damned train song ever written" ~ and Steve Goodman wrote it. He's one of the current "Chicago Gang" of singers/writers, and his music is that special blend of down-home country fun and sophisticated blues called urban folk. Steve records for Buddah Records (Kristofferson produced his first album). Come in and hear him~ he's something special.

Vince Martin
oct. 1-2 (mon.~tues.)

a Coconut Grove legend ~ back again, better than ever!

Teri De Sario
oct. 8~9 (mon.~tues.)

young and fresh and beautiful and very talented ~ you'll fall in love with Teri ~ and her music!

Steve Martin
oct. 8-13 (mon.~sat.)

credits: Midnight Special
In Concert
Tonight (Johnny Carson)
Merv Griffin Show
Mike Douglas Show
The Bitter End (New York)
The Ice House (Pasadena)
~ he's also written for ~
Sonny and Cher
The Smothers Brothers
Glen Campbell

~just your ordinary banjo magic act.

Mike & Barbara Smith~
oct. 3-6, 10-13
(wed.~sat. both weeks)

if you've caught the shows at Bubba's recently, you probably know and love Mike and Barbara already~ if not, you're in for a real treat! You won't find better entertainment anywhere ~as good~maybe but not better!

~shows: mon.~fri. 8:30 & 11:00, sat. 9:30 & 12:00 ~

The flyer at Bubbas. Steve Goodman played the week before me, and later he became a sensational opening act for my show.

pull away, away to El Paso, when there was a knock on his windshield. "We saw you in the hall. Would you like to read for us?" the voice said. He was then cast as the star of the hit television show 77 *Sunset Strip*. My review from John Huddy was the knock on the window just as I was about to get in my car and drive to a metaphorical El Paso, and it gave me a psychological boost that allowed me to nix my arbitrarily chosen thirty-year-old deadline to reenter the conventional world. The next night and the rest of the week the club was full, all ninety seats. Three thousand miles away, Bill McEuen took the review and waved it in the face of every record executive in Hollywood, with no bites.

I continued to appear on *The Tonight Show*, always with a guest host, doing material I was developing on the road. Then I got a surprise note from Bob Shayne: "We had a meeting with Johnny yesterday, told him you'd been a smash twice with guest hosts, and he agrees you should be back on with him. So I think that hurdle is over." In September 1974 I was booked on the show with Johnny.

This was welcome news. Johnny had comic savvy. The daytime television hosts, with the exception of Steve Allen, did not come from comedy. I had a small routine (suggested by my writer friend Michael Elias) that went like this: "I just bought a new car. It's a prestige car. A '65 Greyhound bus. You know you can get up to thirty tons of luggage in one of those babies? I put a lot of money into it. . . . I put a new dog on the side. And if I said to a girl,

'Do you want to get in the backseat?' I had, like, forty chances." Etc. Not great, but at the time it was working. It did, however, require all the pauses and nuance that I could muster. On *The Merv Griffin Show* I decided to use it for panel, meaning I would sit with Merv and pretend it was just chat. I began: "I just bought a new car. A '65 Greyhound bus." Merv, friendly as ever, interrupted and said, "Now, why on earth would you buy a Greyhound bus?" I had no prepared answer; I just stared at him. I thought, "Oh my God, because it's a comedy routine." And the bit was dead. Johnny, on the other hand, was the comedian's friend. He waited; he gave you your timing. He lay back and stepped in like Ali, not to knock you out but to set you up. He struggled with you, too, and sometimes saved you.

I was able to maintain a personal relationship with Johnny over the next thirty years, at least as personal as he or I could make it, and I was flattered that he came to respect my comedy. On one of my appearances, after he had done a solid impression of Goofy the cartoon dog, he leaned over to me during a commercial and whispered prophetically, "You'll use everything you ever knew." He was right; twenty years later I did my teenage rope tricks in the movie *¡Three Amigos!*

Once Johnny joked in his monologue, "I announced that I was going to write my autobiography, and nineteen publishers went out and copyrighted the title *Cold and Aloof.*" This was the common perception of him. But

151
—

Johnny was not aloof; he was polite. He did not presume intimate relationships where there were none; he took time, and with time grew trust. He preserved his dignity by maintaining the personality that was appropriate for him.

Johnny enjoyed the delights of split-second timing, of watching a comedian squirm and then rescue himself, of the surprises that can arise in the seconds of desperation when the comedian senses that his joke might fall to silence. Johnny was inclined toward the sciences, especially astronomy, and his Nebraskan pragmatism—and knowledge of magicians' tricks—guaranteed that the occultists, future predictors, spoon benders, and mind readers never left his show without a challenge. He knew the difference between the pompous ass and the nervous actress and who should receive appropriate consideration. He enjoyed the unflappable grannies who sewed log-cabin quilts, as well as the Vegas pro who machine-gunned the audience into hysterical fits. Johnny hosted authors, children, intellects, and nitwits and treated them all well, and he served the audience with his curiosity and tolerance. He gave each guest—like the ideal America would—the benefit of the doubt: You're nuts, but you're welcome here.

For my first show back, I chose to do a bit I had developed years earlier at the Ice House. I speed-talked a Vegas nightclub act in two minutes. Appearing on the show was Sammy Davis, Jr., who, while still performing energeti-

152

STEVE MARTIN

cally, had also become a historic showbiz figure. I was whizzing along, singing a four-second version of "Ebb Tide," then saying at lightning speed, "Frank Sinatra personal friend of mine Sammy Davis Jr. personal friend of mine Steve Martin I'm a personal friend of mine too and now a little dancin'!" I started a wild flail, which I must say was pretty funny, when a showbiz miracle occurred. The camera cut away to a dimly lit Johnny, precisely as he whirled up from his chair, doubling over with laughter. Suddenly, subliminally, I was endorsed. At the end of the act, Sammy came over and hugged me. I felt like I hadn't been hugged since I was born.

This was my sixteenth appearance on the show, and

On *The Tonight Show* with Johnny and Sammy.

the first one I could really call a smash. The next day, elated by my success, I walked into an antique store on La Brea. The woman behind the counter looked at me.

"Are you that boy who was on *The Tonight Show* last night?"

"Yes," I said.

"Yuck!" she blurted out.

Breakthrough

I DID HAVE A TINY BIT of drawing power, generated through my daytime television appearances and my growing presence on *The Tonight Show*, but mostly my name was a rumor. My dubious status as a headliner led me to a tiny pie slice of a folk club in Greenwich Village, the Metro. Now *I* had an opening act. Still, no one showed up to see me and a new duo, Lindsey Buckingham and Stevie Nicks. I told the club owner that he could let me go if he wanted, that I wouldn't hold him to his contract. He said he wanted me to stay . . . until the next night, when again no one showed up. We parted with a handshake.

In March 1975 my agent, Marty Klein, secured a job in San Francisco, two weeks headlining the Playboy Club for fifteen hundred dollars per week. A big payday, and I was desperate for money. Playboy Clubs always made me nervous. I never seemed to do well in them, but I had no choice. Opening night was on a Monday, which was already unusual; clubs were usually closed on Mondays. I stood at the back of the club and checked out the capacity crowd. Amazed, I said to one of the musicians leaning against the wall, "We got a nice house out there." An odd look crossed the musician's face. "Yeah," he said mysteriously.

156

After I was introduced as Steve Miller, I walked out

onstage and saw a sea of Japanese faces. I attempted a few lines; nothing came back except nice smiles. No one spoke English. It turned out that the bus tours offered a nightclub as part of their packages, but on Mondays the Playboy Club was the only one open, so every foreign tour group was herded into this showroom. Now I understood the musician's wry grin. I gamely went forward, not doing badly because the audience was kind and polite, and my balloon-animal and magic act went over well because it was visual and antic. The next night I went on for the regular audience: death. Comedy Death. Which is worse than regular death. I sank low and, in spite of my declining financial situation, called Marty, saying, "You've got to get me out of here." He did, and I went back the next night to collect my things. My clothes had been stolen. A week later, I took out a bank loan of five thousand dollars.

The euphoria from my week at Bubbas in Coconut Grove and my nice score on *The Tonight Show* had dissipated, and I was marooned in the depression that followed my flop at the Playboy Club. In June 1975 I was booked into the frighteningly named Hub Pub Club, in Winston-Salem, North Carolina. The Hub Pub Club, located in a shopping mall, was trying to be a fancy spot for gentlemen, but the liquor laws in North Carolina limited attendance at nightclubs to members only. About the worst things an entertainer can hear are "members only" and "group tours." While I was onstage doing my act to churchlike silence, a guy said to his date, loud enough

157

that we all heard it, "I don't understand any of this." And at that moment, neither did I.

In spite of the gloom, I had a premonition of success, and in January 1975 I started a short-lived diary. It surprises me that a diary meant to chronicle an important year in my life could contain so many negative passages. My entry for the Hub Pub Club started this way: "This town smells like a cigarette." Then I sank a bit lower: "My material seems so old. The audience indulged me during the second show." Then I really started wallowing in it: "My act might have well been in a foreign language . . . my act has no ending." Next I degenerated into my version of Kurtz's lament, "The horror, the horror," from *Heart of Darkness*: "My new material is hopelessly poor. My act is simply not good enough—it's not even bad."

However, there was one, sole, positive entry in my journal that week. It related to a lonely-guy phone call I had made to a new acquaintance, Victoria Dailey. Victoria was a young rare-book-and-print dealer in Los Angeles whom I had stumbled upon in my collecting quests, and who had her wits about her in the same way that Oscar Wilde had his wits about him. I must have had an intuition about the future depth and scope of our relationship, as I called her long distance from a motel phone, which in those days cost about a million dollars a minute. While traffic whizzed by outside the gray motel room, I churned out my Winston-Salem stories with the same toxicity as the R. J. Reynolds company churned out cigarettes. Victoria used her refined sense of artistic ethics to talk me down from my metaphorical window ledge, and over the next few years we cemented an enduring relationship that has been complex and rewarding. We have been connected over the past thirty years intellectually, aesthetically, and seemingly, gravitationally. In my latest conversation with her, I complimented her recent essay on early Southern California history. I said, "Do you realize you're going to be studied one day?" She replied, "Only one day?"

Two months after Winston-Salem everything was about to change. A few blocks away from San Francisco's Playboy Club, where I had died so swiftly, was a very different kind of club, one that booked current music acts, and where the waitresses were sexy but didn't have to wear bunny outfits. I had played the Boarding House before, but only as a developing opening act. The owner, David Allen, saw that things were different, both with my act and with its reception, and he was ready to try the new and improved me. In August 1975 I was booked to headline, evidence that the Boarding House and the Playboy Club did not speak to each other. My years on the road had produced a change I had only dreamed of earlier: I now had four hours of material from which to pick and choose, and there was more to come.

I opened at the Boarding House on a Tuesday evening to a fair-sized crowd. Headlining there, in friendly and familiar San Francisco, where I had established some kind of beachhead, filled me and the audience with confidence. They had paid to see this show, this particular show, and I was inspired to push the limits even further. What had been deadly at the Playboy Clubs was lively with a younger crowd. I wanted the audience to leave with the feeling that something had happened. The first few minutes into the show, I began to strum the banjo, singing a song that had no particular tune or rhyme:

We're having some fun
We've got music and laughter
And wonderful times

That's so important in today's world

Oh yeah.

It's so hard to laugh
It seems that short of tripping a nun
Nothing is funny anymore

But you know
I see people going to college
For fourteen years
Studying to be doctors and lawyers
And I see people going to work
At the drugstore at 7:30 every morning

To sell Flair pens

Onstage at the Boarding House.

But the most amazing thing to me is
I get paid
For doing
This.

Midweek, before the show, I told the spotlight operator not to change the light no matter how urgently I asked him to do it. Then, onstage, I made a small request for some mood lighting, a blue spotlight. The light stayed white. I slowly grew more and more angry. "Please," I said, "I would really like a blue spot. It's for the mood-lighting thing." I got very serious and murmured under my breath, "I can't even get a light change." John McEuen was sitting in the light booth that night. He said the operator began to believe me and moved to change the spot, but John stopped him. Soon it became clear that it was a gag, because I was reaching new levels of anger as I said how disgusting it was "that I, this entertainer who keeps *giving, and giving and giving, and keeps on giving,* can't seem to get a simple blue spotlight!" The bit ended at an exaggerated level of madness, with me screaming another phrase from my past, *"Well, excuuuse me,"* turning four syllables into about twenty. The audience response was nice enough, but I was surprised weeks later when I heard this expression coming back to me on the streets. It surprised me even more when in another few years it became a ubiquitous catchphrase.

Toward the end of the Boarding House show, I stepped off the stage, saying: "I just want to come down into the audience with my people . . . DON'T TOUCH ME!" I took them into the lobby, where there was an old-fashioned grand staircase. One of the doormen, a very likable and funny guy named Larry who had seen my show all week, happened to come in from the street, carrying a pair of pants on a hanger fresh from the dry cleaner. I looked at him, and he looked back, knowing he was in for it. He had a great sense of humor and didn't mind a bit. I said disdainfully, "Oh, it's Cleanpants. Mr. Cleanpants. You think your pants are so CLEAN. Well, CLEANPANTS, we don't need your type around here. . . . WAIT, CLEANPANTS . . . where ya going? You think you don't need us because your PANTS ARE SO CLEAN?" A better comic foil could not have been found; I still can see Larry standing there holding his dry cleaning and accepting the fake lambasting with bemused patience. And the audience, crowded together in the stairwell and mezzanine, ate it up.

MY SISTER, MELINDA, had gotten married and was raising her two children in San Jose, an hour's drive from San Francisco. My communication with her over the past decade had been minimal. She had made efforts to connect, but my travel kept sweeping me away, and I was most comfortable in the world I had made, detached from home ties. When I first became an uncle, I could have used a self-help book, *So Now You're an Uncle*. Melinda showed up at one of these Boarding House performances, and we visited after the show. It turned out she had been proudly monitoring my career from a distance, saving reviews and magazine stories, but our relationship, because of my familial ineptness, remained awkward and was not yet ready to bloom.

Bill McEuen dragged his Nagra up to San Francisco and started taping my shows in hopes of crafting a record from the material. John Wasserman, the critic at the *San Francisco Chronicle,* offered a rave of the Boarding House appearance that was so enticing it made *me* want to see the show. At the end of the week, I was handed my percentage of the gate, an envelope containing forty-five hundred dollars in cash, a sum I had never seen in one place before, much less in my needy and greedy palm. I walked home in the dark toward my room at the Hotel Commodore— still lugging my banjo, which I never let out of my sight— and fortunately, I was not mugged. There was something about that walk in the night that recalled my contemplative mood of nine years earlier, when I sat in darkness, just a few miles away at the Coffee Gallery, with absolutely no prospects. But now I was about to enter a phase of my life when three things would occur: I would earn money; I would grow to be famous; and I would be the funniest I ever was.

AFTER THE BOARDING HOUSE GIG, I was booked into a club in Nashville called the Exit/In. It was a low-ceilinged box, painted black inside, with two noisy smoke eaters hanging from the ceiling, to no avail. The dense secondhand smoke was being inhaled and exhaled, making it thirdhand and fourthhand smoke. The stage was perfectly situated in the corner of the room.

When I was performing, I could touch the ceiling with my hand, and I had to be careful when jumping onstage not to knock myself out. I was selling tickets without the usual requirement of hit records. The audience was there by word of mouth only, so everything they saw me do was new. The room seated about two hundred and fifty, and the shows were oversold, riotous and packed tight, which verified a growing belief of mine about comedy: The more physically uncomfortable the audience, the bigger the laughs. I continued closing the show by performing outside, which had an auxiliary effect of emptying out the house so the second show could begin. One night at the Exit/In I took the crowd down the street to a McDonald's and ordered three hundred hamburgers to go, then quickly changed it to one bag of fries. Another night, I took them to a club across the street and we watched another act. I was a new-enough performer that there was no overblown celebrity worship, which meant I could do the show and carouse in the streets, uninterrupted by ill-timed requests for autographs or photos. Even though I had done the act hundreds of times, it became new to me this hot, muggy week in Nashville. The disparate elements I'd begun with ten years before had become unified; my road experience had made me tough as steel, and I had total command of my material. But most important, I felt really, really funny.

. . .

I MOVED TO ASPEN, COLORADO, to be closer to my pals Bill McEuen and the Dirt Band. It was there, on the night of October 11, 1975, that I turned on the TV and watched the premier episode of *Saturday Night Live*. "Fuck," I thought, "they did it." The new comedy had been brought to the airwaves in New York by people I didn't know, and they were incredibly good at it, too. The show was a heavy blow to my inner belief that I alone was leading the cavalry and carrying the new comedy flag. *Saturday Night Live* and I, however, were destined to meet.

My performing roll continued. Dave Felton, a highly regarded rock-and-roll journalist, interviewed me for an article in *Rolling Stone*. He did a perceptive job of quoting my act verbatim, using pauses, italics, and sudden jumps into all capital letters. It read funny, even the visual stuff, and rather than kill the act through exposure, he made it a necessity to see in person. Felton wrote, "This isn't comedy; it's campfire recreation for the bent at heart. It's a laugh-along for loonies. Disneyland on acid." On the strength of everything that was happening, Bill McEuen closed a record deal with an uneasy Warner Bros. He took the Boarding House recordings up to his studio in Aspen and began editing them.

I was still adding to the show. My Ramblin' Guy persona had been inspired, way back, by the folksinger Ramblin' Jack Elliott's outlaw stance, then reinforced by the Allman Brothers' hit "Ramblin' Man" and even Joni

Mitchell's "He's a rambler and a gambler and a sweet-talkin' ladies man." It seemed like all the sexy guys were ramblers! I would sing: "I'M RA-uh-AM-uh-AM-uh-AM . . . [long pause] . . . BLIN'!" I liked to give myself heroic qualities that were obviously delusional. I started saying with mock self-importance, "I'm so wild." Then "I'm a wild and crazy guy." Which actually was a bailout if a bit didn't work. The piece developed into this: "Yes . . . I am . . . a wild and craaaazy guy . . . the kind of guy who might like to do annnaything . . . at any time . . . to drink champagne at three A.M. or maybe . . . at four A.M. . . . eat a live chipmunk . . . or maybe even . . . [excitedly] . . . WEAR TWO SOCKS ON ONE FOOT."

Forces converged. The article in *Rolling Stone*, my live performances, appearances on *The Tonight Show*, a modestly produced one-man show on the new and experimental network HBO, and intriguing reviews and press made audiences ignite. The confluence that I had doubted would ever happen through auditions for sitcoms was now happening outside of Hollywood's control. My audience was developing more like a rock-and-roll band's than a comedian's: I was underground and on the road.

Outside of the big cities, I was playing concerts seating about five hundred people, a small number, but they were avid. Aggressive fans, sometimes wearing arrows through their heads or balloon hats, were gathering outside the stage door after the shows, and I had to have a guard walk me safely to my car. After a show at a college in Boise,

Idaho, I said to the two student escorts, "Stand close, I'll sign a few autographs, but we should keep moving toward the car." I pushed open the stage door. A rush of Idaho silence. Nobody. Nothing but twinkling stars. Idaho hadn't gotten the word yet. The two students looked at me with disgust.

Some promoters got on board and booked me into a theater in Dallas. Before the show I asked one of them, "How many people are out there?" "Two thousand," he said. Two thousand? How could there be two thousand? That night I did my usual bit of taking people outside, but it was starting to get dangerous and difficult. First, people were standing in the streets, where they could be hit by a car. Second, only a small number of the audience could hear or see me (could Charlton Heston really have been audible when he was addressing a thousand extras?). Third, it didn't seem as funny or direct with so many people; I reluctantly dropped it from my repertoire.

I now had the luxury of performing only one show per night, which meant that after a dozen years of two, three, and even five shows per day, I no longer had to include a weak bit in order to fill time. I cut lines that I loved but which rarely worked, such as:

"I think communication is so firsbern."

Or:

"I'm so depressed today. I just found out this 'death thing' applies to me."

168

And:

"I have no fear, no fear at all. I wake up, and I have no fear. I go to bed without fear. Fear, fear, fear, fear. Yes, 'fear' is a word that is not in my vocabulary."

Or this weird one:

"I just found out I'm vain. I thought that song was about me."

I continued doing *The Tonight Show* and performing in concert. Before a show in Milwaukee, I asked the promoter, "How many are out there?" Three thousand. Three thousand? It didn't seem possible. I worried about being seen at such distances—this was a small comedy act. For visibility, I bought a white suit to wear onstage. I was conflicted because the white suit had already been used by entertainers, including John Lennon. I was afraid it might seem derivative, but I stayed with it for practical reasons, and it didn't seem to matter to the audience or critics. The suit was made of gabardine, which always stayed fresh and flowed smoothly with my body. It got noticed in the press because it was three-piece, which appeared to be a symbol of conservatism, but I really wore the vest so my shirt would stay tucked into my pants. How could I "look better than they do" if my shirt was blousing out between my belt and my suit button? I was now coming up with jokes about the increased size of the house. My opening was the magic dime trick, in which I would claim to change the date of a dime. Then I would ask the back row what they'd paid to get in. They would shout it out, and I would laugh hysterically, implying that they were getting screwed.

169

Lorne Michaels, the producer of *SNL*, inquired about my hosting the show. Yes and yes, I said. I flew to New York a few days early, and Lorne walked me into the busy studio on Saturday afternoon. Gilda Radner's cheery lilt and Laraine Newman's alto voice crisscrossed as they rehearsed a sketch. Chevy Chase noodled on a piano in a corner. Danny Aykroyd and John Belushi, one a virtuoso and one a hurricane, energetically entertained each other while the cameras swung around the studio, and the dominant sound was the resonance of Danny's big laugh. Belushi turned out to be the nicest rowdy person I ever met. Both scary and down-to-earth, he once told me, "I never yell at the staff, only the department heads."

In Lorne's office later that day, the leather-clad Danny Aykroyd told me he had been up all night riding his motorcycle, and when it had stalled at four A.M., he had thumbed a ride. When the car got up to speed, the driver pushed him out of the moving vehicle, and he rolled onto the rainy streets of Manhattan. I pictured Danny bouncing down the wet pavement and then said the only thing that came to mind. I asked him if he wanted to go to Saks and shop for clothes. He said, as friendly as he could, "Uh, man, that's not my thing." We liked each other, but we were different.

I first appeared on *Saturday Night Live* in October 1976. I felt powerful butterflies just prior to being introduced, especially when I reminded myself that it was live, and anything that went wrong stayed wrong. But it is possible to will confidence. My consistent performing schedule had kept me sharp; it would have been difficult to blow it. I did two monologues straight out of my act; some sketches, including *Jeopardy! 1999* (remember, this was 1976); and a spoof commercial where I pitched a dog that was also a watch, called Fido-Flex. The show turned out well, though I didn't realize how well. The next Monday I had a concert in Madison, Wisconsin. It would be my first show after the *SNL* appearance. "How many are out there?" I asked. Six thousand. Six thousand? At least twice the normal. I walked onstage and was greeted with a roar of such intensity that I remember feeling both pleasure and fear. In response to the deafening approval, I was, like an athlete at the college play-offs, flooded with adrenaline. I made quick adjustments for the thundering cheers and the increased audience size. I bore down. My physicality intensified and compressed—smaller gestures had greater meaning—and my comedy became more potent as I settled deeper into my own body. I opened the show with this line: "I have decided to give the greatest performance of my life! Oh, wait, sorry, that's tomorrow night."

My fame knocked on my parents' door. They couldn't help hearing about their son. My father, though, was not impressed. After my first appearance on *Saturday Night Live,* he wrote a bad review of me in his newsletter for the Newport Beach Association of Realtors, of which he was president: "His performance did nothing to further his career." Later, shamefaced, my father told me that his best friend had come into his office holding the newsletter, placed it on his desk, and shaken his head sternly, indicating a wordless "This is wrong." I believe my father didn't like what I was doing in my work and was embarrassed by it. Perhaps he thought his friends were embarrassed by it, too, and the review was to indicate that he was not sanctioning this new comedy. Later, he gave an interview in a newspaper in which he said, "I think *Saturday Night Live* is the most horrible thing on television." I suppressed anything I felt about his comments because I couldn't let him have power over my work. After all, I explained to myself, the whole point of this comedy was to turn off the older crowd while reeling in the young. But as my career progressed, I noticed that my father remained uncomplimentary toward my comedy, and what I did about it still makes sense to me: I never discussed my work with him again.

But my mother was aglow. She had a continuing fascination with celebrities, and now she had one of her own. She was never moved by *what* I was doing (in an interview she said, "He writes his own material, I'm always telling him he needs a new writer"), but she was very involved with *how* things were going. She kept up with every little appearance and success and reported anything positive her friends had said to her, though sometimes she couldn't discern the fine line between a compliment and an insult. After I'd started making films, she once told me, "Oh, my friends went to the movies last weekend, and they couldn't get in anywhere so they went to see yours, and they loved it!"

I was a newly minted star when we were driving through Beverly Hills and she said, "Get out and walk down the street so I can watch people look at you." I gently declined, explaining to her how uncomfortable it would make me feel, but it never sank in. Another time she said, "I was in line at the supermarket yesterday, and when they found out I was your mother . . . !" I keep puzzling over the exact phraseology my proud mama must have used to work her information into normal supermarket discourse.

Money trickled her way—I was able to give her a monthly clothes allowance—and she was ecstatic. She became a regular at Neiman Marcus and loved that she was modestly famous as she browsed the racks of her favorite designer, St. John. When our mother died, my sister, Melinda, had an idea. She suggested our mother be buried on a hillside, in a plot overlooking the upscale Fashion Island shopping center in Orange County. And that is exactly what we did.

My first album, *Let's Get Small*, released in 1977, sold a million and a half copies. The material was so vivid to Bill and me that we naively included bits that were largely visual. The uninitiated heard clanks and spaces that brought forth laughs, and this minus turned into a plus, as the transitions seemed more surreal than they already were. Audiences were intrigued to see live what they could only hear on the album, and the theaters filled.

During my third appearance on *Saturday Night Live* I incorporated a line from my act, "I'm a wild and crazy guy," into Danny Aykroyd's idea (along with Marilyn Miller and James Downey) about two Czechoslovakian brothers. We caught the public's fancy, which gave me my second ticket into catchphrase heaven. My second album, *A Wild and Crazy Guy*, released in 1978, was being

Danny Aykroyd and me as the Czech brothers.

STEVE MARTIN

promoted every time we did the sketch on the show. It sold two and a half million copies and went to number one on the charts. Well, okay, number two. Promotion was becoming a regular part of the job, and when I did *The Tonight Show* it was understood that either I or Johnny would hold up an album for all to see. After *A Wild and Crazy Guy* blistered the record charts in 1978, I was on the cover of *Rolling Stone* and *Newsweek*.

I hadn't significantly collaborated with other performers since my days at the Bird Cage. My appearances on *SNL,* whether I was dancing with Gilda Radner, clowning with Danny, pitching show ideas with Lorne and the writers, or simply admiring Bill Murray, were community comic efforts that made me feel like I had been dropped off at a playground rather than the office. Watching the gleam in your partner's eyes, acting on impulses that had been nurtured over thousands of shows, working with edgy comic actors—some so edgy they died from it—was thrilling. We were all united in one, single goal, which was, using the comedian's parlance, to kill.

The record sales and the appearances on *SNL* compounded the size of the live audience. How many tickets sold? I asked in Toronto. "Fifteen thousand," they said. In St. Louis, I was told, "Twenty-two thousand." The act was on fire. My set lists from the period, now tattered and yellowed, remind me of forgotten routines: I would sing "I Can See Clearly Now" and walk into the mike. I would juggle kittens (swapping the one real kitten for a stuffed look-alike); I would stand in spilled water and touch the mike, faking an electric shock, then do it again as though I had enjoyed it. I had a long routine (for me) in which I confessed my weird sexual fetish, "I like to wear men's underwear."

There were more:

"I know what you're thinking," I would say conspiratorially, "you're thinking, 'Steve, how can you be so fuckin' funny?'"

In my opening seconds, I would say, "It's great to be here," then move to several other spots on the stage and say, "No, it's great to be here!" I would move again: "No, it's great to be here!"

Shouting to the audience, "Everybody put your hands together!" I would put my hands together and hold them there, making only one clap, saying, "Now keep them together!"

"Hello, Crime Stoppers! [audience: "Hello, Steve."] Let's repeat the Crime Stoppers' oath: 'I promise not to depreciate items carried forward from one tax year as nondepreciable items!'"

"I've learned in comedy never to alienate the audience. Otherwise, I would be like Dimitri in *La Condition Humaine.* . . ."

"A lot of people wonder if Steve Martin is my real name. Well, I did change my name for show business. My real name is Gern Blanston. So please, just call me . . . [long pause] . . . Gern." Don't ask me why, but this was funny at the time. There is even a Gern Blanston website, and for a while there was a rock band that used the name.

"I'm so mad at my mother, she's a hundred and two years old, and she called me the other day. She wanted to borrow *ten dollars for some food!* I said, 'Hey, I work for a living!'"

I would stand onstage and tune my banjo, but my hand would be about a foot away from the tuners, twisting in the air. I would act as though I couldn't figure out why it wouldn't go in tune.

And my closer, "Well, we've had a good time tonight, considering we're all going to die someday."

Moovin' and groovin' onstage.

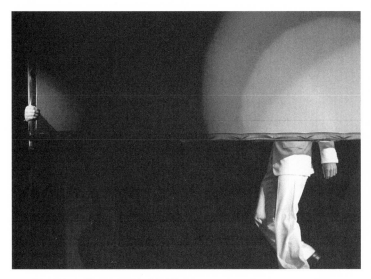

I loved performing this bit. There was a movie screen onstage, and I would go behind it and attach a fake rubber hand to it as though the hand were mine. Then I would slowly move backward, making it appear as if my arm was stretching.

IN THE LATE SEVENTIES, I continued to tour. My schedule was this: After sleeping all night on a band bus, I would arrive at the hotel around seven A.M. and collapse in a groggy half-sleep until four P.M. Then I would have a room-service dinner, and the only thing on the hotel menu that fit my fish-a-tarian diet was breaded fried shrimp with the texture of sandpaper, really just a ketchup delivery system. Following that, I would dumbly watch the five-thirty P.M. airing of *The Brady Bunch* (this showing, it seemed, was universal), then I would do the show. We—my roadie, Maple, and the sound team— were moving with such clockwork that some nights it

178

Date	CITY	Time	Hotel	TRANSPORTATION	FACILITY	REMARKS
SEP. 8 fri.	FRESNO CA.	7:30 A 10:30	Smuggler's Inn 209-226-2200	lv. Airesearch LAX (Lacy Avn) 4:34 at 1:00 PM lv. Beechcraft West arr. Airesearch 1:45	(CAL. ST. UNIV.) Amphitheatre	2 SHOWS (outdoors) 989-2900 LEAR: Lacy Aviation & 5 hrs. drive from LA
9– sat. thru' 17 sun.	UNIVERSAL CITY CA.	8:15 nightly			Universal Amphitheatre	w. Blues Bros. maple: Trop. 213-652-5720
25 mon.	Burbank Ca.	5:30		—26th tue:— LAX-LAS 7:15-8:05 WA#232	NBC The Tonight Show	
27 wed.	SALT LAKE CITY UT.	7:00 A 10:00	Hotel Utah 801-531-1000	LAS-SLC 10:30-12:34 WA #406	(UNIV. of UTAH) Special Events Center	2 SHOWS (MOUNTAIN TIME)
28 thu. CHICAGO 29 fri. IL.		7:30 A (10:30)	Ritz-Carlton 312-266-1000	SLC-ORD 9:40-1:25 UA #276	International Amphitheatre	2 SHOWS (FRIDAY) DONAHUE FRI: 9:45am (CENTRAL TIME)
30 sat.	KANSAS CITY MO.	8:00	Crown Centre 816-474-4400	ORD-MCI 12:00-1:16 TW #163	Kemper Arena	
OCT. 1. sun.	ST. PAUL MN.	7:30	Radisson 612-222-7711	MCI-MSP 11:10-12:15 BN #124	Civic Center Arena	
2 mon.	LEXINGTON KY.	8:00	Hyatt Regency 606-233-4111	MSP-ORD 10:25-11:33 NW# 426 ORD-LEX 1:11-3:09 DL #145	Lex. Center Arena	meet bus: overnight to Greensboro (eastern time)
3 tue.	GREENSBORO N.C.	8:00	Howard Johnson's (coliseum) 919-294-4920	overnight	Coliseum Arena	
4 wed.	PITTSBURG PA.	8:00	Hyatt House (Chatham Center) 412-391-5000		Civic Arena	
5 thu.	COLLEGE PARK MD.	7:30	Madison (washington d.c.) 202-785-1000	≈5hr.	(UNIV. OF MD.) Cole Fieldhouse	crew: Sheraton N.E. 301-459-6700
6 fri. UNIONDALE 7 sat. NY.		7:30 A (10:30)	Carlyle (N.Y.) 212-744-1600	≈5hr. overnight	Nassau Veteran's Mem. Coliseum	crew: 2 shows Holiday Inn FRI Hemp stead 516-486-4100
8 sun. BOSTON 9 mon. MS.		7:30 A 10:30 nightly	Hyatt (cambridge) 617-492-1234	≈5hr.	John B. Hynes Veteran's Auditorium	2 show sun. mon: 3 shows 4:00-7:30-10:30
10	NEW HAVEN	8:00	Sheraton	≈2hr.	veteran's mem. Coliseum	

One month's itinerary; design by Maple Byrne. Even though it indicates two shows at the Nassau Coliseum, a third was added. I remember nothing on this schedule except the Universal Amphitheatre—because it was in my hometown and opening the show were my friends the Blues Brothers—and the Nassau Coliseum, because of the harrowing helicopter ride to get from Manhattan to Long Island, with jets from LaGuardia Airport streaking all around us.

seemed as though we were rolling down the highway for the next town before the applause had stopped in the arena.

Sixty cities in sixty-three days. Seventy-two cities in eighty days. Eighty-five cities in ninety days. The Coliseum in Richfield, Ohio, largest audience in one day, 18,695. The Chicago International Amphitheatre: twenty-nine thousand people. Stealth limousines and subterranean entrances. I played Nassau Coliseum in New York. How many tickets sold? Forty-five thousand. I was astonished that popular culture had fixed its attention so intensely on my little act. This lightning strike was happening to me, Stephen Glenn Martin, who had started from zero, from a magic act, from juggling in my backyard, from Disneyland, from the Bird Cage, and I was now the biggest concert comedian in show business, ever. I was elated. My success had outstripped my wildest aspirations. I had hit a gusher, and I stopped checking prices in restaurants, hotels, and clothing stores. I bought my first house, and then I bought my second house, skillfully negotiated by my father. My wisecrack about success was "We'll offer you fifty thousand dollars to go stand over there." "I can't," I would say, "I'm getting seventy-five thousand to stand right here." I had a line: "I think I'm spending my money wisely. . . . I just bought a three-hundred-dollar pair of socks. And last week I got a gasoline-powered turtleneck sweater."

Standing Down

THE ACT WAS SHIFTING into automatic. The choreography was in place, and all I had to do was fulfill it. I was performing a litany of immediate old favorites, and the laughs, rather than being the result of spontaneous combustion, now seemed to roll in like waves created far out at sea. The nuances of stand-up still thrilled me, but nuance was difficult when you were a white dot in a basketball arena. This was no longer an experiment; I felt a huge responsibility not to let people down. Arenas of twenty thousand and three-day gigs of forty-five thousand were no place to try out new material. I dabbled with changes, introducing a small addition or mutation here and there, but they were swallowed up by the echoing, cavernous venues.

Onstage, Syracuse, New York, 1978, as King Tut.

STEVE MARTIN

Though the audiences continued to grow, I experienced a concomitant depression caused by exhaustion, isolation, and creative ennui. As I was too famous to go outdoors without a discomforting hoopla, my romantic interludes ceased because I no longer had normal access to civilized life. The hour and a half I spent performing was still fun, but there were no band members, no others onstage, and after the show, I took a solitary ride back to the hotel, where I was speedily escorted by security across the lobby. A key went in a door, and boom: the blunt interior of a hotel room. Nowhere to look but inward. I'm sure there were a hundred solutions. I could have invited friends to join me on the road, or asked a feel-good guru to shake my shoulders and say, "Perk up, you idiot," but I was too exhausted to communicate, and it seemed like a near-coma was the best way to spend the day. This was, as the cliché goes, the loneliest period of my life.

I was caught and I could not quit, because this multi-zeroed income might last only a moment. I couldn't imagine abandoning something I had worked so hard to craft. I knew about the flash in the pan, I had seen it happen to others, and I worried about it happening to me. In the middle of all this, I saw that the only way I could go, at best, was sideways. I wasn't singing songs that you hum forever; I was doing comedy, which is as ephemeral as the daily newspaper. Onstage I was no longer the funniest I ever was; my shelf life was expiring. I recently found a discarded joke among my papers: "You might think I'm making a lot of money, but you have to understand my expenses. Twenty percent to a manager, ten percent to an agent, thirty percent to travel, and .000000005 percent to develop new material." It was 1979, and I was already booked for the next two years.

The prospect of the remaining stand-up dates loomed over me. The glowing reviews changed; I was now a target. Critics who once lauded me were starting to rebel. Easy headlines appeared: STEVE MARTIN, A MILD AND LAZY GUY. I received a bad review in a local newspaper before I even performed. The backlash had begun. My tired body had rebelled, too. One summer night I was midway through my show in a southern college gymnasium when the temperature reached 120. In a resurrection of my old anxiety, my heart began to skip beats, and I panicked. I abruptly walked offstage and went to a hospital, where I was given a well-attended celebrity EKG. Fine. Stress and heat, I was told, but as I was lying on a gurney, with the sheet up to my neck but not quite over my head, confident that I was dying, a nurse asked me to autograph the printout of my erratic heartbeat. I perfunctorily signed to avoid further stress. The concept of privacy crystallized at that moment and became something to protect. What I was doing, what I was thinking, and who I was seeing, I now kept to myself as a necessary defense against the feeling that I was becoming, like the Weinermobile, a commercial artifact. Once, in Texas, a woman came up to me and said, with some humor and a lot of drawl, "Are you that Steve Martin thang?"

Being the good Baptist-raised boy I was, I honored all my contracts and did the shows, though with mounting frustration. The act was still rocking, but audience disruptions, whoops and shouts, sometimes killed the timing of bits, violating my premise that *every moment mattered*. The days of the heckler comebacks were over. The audiences were so large that if someone was calling or signaling to me, only I and their immediate seatmates could hear them. My timing was jarred, yet if I had responded to the heckler, the rest of the audience wouldn't have known what I was talking about. Today I realize that I misunderstood what my last year of stand-up was about. I had become a party host, presiding not over timing and ideas but over a celebratory bash of my own making. If I had understood what was happening, I might have been happier, but I didn't. I still thought I was doing comedy.

During this time, I asked a woman to dinner, and she accepted. After the salad course, she started talking about her boyfriend.

"You have a boyfriend?" I asked, puzzled.

"Yes, I do."

"Does he know you're out with me?" I asked.

"Yes, he does."

"And what does he think of that?"

"He thinks it's great!"

I was now famous, and the normal rules of social interaction no longer applied.

185

Suddenly, restaurant reservations were always available, and VIP considerations made hassles with travel, long lines, and rude salesclerks vanish. Waiters were cordial and prompt. Every call was returned, there was no further need for ID, and I was able to meet artists whom I admired. I was surprised by James Cagney's noblesse oblige phone call to my New York hotel room just to say hello, and by Cary Grant's friendly backstage chat at the American Film Institute's salute to Gene Kelly, during which he seriously charmed my girlfriend.

But guess what. There was a dark side. A regular conversation, except with established friends, became difficult, fraught with ulterior motives, and often degenerated into deadening nephew autograph requests. Almost every ordinary action that took place in public had a freakish celebrity aura around it. I would get laughs at innocuous things I said, such as "What time does the movie start?" or "Hello." I would pull my hat down low on my head and stare at the ground when I walked through airports, and I would duck around corners quickly at museums. My room-service meal could be delivered by four people wearing arrows through their heads—funny, yes, but when you're dead tired of your own jokes, it's hard to respond with the expected glee. Cars would follow me recklessly on the freeway, and I worried for the passengers' lives as the driver hung out the window, shouting, "I'm a wild and craaaazzzzyy guy!" while steering with one hand and holding a beer in the other. In a public situation, I was expected to be the figure I was onstage, which I stubbornly resisted. People were waiting for a show, but my show was only that, a show. It was precise and particular and not reproducible in a living room; in fact, to me my act was serious.

Fame suited me in that the icebreaking was already done and my natural shyness could be easily overcome. I was, however, ill suited for fame's destruction of privacy, for the uninvited doorbell ringers and anonymous phone callers. I had never been outgoing, and when strangers approached me with the familiarity of old friends, I felt dishonest if I returned it in kind.

When I got divorced in 1992, a tabloid reported that I would practice my routines in front of a mirror, and if they weren't going well, I would find my wife and scream at her. At the time, as I was naturally sensitive about the divorce, this lie seemed almost actionable. And once, on a local Los Angeles news show dealing with "celebrity assassinations," I was shown getting out of a car while crosshairs were superimposed over my head along with the sound effect of a rifle crack. In spite of these examples, I have been treated fairly for most of my career in showbiz, probably by being dull and dreary and failing to excite the needle on the gossipometer. I admit that I'm a lousy interview. My magician's instincts make me reluctant to tell 'em how it's done, whether it's a movie, book, play, or any aspect of personal life. Sometimes a journalist will lean in and say, "You're very private." And I mentally respond,

"Someone who's private would not be doing an interview on television."

Time has helped me achieve peace with celebrity. At first I was not famous enough, then I was too famous, now I am famous just right. Oh yes, I have heard the argument that celebrities want fame when it's useful and don't when it's not. That argument is absolutely true.

I WAS DETERMINED to parlay my stand-up success into motion pictures while I still had some clout. A movie career seemed to foster longevity, whereas a career as a comedian who had become a fad seemed finite. Plus, the travel was exhausting me, and I swooned at the idea that instead of my going to every town to perform my act, a movie would go while I stayed home.

I had an idea for a film. It came from a line in my act: "It wasn't always easy for me; I was born a poor black child." That was the idea, and that was all I had. I knew only that I wanted the movie to have the feel of a saga, and I toyed with story ideas.

I was hot enough to get in any door, or so I thought. Bill McEuen had a relationship with David Picker, then the head of Paramount Pictures. This was not a time when it was automatic that a popular comedian could land a movie deal, so the prospect was considered carefully by the studio. I gave them the notes on a screenplay I had dabbled with.

We see Steve sitting on the porch of a ramshackle
tenement farm in Tennessee. He is his white self while
his black family members do chores about the yard. His
mother, a big black woman à la Hattie McDaniel, sits
on the porch and sings the blues. Steve says things like
"Gosh, Mom, that's really great blues you're singing!"
His family relationship is very close with his black brothers
and sisters, so when he makes a decision to go on the road
after hearing the music of Lawrence Welk on the radio, it
is a sad occasion. There is a tearful farewell, and Steve sets
off hitchhiking in the front of the family house and gets a
ride about two hours later. His family stands outside with
him in awkward silence while he waits for a ride.

The notes continue to describe a series of odd jobs that
"Steve" gets on his journey: a ranch hand who practices
roping fence posts and ends up with a herd of fence posts;
a buffalo counter in Beverly Hills who stands on Rodeo
Drive—after several days, a buffalo finally walks by, and
"Steve" takes out a clipboard and writes down, "One." My
list of odd jobs went on: "My third job, perhaps the weird-
est of all, was standing on my head in a river." None of
these odd jobs ended up in the movie, which was ultimately written and rewritten many times with Carl Gott-
lieb and Michael Elias. Eventually, Bill McEuen and David
Picker, who by now had left the studio, moved the film to
Universal after Paramount passed.

Carl Reiner, who, in a six-year burst of comic perfection, wrote and produced television's *The Dick Van Dyke Show,* was our lucky choice as director. Carl and I met constantly. His memory was sharp as cheddar, and he would spontaneously relate anecdotes relevant to our work. One day I mentioned concern over my lack of concrete talents. Carl told me about his first appearance on *The Sid Caesar Show,* a sketch in which he spoke a long stretch of German-sounding gibberish. The next day his mother called and said, "Carl, I was with some ladies in the park, and they said they didn't know you spoke German." Carl said, "Ma, that's why they hire me, because I *can't* speak German." Carl's mother then said, "Well, the ladies don't have to know that."

We were still mulling over titles for the movie. One day I said to Carl, "It needs to be something short, yet have the feeling of an epic tale. Like Dostoyevsky's *The Idiot,* but not that. Like *The Jerk.*" The title, after a few more days of analyzing, stuck.

I was injecting stage material into the screenplay, including a bit that was taken directly from the end of my act, first developed at the Boarding House. Onstage, I would exit through the audience, saying, "I'm quitting, I'm leaving and never coming back, and I don't need anything, nothing at all, well, I need this ashtray." I would collect doodads from the tabletops until I finally disappeared out the door. The bit appears in the final film as I forlornly leave Bernadette Peters and my movie mansion:

"Well, I'm gonna go then! And I don't need any of this! I don't need this stuff [*I push all of the letters off the desk*], and I don't need you. I don't need anything except this [*I pick up an ashtray*], and that's it and that's the only thing I need, is this. Just this ashtray. And this paddle game, the ashtray and the paddle game and that's all I need. And this remote control. The ashtray, the paddle game and the remote control, and that's all I need. And these matches. The ashtray, and these matches, and the remote control and the paddle ball. And this lamp. The ashtray, this paddle game and the remote control and the lamp and that's all I need. I don't need one other thing, not one—I need this! [*I pick up a magazine.*] The paddle game, the remote control, and the matches, for sure. And this! [*I pick up a chair.*] And that's all I need. The ashtray, the remote control, the paddle game, this magazine, and the chair. Well, what are you looking at? What do you think I am, some kind of a jerk or something?"

It was a joy to work on the movie and the script. Our goal in writing was a laugh on every page. But my favorite line in the movie was an ad lib, one that is mildly obscured by traffic noise in the finished film. My character, Navin Johnson, is hitchhiking in Missouri, headed for the big city. A car pulls over, and the driver asks, "St. Louis?" "No," I answer, "Navin Johnson."

We made the film and went off to preview it in St. Louis. As much as I loved the comedy in the movie, my favorite moment was when Bernadette Peters and I sang a simple song on a beach, "Tonight You Belong to Me," a tune that was a hit in the twenties and again in the fifties, when it was recorded by two adolescent sisters called Patience and Prudence. I thought the scene was touching, and I couldn't wait for it to come on-screen, hoping the audience would be as affected as I had been. The movie was rolling along with lots of laughter. Then the song came on. Mass exodus for popcorn. Song over, audience returned for more laughs. After the screening, I got a left-handed compliment of juicy perfection: A woman approached me and said, "I *loved* this movie. And my husband loved it, and he hates you!"

The world of moviemaking had changed me. Carl Reiner ran a joyful set. Movies were social; stand-up was antisocial. I was not judged every day by a changing audience. It was fun to have lunches with cast and crew and to dream up material in the morning that could be shot seven different ways in the afternoon and evaluated—and possibly perfected—in the editing room months later. The end of a movie is like graduation day, and right or wrong, we felt we had accomplished something wonderful. I got another benefit: my daily observation of Carl Reiner. He had an entrenched sense of glee; he used humor as a gentle way of speaking difficult truths; and he could be effortlessly frank. He taught me more about how to be a social person than any other adult in my life.

The Jerk, receiving one lone good review from a small

paper in Florida and getting dismissive and sadistic reviews from the rest of the country, made one hundred eighty million dollars in old money. It was recently voted among the American Film Institute's top one hundred comedies of all time, he said smugly. Because it was a hit, my life changed, though again, my father was not impressed. I had invited him to the premiere. The Bruin Theatre in Westwood, next to UCLA, was ringed outside with spotlights drawing figure eights in the sky and packed inside with clamoring, vocal fans. Press crews lined the red carpet, and it took us forty-five minutes to get from the car to our seats. The movie played well, and afterward my friends and I took my father to dinner at a quiet, old-fashioned eatery that didn't offer "silly" modern food. He said nothing about the film; he talked about everything but the film. Finally, one of my friends said, "Glenn, what did you think of Steve's movie?" My father chuckled and said, "Well, he's no Charlie Chaplin."

My body was on the road but my heart was elsewhere. I continued to fulfill my contracts, mostly weekly gigs where I was allowed to "sit down," a term meaning the performer wasn't having to travel to a different town every night. Working in Vegas for several weeks, I taped tinfoil over the windows in my rental house so I could adjust to the city's all-night schedule. According to scientists, no sunlight for two weeks can do things to a person, such as make you insane. I fell into a depression that might be called self-indulgent but was real just the same.

The Jerk had been a smash hit, but my comic well was dry; the movie represented my small act's ultimate expression. My cheap cassette player, which I now used to play thirties songs from *Pennies from Heaven*—the dark, audience-jolting drama that I chose to do next—was my only solace inside the blacked-out bedroom.

In 1981 my act was like an overly plumed bird whose next evolutionary step was extinction. One night in Las Vegas, I saw something so disturbing that I didn't mention it to my friends, my agent, or my manager. It was received in my mind like grim, inevitable news. I was onstage at the Riviera showroom, and the house, as usual, was full. The floor tables were jammed, and the club was ringed with tiers of booths. There were soft lights around the interior wall, which silhouetted the patrons in halos of light. My eyes scanned the room as I worked, seeing heads bobbing and nodding; and then, in one booth in the back, I saw something I hadn't seen in five years: empty seats. I had reached the top of the roller coaster.

I had a week's job in Atlantic City. The shows were still sold out, but I was exhausted, physically and existentially. When I performed the song "King Tut," a guitar suspended on wires (a beautiful, mirrored Fender Flying-V) would descend from the rafters. I would then "Tut walk" over and strum it only once, and it would ascend back into the ceiling, creating the shortest guitar solo in the history of show business. For the third night in a row, the guitar failed to descend, leaving me horribly stuck. I guessed that I hadn't greased the right union guy. The act ended normally, and I exited the stage and felt something rare for me: rage. In the wings, I began swearing to myself. I ripped off my coat and threw it against a wall. Of course, my fury was not from the failure of the King Tut guitar to descend from the ceiling— it was that over the last few years I had lost contact with what I was doing, and I was suffering an artistic crisis that I didn't know I had a capacity for. I went to my dressing room, opened my travel-weary black prop case, and stowed away my magic act, thinking that one day I would open it and look at it sentimentally, which for no particular reason, I haven't. I never did stand-up again.

IN THE EARLY 1980s, a friend whose father had been killed crossing the street and whose mother had committed suicide on Mother's Day advised me, "If you have anything to work out with your parents, do it now. One day it will be too late." This thought nagged at me and I began a fifteen-year effort to reconnect with my parents. I took them to lunch almost every weekend, probing them for anecdotes about our life together, and these consistent visits made us closer. My father enjoyed dealing with fanmail requests and used his real estate expertise to help manage my vacation home. In the 1990s, my father's attitude toward me began to soften. I had written *Picasso at the Lapin Agile,* a play set in 1905 about a hypothetical meeting between Picasso and Einstein. My father flipped over it, bragging to his friends and telling me I should win a Pulitzer Prize. He was laughing more, too, enjoying pranks on telemarketers and mail solicitors, and he exhibited his charitable streak by delivering Meals on Wheels, a service that provides food to the elderly. I began to appreciate him more as his humor started to shine through. Though he was experiencing disturbing health issues, he took my twenty-five-year-old nephew, Rusty, to a car dealer to help him negotiate a price. After a few offers and counteroffers, the dealer looked at the purchase order and said, "I don't know, I'm not really comfortable with this."

"You're uncomfortable? You're uncomfortable?" my father said. "I'm the one with the catheter in my peter."

After our lunches, my parents, now in their eighties, would walk me to my car. I would kiss my mother on the cheek and wave awkwardly at my father as we said goodbye. But one afternoon, perhaps motivated by a vague awareness that time was running out, we hugged each other and he said, in a voice barely audible, "I love you." This would be the first time these words were ever spoken between us. Several days later, I sent him a letter that began, "I heard what you said," and I wrote the same words back to him.

My father's health declined further, and he became bedridden. There must be an instinct about when the end is near; Melinda and I found ourselves at our parents' home in Laguna Beach, California. I walked into the house they had lived in for thirty-five years, and my tearful sister said, "He's saying goodbye to everyone." A nurse said to me, "This is when it all happens." I didn't know what she meant, but I soon understood.

I was alone with him in the bedroom; his mind was alert but his body was failing. He said, almost buoyantly, "I'm ready now." I sat on the edge of the bed, and another silence fell over us. Then he said, "I wish I could cry, I wish I could cry."

At first I took this as a comment on his condition but am forever thankful that I pushed on. "What do you want to cry about?" I said.

"For all the love I received and couldn't return."

I felt a chill of familiarity.

There was another lengthy silence as we looked into each other's eyes. At last he said, "You did everything I wanted to do."

"I did it for you," I said. Then we wept for the lost years. I was glad I didn't say the more complicated truth: "I did it *because* of you."

Our father's sickness reunited me and my sister. When we visited our ailing parents, we did something we had never done in our lives: talked. We had something uniquely in common, and each conversation turned to our past, as though we had found a mine with a rich vein. I was surprised that our views of the household jibed. I had thought I was the only outsider, but no, she was, too. She was aware of the tension and fear that had made home life so miserable and the outside world so appealing. When she confirmed our father's unprovoked hostility toward me, I was shocked. Somehow I thought I had made it up, had caused it, or had an innate, unlikable quality that riled him.

Together again.

STEVE MARTIN

My father died in 1997, and my mother, for a short time, became a stylish matriarch. She immediately cut off all the consistent small loans my father had continued to make to a few friends; to her they were freeloaders. But she didn't have long to enjoy her single life. Having few interests to sustain her, over the next few years she fell into a vacant, mental decline. I continued my visits with her, and always when I walked into the room, her blue eyes lit up and her face brought forth a smile. I was, after all, her son.

She began to alternate between lucidity and confusion, creating moments of tenderness and painful hilarity. She told me she thought Glenn had treated me unfairly, that she wished she had intervened. She said when I was a child, she hugged me and kissed me a lot, something I did not recollect. Then she took a long pause. She looked at me, quietly puzzled, and said, "How's your mother?"

Another day, curious about an old family rumor, I asked her if she ever had a miscarriage. "No, I never did." Then my ninety-year-old mother added, "Knock on wood."

One emotional afternoon I told her that I loved her and I thanked her for bringing me into the world. Her eyes moistened, and she said, "This is the highest moment of my life." I asked her if she had any regrets. She said, "I wish I had been more truthful," a comment regarding, I believe, her lifelong subordination to my father. She expressed embarrassment that she was dying, saying, "I hate to be silly." In February 2002 she lay on a bed in the house, not able to speak, but with her eyes smiling. Her saintly Filipino nurse, Mila, was daubing her head with a damp towel and was, in an eerie recall from my childhood, singing to her "America the Beautiful." Then Mila quietly left the room. I moved closer and said goodbye to my mother. I put my arms around her and, surprising myself, choked out, "Mama, Mama, Mama," a term I hadn't used since childhood. I kissed her on the cheek, and her skin felt cool and young. She seemed to pass into a trance, and eventually, I left the house.

I drove toward home and on the way felt a sentimental urge to stop by the Bird Cage. It had been thirty-one years since I had left the little theater where I got my start. I cruised the main gate, but the lines were long. I almost went home but decided to try the employee entrance in the back. I pulled in to a parking space wondering if they were going to throw me out, but an elderly security guard immediately said, "Hi, Steve." He was saying hello to me not as a celebrity but as someone he remembered from thirty years ago. A few hand waves were telegraphed from security guard to security guard, and I found myself entering the grounds through the employees' gate.

Knott's had expanded over the decades, giving it the qualities of a tree trunk: The newest developments were on the outside, with the oldest buildings still standing at its core. As I moved toward the theater, I felt a peculiar sense of passing through rings of time. The newer

Knott's gave way to the seventies Knott's, which gave way to the Knott's of the sixties, fifties, and forties. I was time-traveling, not in an exotic Wellsian time machine, but with every footstep.

The deserted lobby of the Bird Cage looked as though time had stopped the day I left. On the walls were photos from various productions, some of which included me as resident goofball. On one wall were hall-of-fame eight-by-tens of graduates, including me, John Stuart, and Kathy Westmoreland. Stormie's photo was from the period: She was probably twenty when it was taken. It was hung at eye level, and I had the feeling of staring into her face, just as I did then.

I tugged on the theater door; it was locked. I was about to give up when I remembered a back entrance in the employees-only area, a clunky, oversize wooden gate that rarely locked because it was so rickety. I sneaked behind the theater and opened the door, which, for the millionth time, had failed to latch. The darkened theater flooded with sunlight, and I stepped inside and quickly shut the door. Light filtered in from the canvas roof, giving the Bird Cage a dim, golden hue. There I was, standing in a memory frozen in amber, and I experienced an overwhelming rush of sadness.

I went backstage and had a muscle memory of how to raise and lower the curtain, tying it off with a looping knot shown to me on my first day of work. I fiddled with the sole lighting rheostat, as antique as Edison. I stood on the stage and looked out at the empty theater and was overcome by the feeling of today being pressed into yesterday. I didn't realize how much this place had meant to me.

Driving home along the Santa Ana freeway, I was still unnerved. I asked myself what it was that had made this place capable of inducing in me such a powerful nostalgic shock. The answer floated clearly into my consciousness as though I had asked the question of a Magic 8-Ball: I wanted to be there again, if only for a day, indulging in high spirits and high jinks, before I turned professional, before comedy became serious.

I ALWAYS GAVE MY PERFORMANCES, even my five-minute talk show appearances, a beginning, a middle, and an end. It turned out that my stand-up career took that shape, too. I was in a conversation a few years ago with a friend, the painter Eric Fischl. We were comparing psychoanalysis with the making of art. I said, "Both require explorations of the subconscious, and in that way they are similar." He agreed, thought about it, then added, "But there is a fundamental difference between the two. In psychoanalysis, you try to retain a discovery; in art, once the thing is made, you let it go." He was right. I had not looked at or considered my stand-up career until writing this memoir; I had, in fact, abandoned it. Moving on and not looking back, not living in the past, was a way to trick myself into further creativity.

My career in stand-up gave me a vestigial sense of the crowd that I have relied upon over the last twenty-seven years. In the world of filmmaking, where there is no audience, where, in fact, quiet on the set is required, I sometimes try to determine if a particular idea is funny. I picture myself at the back of a darkened theater, watching the bit in question unspooling on the screen, and somewhere, in the black interior of my brain, I can hear the audience's response. Thankfully, when the movie is finally screened, I discover that my intuition is not always right. If it were, there would be no surprises left; I would be living in a dull comedy heaven.

I do not know if my act holds up these many years later. It is not for me to decide or even think about. Sometimes I hear or see a piece of the old show, and it sounds funny; sometimes I don't get it and can't figure out what all the fuss was about. I did, however, in the course of writing this memoir, come across routines and ad libs, long forgotten, that made me smile, like this description of a radio show in Austin, Texas, in the seventies, remembered by the host Sonny Melendrez:

"Steve Martin came directly from a recording session to debut his *Let's Get Small* album on my show. Before he left, he got very serious, and I truly thought we were seeing another side of him. He launched into a monologue of what seemed like sincere words of friendship. It

203

took me by surprise, given the hour of silliness that had just taken place. 'Could this be the real Steve Martin?' I thought."

"Sonny, you know, I've listened to you for years, and I really feel like you've become my friend. I feel like I can ask you this question."

"Sure. Steve, you can ask me anything."

"What time is it?"

Acknowledgments

TWENTY YEARS AGO, I looked at the collected flotsam of my life and sent it off to an archivist, Candace Bothwell, who did an outstanding job of sequencing and preserving whatever she could. Later, I collected other cardboard boxes from my parents' house, some moldy from garage floods. Inside were sedimentary layers of collected junk, ephemera, snapshots, and yellowed newspaper clippings. Like a geologist, I was sometimes able to date items by their position in the stack. As much as I enjoyed the writing of this book, researching it was a new thrill for me. Finding a photo that confirmed a dim recollection of days gone by hooked me on the detective work, and the legwork—marching from my desk back and forth to the archival boxes—gave me something to do besides type, think, worry, and cry.

This book has allowed me to contact old friends and dig through their memories and memorabilia. All contacts

205

have been pleasant and some quite moving. The arrival of a package of photos or copies of letters offered by a friend was like having an archaeological dig brought to my own home. People to whom I am grateful include, in no particular order, Gaylord Alexander, George and Carole McKelvey, John McClure, Nina Raggio, Gary Mule Deer, Dave Archer, John McEuen, Ivan Ultz, Dean Carter, Nick Pileggi, Kathy Westmoreland, Mitzi Trumbo, Melinda Dobbs, Stormie Omartian, Phil Carey, Bob Shayne, Betty Buckley (not the actress), Maple Byrne, and many others. They all helped fill in the past. In distilling my life, or a portion of my life, I may have left out people who had a crucial impact on me. Victoria Dailey deserves her own biography in order to tell the story of my debt to her, and Lorne Michaels deserves a bio, too, but he's already the subject of about ten.

Two valuable editors helped shape this book, Bill Phillips and Nan Graham, without whom I would still be wondering, "Where did I go wrong?" My representative, Esther Newberg, gave me tough love when she could have said, "You're beautiful, Stevie baby, you're beautiful." I also have to thank the host of friends I have used through the years as readers. I'm sure they're grateful that I have finally learned an important rule: You can't ask a friend to read your manuscript twice. I would string them out through the writing stages from clumsy first draft to shiny final, knowing I only had one shot at them, and, after the manuscript had improved, I always felt bad that a particular friend had read it when it stank. My thanks extend to Rebecca Wilson, Geoff Dyer, Nora Ephron, April Gornik, Eric Fischl, Adam Gopnik, Bruce McCall, Joan Stein, Ricky Jay, Mike Nichols, David Geffen, Pete Wernick, Anne Stringfield, and finally, the Internet: I have learned that people are uploading their lives into cyberspace and am convinced that one day all human knowledge and memory will exist on a suitable hard drive which, for preservation, will be flung out of the solar system to orbit a galaxy far, far away.

Photograph Credits

Photographs were provided courtesy of the author except for the following:

Page 6: © Morris Lafon

Pages 58 and 61: © Dean Carter

Page 69 and 94: © Mitzi Trumbo

Pages 77 and 82: © Nina Raggio

Page 93: © Cleo Trumbo

Pages 114 and 116: © Henry Diltz

Page 118: © William E. McEuen

Page 155: © Norman Seeff

Page 174: © 1978 Edie Baskin

Page 178: © John Malmquist/pixdude.com

Page 182: © Bill Thompson

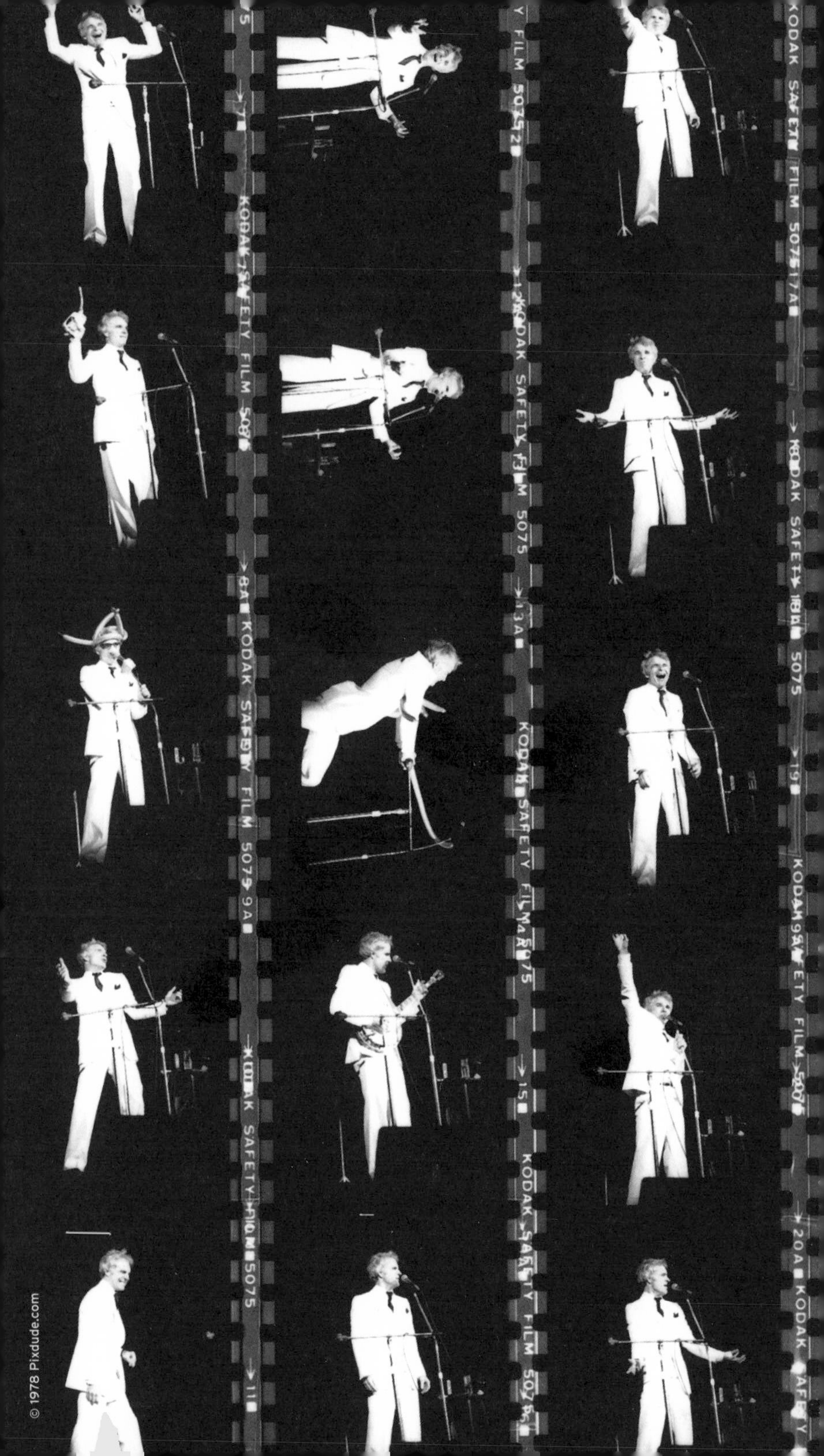
KODAK SAFETY FILM 5075